THE ESSENTIAL SOL STONE

Best wishes for your good health, happiness and success.

Sol Stone
New York

THE ESSENTIAL SOL STONE

INTIMATE MAGIC *with the* SOL STONE TOUCH

STEPHEN HOBBS

ILLUSTRATIONS BY CASSIDY J. ALEXANDER

EDITED BY RICHARD KAUFMAN

PUBLISHED BY
MEIR YEDID MAGIC

The original hard cover edition of this book was Copyright in 2010 by Penny J. Alexander and published by The Alexander Studio.

Patter Punches was Copyright and published in 1947 by Abbott's Magic Novelty Co. The Patter Punches booklet by Sol Stone is reprinted with permission from Greg Bordner and the Abbott Magic Company.

Book design by Thomas Baxter.

Cover designed by Martin Korstanje.

Illustrations by Cassidy J. Alexander.

Library of Congress Cataloging-In-Publication Data available from the publisher upon request.

ISBN-13: 978-1-7335972-1-0

ISBN-10: 1-7335972-1-2

First Edition

Printed in the United States

Published by

MEIR YEDID MAGIC

E-mail: meir@mymagic.com

Web: www.MyMagic.com

Dedication

This book is lovingly dedicated to my wife Alice, our sons Robert and Lawrence, our daughter-in-law Phyllis, our grandson Joshua and our granddaughter Shelby, who have enriched my life immeasurably.

Sol Stone

TABLE OF CONTENTS

FOREWORD

I first saw Sol Stone from across the room at Lou Tannen's magic shop at 1540 Broadway. I must have been 14 or 15 years old, so that would make it 1972 or 73. He was reading a magazine—perhaps the latest issue of Genii or The Pallbearers Review. At first I thought it was George C. Scott (Sol looks a lot like him to me), which wasn't such an odd thought because lots of celebrities came up to Tannen's in those days: Orson Welles, Hugh O'Brien, Dick Cavett, and others I've forgotten.

While I had been hanging around at Tannen's for about 6 months, my friend Gene Maze had been trying to talk me into going to the Governor's Cafeteria, where everyone went after Tannen's closed at 3 p.m. on Saturday afternoons. A shy kid, I found the idea terrifying, but after much encouragement from Gene and another friend, Rene Clement, off I went.

People tended to cluster into groups at certain tables, and usually sitting with Gene and Rene were Ben Lichtenstein, Buddy Anckner, Max Abrams, Sol Stone, and Gerry Deutsch. Sol introduced himself to me almost immediately and said he was working on the famous Sack Dice Routine. Coincidentally, this routine appears in one of my favorite books, Bruce Elliott's Classic Secrets of Magic, and it was something I knew well (at least as well as any young teen could). Sol was very gracious in talking about it and he immediately made me feel like one of the group. In retrospect I can clearly see that this wasn't happenstance, and he had gone out of his way to make me welcome.

And then he showed me some coin magic. My oh my, what a beautiful light touch he has—like an artist's hands sliding across a smooth piece of marble.

So, it was obvious right away that Sol was a lovely, generous man who did absolutely wonderful coin magic. It turns out that Sol was, for lack of a better word, an "old fashioned" coin man—his methods were much more like those of Vernon and Leipzig than those up and coming, the next generation.

A few years later, in 1979, I started writing a large book called CoinMagic. There were so many guys doing great coin magic in New York City at the time that it seemed like a crazy idea not to do it. Sol, David Roth, Geoff Latta, Derek Dingle; all contributed greatly to my book, each with their own completely different styles of magic using that most common object: pocket change.

In the late 1980s I thought that Sol should have all of his material collected in one book, and hired Stephen Hobbs, then living in New York City, to write it. Things proceeded in fits and starts and sometime between 1995 and 1997 I eventually took about 400 photographs of Sol's hands for the illustrations. And then in 1998 I purchased Genii, The Conjurors' Magazine, from the Larsen family. All my book projects languished.

About four years ago David Alexander, having recently moved from California to Illinois, had the itch to publish some books on magic. David was a good and intelligent friend, and when I mentioned that Sol's book needed to be illustrated and published, he was enthusiastic and we struck a deal. David's wife Cassidy (also called "Penny") did the wonderful drawings ... and then David died suddenly and unexpectedly in December, 2010. It was a great shock to all of us who knew him because he was so busy, with so many plans for the future.

Cassidy, a remarkable woman, has soldiered on with this project, not only to rescue her own work, but also that of David and Sol, the latter having waited patiently for many years to see his book finally reach publication.

Sol has remained remarkably youthful throughout the years, and has never lost that golden touch—so soft and gentle—that made his effects look so utterly effortless and magical. I hope this book, filled with so many miracles, is greeted with the enthusiasm it deserves.

Richard Kaufman
Washington, DC
March, 2012

PREFACE

Sol Stone and David Alexander first crossed paths in Acapulco back in the 1960s. Sol's son and daughter-in-law had taken their honeymoon in Acapulco and had seen David performing at the Marriott Hotel. David was living in Mexico at the time, as he had two long-term gigs back to back. They both enjoyed his performance very much and immediately upon returning home told Sol about the wonderful magician they saw.

Not long after, Sol decided to take his wife on a vacation to Acapulco to see this young performer. They hit it off and spent most of the week together. David was charming, kind and bright. They talked magic and more. David showed the two of them all around Acapulco to places that they would never have seen otherwise. At that time, David was going through a break-up and was pretty down. Sol helped him through it with kindness and words of wisdom which David never forgot.

Although their paths did not cross again, when David got a chance to publish Sol's book he decided the karma was right. (Of course, having run his own book publishing business and being married to a capable artist didn't hurt either.) When he called Sol and informed him that he had just bought the rights to the book, they had a chance to reconnect. David told Sol how much his wise counsel had helped him, not only at the time, but also later on when it helped him to pick out his next (and last) wife and have a happy marriage, which Sol was pleased to hear.

It is unfortunate that David did not live to see the project through, but I felt it was important for this book to be published, not only to fulfill Sol Stone's wishes and those of the author and editor, but also to complete what David and I had started. With tremendous help from Tom Baxter, I was finally able to bring this book to light. I hope that you will enjoy it.

Cassidy J. Alexander
Aurora, Illinois
March, 2012

INTRODUCTION

I REMEMBER one of my first visits to Reuben's Deli — the Saturday hang-out for New York magicians — after moving to the Big Apple. I witnessed a skillful and smooth demonstration of a series of Sol Stone effects that I recognized from ***CoinMagic***. The performer was good — very good in fact — but it never occurred to me that it might be Sol Stone himself. Why? Because I knew that Sol Stone was an "older" man of at least seventy, while the performer I was watching was at best in his mid-fifties.

It was, of course, Sol Stone. Over time I learned that Sol's youthfulness—both in body and spirit—were only one aspect of this truly unique individual. Another was the remarkable magic that he performed. I will gladly go on record as stating that although I have seen many good, and a few great, magicians, I have never seen anyone whose "touch" with coins is as soft and gentle as Sol's.

Recently there has been some debate as to the meaning of Dai Vernon's famous statement: "Be natural." Some have argued that there is no objective, universal criteria for naturalness, that naturalness is best defined in terms of the individual's own actions. In other words, what is natural will differ from person to person and is perhaps best defined in terms of subjective consistency. For the most part, I agree with this line of thinking. And yet, if I had to identify one individual who best exemplifies what I intuitively call *natural*, I would point to Sol Stone.

I consider Sol to be one of the true masters of "intimate magic"—magic performed for one or two people, often spontaneously, in a casual and informal setting. Intimate magic places a premium upon establishing a rapport with the audience, on charming them and encouraging them to enter your world for at least a few moments. It is simultaneously child-like and very mature. Fancy flourishes, studied performances, and long, drawn-out effects are anathema in this environment.

I have lost track of how many times I have watched Sol in Reuben's Deli making an out-of-town magician feel at home—demonstrating a few effects and then encouraging the visitor to perform in what may be described as an intimidating situation ("I'm in New York! These guys must be good!").

Sol's friendly, unassuming manner immediately sets the guest at ease. Indeed, it probably reduces his expectations. It doesn't seem possible that anyone so nice could be so good.

As this project was progressing I spoke to many individuals who knew Sol and were familiar with his work. Without exception, they each asked, "How are you going to capture the 'Sol Stone Touch' on paper?" The answer is, ultimately, that I can't—I can talk about it, I can try to define it, I can give metaphors for it, but in the end you have to see it to appreciate it. I have decided not to worry about this too much. I have tried to describe the effects to the best of my ability without repeatedly saying, "Sol does this incredibly smoothly, you should too." Just remember, Sol does it all smoothly, softly, and naturally.

Sol has a very "behind-the-scenes" reputation. In part this is because he abandoned his semi-professional status as a performing magician when he became a practicing psychologist in 1957. Sol has also avoided lecturing for magicians. In fact he has only given five lectures in his life, and three of those were in Japan! This does not mean that Sol is not generous with his advice and time -- he freely gives of himself when asked to do so. It's just that you have to travel to New York and Reuben's Deli to meet him. One of my hopes is that the publication of this book will encourage Sol to do a few more lectures so that others can see and more fully appreciate his magic.

Many of Sol's magical creations have seen publication, in various forms and at various times, in magazines and books. Chief among these are Harry Lorayne's periodical ***Apocalypse*** and the section devoted to him in Richard Kaufman's ***CoinMagic***.

A list of Sol Stone in print can be found in the Appendix. No excuse is offered for re-describing items here, other than that it seems appropriate to gather Sol Stone's best effects in a single volume. All of the items have been completely rewritten and often incorporate new improvements and updated handlings. I have generally chosen to describe only Sol's most recent, preferred handling, leaving it to those who are interested to ferret out previous incarnations in the literature. One benefit of rewriting this material is that it allows me to extract certain basic sleights that Sol repeatedly uses (e.g., the **Pivot Vanish** and its variations) and describe them in isolation. This in turn streamlines the descriptions of many of the routines, simplifying the learning process.

Finally, there is the pleasant task of extending thanks. First, to Sol Stone himself, for trusting me to describe a lifetime of magic, for being an inspiration and role-model when it comes to things magical, and for waiting so patiently for publication. Second, to Richard Kaufman for instigating and funding the original project. Third, to the late David Alexander for rescuing the manuscript from a very dusty shelf, and to his wife, Cassidy Alexander, who has heroically assumed responsibility for its completion and whose amazing illustrations have brought Sol's magic to life. Finally, to Shannon, whose support and love I appreciate beyond words.

Stephen Hobbs
Seattle, Washington
March, 2012

Childhood Memories: 1922 - 1936

Sol Stone was born in Brooklyn, New York on November 24, 1922. He is the oldest child of Sam and Ray (Rachel) Stone, whose families came to the U.S. in the early years of this century in search of better lives for themselves and their children and to escape from the religious persecution, rape and murder then prevalent in Poland and Russia.

Sol's father worked in a hat factory. This was seasonal work and money was tight during the off-season. He studied English at night until he was fluent enough to obtain a permanent job with the Metropolitan Life Insurance Company. He was so happy to be out of the factory and working with people that he stayed with this firm until his retirement.

In 1929, when he was seven years old, Sol's father took him to see the Howard Thurston show. At this time, Thurston was the preeminent illusionist in the United States. He was pleasant, obviously enjoyed children, and made everyone in the audience feel as though he was a friend entertaining them personally. Moreover, Thurston was both well-educated and a perfectionist when it came to his art. His stage show was large and impressive. With one notable exception, however, Sol's memory of Thurston's show has dimmed over the past sixty-five years.

What Sol does remember, and it is a memory that has stayed with him his entire life, is the platform attraction in the lobby, prior to the show. There, balanced on a sword that was resting across the arms of a chair, was a women's head. As Sol and his father approached the platform, the head looked at Sol and said, "Hello, little boy. What's your name?" Sol's mouth fell open; he was so stunned that he could hardly speak. Eventually, he mustered up the courage to state his name and ask a few questions...

"How do you eat?" he asked.

And the head replied, "People feed me."

"Where do you sleep?" Sol inquired.

"In that box on the table," came the reply.

And then, "How do you go to the bathroom?"

"I can't answer that!" was the shocked response.

The talking head was the most amazing thing that Sol had ever seen. Sol's sense of wonder (as well as a rather perverse sense of humor) were ignited at that moment and are still burning.

Returning home, Sol told his mother all about the show. She suggested that the library might have some books on magic. Soon, Sol was reading everything he could find on the subject and persuading his friends and relatives to teach him whatever tricks they knew. These were mostly card tricks with a lot of counting and dealing, which perhaps accounts for his preference for coin magic and his strong dislike of convoluted card effects.

Sol slowly improved and became more and more proficient at the small effects he learned. During this period he read T. Nelson Downs' classic ***Modern Coin Manipulation***. The book made a strong impression and undoubtedly contributed to Sol's interest in coin magic. In later years, Sol met magicians who knew Downs and were able to demonstrate many effects from Downs' repertoire. Sol also read Professor Hoffman's ***Modern Magic*** and S.W. Erdnase's ***The Expert at the Card Table***, both of which contributed significantly to his understanding of magic and magicians.

Sol also saw two well-known magicians perform at Coney Island, Brooklyn, New York, during these years. Jean Hugard performed his Chinese act in his own little theater in Luna Park. Among his effects were the "Floating Ball," the "Chinese Linking Rings," the "Birth of a Pearl," and the "Chinese Water Fountains."

Al Flosso did his comedy version of the "Miser's Dream" in the World Circus Side Show. It was the first time that Sol had seen this effect performed and he fell in love with it. He told Al how much he had enjoyed his show and Al told him his philosophy of performing: "Hit 'em in the head, tie 'em in a knot, and get off."

These experiences and many more, helped to transform a childhood hobby into a life-long passion.

PRE-WORLD WAR II: 1936 - 1942

Sol's high school and early college days were during the height of the Depression. During this period, Sol used magic for two primary purposes: to make money and to meet girls. Sol admits that he was a shy teen-ager, and he used magic to break down barriers and establish conversations at high-school parties. His repertoire at that time is informative -- sponge balls (ending of course with the appearance of a ball in a girl's hand), the vanish of a small glass of water (using a rubber ball on a pull — Sol says that this got an even better reaction than the sponge balls, knife-thru-coat, and a few card tricks designed for maximum audience involvement.

Magic was also proving to be an important source of income. Sol started out doing birthday parties and performances for fraternal organizations at $3 for a twenty minute show. By comparison, during the winter Sol would have to shovel three driveways clear of snow to earn $3. Obviously, magic was the better deal. To put this in perspective, when Sol began attending Brooklyn College in 1940, he was living on a $1 a week allowance — which included 10 cents a day for trolley car fare (a nickel each way to and from school) and 35 cents a week for chocolate milk in the cafeteria (to supplement the cheese sandwich he brought from home). The extra 15 cents left over at the end of the week allowed Sol to visit the magic stores in Manhattan and look around. Obviously, there was not a lot of money to spare, so after a $3 show he was flush.

By comparison, top magical performers during the 1930's — such as Nate Leipzig, Tommy Martin, Paul Le Paul and Jack Gwynne — were making up to a $1000 a week. Not bad money, even by today's standards. There was a second tier of magicians who were pulling in roughly half of what the top performers made on a regular basis. Of course, most performers were not making anything near this amount.

On the positive side, undergraduate schooling at the public colleges at the time was considered a practical method of educating and absorbing emigrant children into the economy. Children of poor families went virtually free. Sol notes that if this were not the case most families, including his own, could not have afforded to send a student to college. As it was, Sol does not remember paying more than $30 a year in registration fees plus cost of his books. After the war, his school costs were covered by the G.I. Bill.

War Years: 1942 - 1947

Sol began serving in the Army Air Corps in January, 1943. He had enlisted the year before, when he was nineteen years old, and received his initial training as navigator. Sol's wife, however, was now pregnant, and wanting to finish his tour of duty as quickly as possible, Sol took additional training in Italy to become a Group Lead Navigator. Group Leads were trained in both navigation and radar bombardment. More importantly, Group Leads were allowed to fly many more missions than regular crew members. By flying as many missions in as short a time as possible, Sol hoped to return to the States in time for his wife's delivery.

Sol flew twenty-five heavy bombardment missions over Germany before he was shot down. He would fly two or three missions in a row — each lasting fourteen or more hours — and then would collapse for a day of rest. He had about a month remaining on his tour —five more missions — when, on his twenty-sixth mission, his plane suffered a crippling hit to its left-wing engines and main gas line. Lacking enough fuel for the return flight over the Alps and to safety in Italy, the crew decided to head east and try for an emergency landing in Soviet Russia. They almost made it.

Instead, lack of fuel forced them to crash land in a field in Hungary, which for all practical purposes represented the edge of the Eastern Front at the time. As Group Lead, it was Sol's responsibility to destroy the onboard radar so that this "secret weapon" would not fall into the hands of the Germans. With the radar destroyed, Sol and his crew beat a hasty retreat away from the plane which was awash with leaking gas, fearing that it might explode. No sooner had they made it to the cover of some nearby trees than a German search party arrived at the field and began inspecting the plane and searching for the missing crew.

Sol and his crew remained hidden in the woods. Twenty minutes after their arrival, the Germans suddenly became extremely agitated; they ran for the road and left in a hurry. Ten minutes later, a Russian Infantry Patrol was seen advancing down the road. Sol and his friends came out from the woods, waving their hands and shouting in broken Russian, "American Flyers!" The haste with which the Germans abandoned their position is perhaps understandable, given the Russian motto of "two eyes for an eye" as they moved into Germany.

The Russians welcomed the Americans. They were sent behind the front lines, and then a round-about route was arranged for their return to Italy. This began a thirty-eight day odyssey that Sol refers to as "bumming his way through the Balkans." They were sent first to Hungary, and from there to Northern Yugoslavia, across the full breadth of Romania, and into Odessa, Russia. Here they waited to be picked up by a British merchant ship — the first ship, in fact, to make it into the Black Sea after the Axis blockade of the Dardanelles was broken by the Allies. The ship returned them to Italy and Sol rejoined his flight group.

Sol had been declared missing in action after he was shot down. While he was still traversing the Balkans, his wife went into labor. She was about to deliver, still assuming the worst about her missing husband, when a neighbor rushed to the hospital with the news that a telegram had just arrived saying that Sol was alive and unhurt.

Sol learned of his son's birth by letter a few days after he returned to Italy. The entire episode received considerable attention in the newspapers — presumably with the intent of giving hope to others who had received missing-in-action telegrams.

The trip through the Balkans was, amazingly, a magically fruitful time for Sol. While it would be an exaggeration to say that "magic saved his life," his impromptu performances broke down language barriers and helped to make Sol and his crew welcome. It even earned them a meal or two in thanks. Sol actually developed his "**Fifty-One Cent**" routine during the journey. Finally, while traveling through Romania, Sol discovered that certain Romanian coins were magnetic. He saved some of these and upon his return to the States was perhaps the first, if not the only magician to have a magnetic coin. This led to the development, immediately after the war, of "**The Jarred Coin**" and other similar routines.

Sol made it back to Italy nine or ten days before the end of the war in Europe. He was not allowed to fly any more combat missions in the European Theater (if you were shot down twice over Russian controlled territory, the Soviets considered you a spy). He did volunteer to fly supply missions, and actually flew one before Germany surrendered. He then returned to the States and, after a month of leave, was sent to Florida as an Air Force radar instructor. He was about to be transferred to the Pacific when the Japanese surrendered. Sol was then transferred to Mitchell Field on Long Island, New York where he remained on active duty for two more years, mustering out in 1947.

Brooklyn College: 1947 - 1957

After he left the Air Corps, Sol finished up the remaining credits required for his Bachelor's degree. Then he started work on his doctorate, while working full-time as a placement and career counselor at Brooklyn College to support his family. Finally, after three years, having accumulated enough graduate credits, he moved into clinical psychology. Sol received his Ph.D. in 1957.

While he was at Brooklyn College, Sol worked children's birthday parties and club dates as a magician. He was registered with the Speaker's Bureau, and often worked on their behalf. After 1945, the Speakers Bureau paid $30 for a talk on career counseling and the same for a twenty-minute magic show. While Sol never considered himself a "high-priced professional" this was still nothing to sneeze at. As a placement counselor Sol was making $1860 a year, down from $448 a month as a captain on flying pay. So $30 for a twenty-minute show on Sunday morning was a substantial amount of cash.

PRIVATE PRACTICE: 1957 - PRESENT

In 1957, Sol went into private practice as a clinical psychologist while still retaining his position on the faculty at Brooklyn College. At that time Sol ceased to work as a paid performer. It was not that the extra money might not have been useful, but as Sol says, "It's not good business to let the clients see their therapist hustling for money." He continued to enjoy and practice magic, and developed many of the routines described in this text, because it had always been his hobby. After thirty-three years Sol retired from his position at Brooklyn College in 1980. He no longer maintains a private practice, but worked part-time as a consultant for the Metropolitan Life Insurance Company. Sol retired in 2000.

As a rule, Sol did not perform magic for his patients. Occasionally, however, magic proved to be a useful therapeutic tool. The most interesting — and bizarre — incident occurred in the late 1950s. A young school teacher was referred to Sol and confessed that she felt that she was going crazy. When Sol asked why, she replied that her roommate's shoes were answering questions — that is, they were moving by themselves and tapping out responses. After a few minutes of gentle questioning, Sol became convinced that the she really felt that she was losing her mind.

Sol soon deduced that the teacher's roommate — who must have been a most sadistic person — had tied a thread to her shoe and run it to the bed where she slept. She could then have the shoes tap out "yes" or "no" answers to questions. Unfortunately, the roommate never told the teacher that it was only a trick and not a supernatural manifestation. After several weeks of therapy, the schoolteacher wisely decided to leave her roommate, recognizing that the relationship was, at best, unhealthy. Sol's dilemma in the first session, however, was how to reassure his patient.

Sol's solution was to perform the **Rising Bill**. At the time, he always had the effect hooked up and ready to go, with the thread permanently attached to the bill in his wallet. He removed the bill and dropped it into a flower vase on his desk. A few magical gestures and the bill slowly rose in the vase.

"Don't be alarmed," Sol said. "This is not supernatural at all. I am making it look like something supernatural for you, arousing your sense of wonder. I am not doing it to make you crazy, but to dis-abuse you of a dangerous notion. Normally, I would do this simply to entertain you, to give you a respite from the stresses and strains of every-day life."

Although Sol never revealed the secret, the patient was immensely relieved. Sol simply persuaded her that what he was doing was a trick, as opposed to the actions of her "friend" which were done to harass or to get some sort of perverse hold on her.

Theories

In his many years as a magician, Sol has slowly developed his own ideas and theories about what constitutes good magic. Of course, this is ultimately a very personal process — each performer must decide for himself what works for him and what aspects of the art he wants to emphasize. In the final analysis, I am not sure that there are right or wrong answers or hard and fast rules in this regard. The process of choosing is as important as the choices themselves. Indeed, it is the very act of making such decisions that lies at the heart of the artistic process.

Sol's "theories" did not come to him overnight. He admits that as a kid he was no different than everyone else. In particular, like many neophyte magicians, he was obsessed by method while overlooking the importance of effect. After World War II, however, Sol's ideas about magic slowly began to crystallize, perhaps aided by his ongoing studies in psychology, and he began to realize that the reaction of the audience was more important than his own feelings concerning a trick or routine. He started making note of those effects that appeared to reap the best audience reaction and to make decisions about what type of magic he wanted to perform. As he focused more and more on what pleased and fooled an audience, he began to eliminate many of the routines in his repertoire.

Sol's choices may not be your choices but, by describing the beliefs that underlie his decisions, I hope to provide some insight why Sol performs certain effects and the manner in which he performs them.

Sol believes that the art of magic has a basic and all-important goal— to amaze and delight people. The first thing to note about this simple observation is that it focuses on the audience — the people watching the magic — and not on the performer. Forgetting the importance of the spectator or, even worse, believing that the spectator is unimportant or inconsequential, is guaranteed to lead to weak, uninteresting magic.

All of the following observations are based on Sol's conviction that the audience must come first.

The next thing to note is that the only thing the audience sees is the effect! The spectators should be completely unaware of the method or technique involved in bringing about the magic. Sol finds it somewhat bizarre in this regard that most books on magic place their emphasis almost entirely on method. True, the effect is often (but not always!) summarized at the beginning of the description; but after that it is the method that is stressed. This overemphasis on method is bound to confuse or mis-lead both novices (being exposed to magic for the first time) and experts (who observe it almost without exception in the hundreds of books on their shelves). Remember: magicians are impressed by clever methods; lay people are only interested in magical effects! Performers should keep this in mind and select only those effects which please their audience.

This is not to say that method or technique is unimportant. As Jon Racherbaumer has pointed out, "method affects effect" — which is simply a pithy way of saying that it is important to have good technique and to use soundly constructed routines. But we must never forget the ultimate goal: to entertain the audience.

Sol is fond of using Max Malini as an example in this regard. Malini would take the simplest and most direct effect possible (one that any audience could follow) and he would use the most straightforward method (executed with superb timing and misdirection) and it would look like a miracle because he was always emphasizing and selling effect.

In his effort to emphasize the effect and to entertain the audience, Sol often invents little stories around which the magic is woven. Sol's stories are not long, involved presentations. Rather, they are a hook or brief statement that serves two purposes. First, the story moves the effect out of the realm of simple puzzles or tricks. Second, the story draws the audience into the performance and prevents them from being passive observers.

Ideally, the story allows the audience to become actively involved, even if in only a small way, in the performance. In Sol's words, "You invite them to step onto your magic carpet and fly away with you to magic land — even if it's only for thirty seconds."

Sol notes that when you are developing presentations of any sort, it is important to link them to who you are at your current stage of life. Sol's presentations as a shy teenager trying to pick up girls at a party are obviously different than the presentations he uses today. If Sol tried the "holding hand" presentation he used as a teen-ager he would be considered a "dirty old man" instead of a "romantic adolescent."

Related to the issue of method vs. effect is the question of effort. Sol believes that many magicians spoil the effect and convey an undue emphasis on method because they work too hard. Their technique is obvious because every step is a struggle that is visible to the audience. Worse, this vast expenditure of effort is often wasted on weak or trivial effects. There is simply no excuse for magicians to rely on weak effects when there are so many good ones to choose from. Sol is fond of saying: "If you labor like a mouse and give birth to an elephant, it's magic; but if you labor like an elephant and give birth to a mouse, it's tragic." The moral: If you don't want to do tragic magic, avoid laboring like an elephant.

Sol contends that a magician has to do things that are visually magical. For Sol, if the effect lacks a visual component, it is simply not magic. To help explain his thinking, Sol uses a metaphor employed by J.W. Sullivan, a well-known mathematician, who wrote a biography of Beethoven. Sullivan argued that music transfers the composer's emotions to the listener directly, without the intercession of thought. The music travels "through the ears and directly to the heart."

Sol believes that magic should arouse the audience's emotions in the same way — except that the input is through the eyes and not the ears. The logical extension of this theory (one with which not everyone will agree) is that certain effects are not inherently magical. For example, Sol believes that the term "mental magic" is something of an oxymoron. Mental magic may be intellectually stimulating, but (with the possible exception of telekinetic effects) it is not visually interesting. Thus, for Sol, it does not really qualify as true magic.

Of course, Sol would be the first to admit that strong personalities can overcome this deficiency and perform entertaining mental magic. Its just that they start at a disadvantage.

Unlike many magicians, Sol does not believe in repeating an effect. That is, Sol prefers effects in which the production, vanish, transportation, or transposition happens once only. He believes that the law of diminishing returns sets in after the first effect. The biggest surprise happens at the moment the effect first occurs. Subsequent repetitions of the effect are anti-climatic, even when accomplished by different methods. It takes a very entertaining performer to keep an audience interested when the same effect is repeated three or four times.

Maskelyne believed that a weak effect could be strengthened through repetition. This might be so on stage or in the hands of the right performer. Sol, however, feels that the better course is to choose not to do weak effects at all, and as a result free you from the compulsion to repeat them. Thus, Sol no longer does **Coins Thru Table** or the classic **Flying Eagles** effect — every count and display has become, in Sol's mind, unnecessarily repetitious.

Thus, for example, in the effect where Sol breaks a silver dollar into two fifty-cent pieces Sol usually stops at that point. He may then use the two fifty-cent pieces in another routine.

Later he might take the two coins, rub them together, and produce the silver dollar — bringing him back to the starting point. In other words, Sol would rather do three apparently separate effects than repeat the same effect three times.

Of course, there are exceptions to this general rule. If you have charm and strength of personality of, say, a Daryl Martinez, you can repeat an effect two or three times without boring audience. But most of us do not have either the personality or acting ability to carry this off.

Sometimes the plot or story allows for the repetition of the effect. Thus, in Sol's "**The Chaperone**" a ball jumps from the pocket to the hand three times in accordance to the plot of a simple story. Likewise, Sol believes that the underlying concept of the classic effect "**Sympathetic Coins**", is a "gathering of the clans" and that the effect is so quick and visual that it can safely be repeated until all the coins have gathered in one place.

It is critically important to learn whenand for how long to perform. A little bit of magic well done, when the audience is interested in seeing it, goes a long way to eliminating boredom and stimulating playfulness and creativity. Even a good magician, however, can sour his family and friends by giving them too much of a good thing. Sol is a firm believer of performing only when coaxed to do so, doing a couple or three short effects, and stopping.

Amateur performers usually seek many different tricks to show the same audience — that is, to show the same small circle of family, friends, or fellow magicians. As a result, they don't do any of their effects really well, primarily for lack of practice. Professional performers, on the other hand, usually show the same trick to many different audiences, allowing them to smooth out the rough spots and present them entertainingly and smoothly. Sol strongly believes that amateurs who emulate professionals by limiting their repertoires and seeking different audiences serve the art of magic well.

Card Routines

Today, at Reuben's Deli in New York, where Sol can be found most every Saturday, magicians chuckle when Sol brings out a deck of cards. They are so used to seeing Sol perform coin magic, that a card trick is simply incongruous. In his early days, however, Sol frequently performed card tricks. He still handles playing cards with a soft and gentle touch that many "card workers" would do well to emulate. Included here are some of Sol's favorite card routines. Unlike the coin effects described later in this book—where I have been at pains to detail all necessary sleights—in describing these effects I will assume some knowledge of basic card technique.

HOLD MY HAND

This routine was developed by Sol in his teens with a very specific goal in mind: to give him the opportunity to hold hands with a pretty girl. Sol does not claim originality for the method. The routine combines ideas from two different tricks that Sol learned independently, although he no longer recalls who taught him the specific effects.

This is almost self-working. All you must do is secretly glimpse and remember the card second from the face of the deck (the force card). At the start of the performance, you can casually execute a simple false shuffle that keeps the bottom two cards in place.

Turn to the spectator who is the object of your desire (we will assume a girl) and ask for her help in the experiment. State that you want her to have a small packet of cards and ask her to say "stop" at any point as you slowly riffle up the outer end of the deck with your right first finger. She can stop you at any time, but you emphasize a "small packet" because the trick will move faster if she has only ten to fifteen cards. Give the spectator all the cards below the point at which she stopped you.

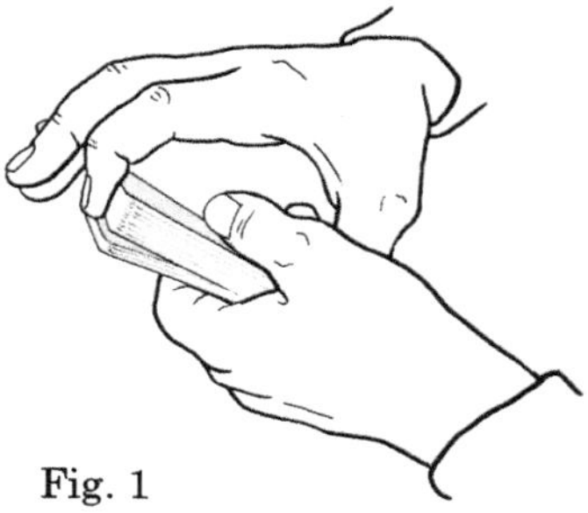
Fig. 1

Say, "*I want to have as many cards as you have. So would you count your cards to the table, one at a time, and I will count an equal number of cards from the top of the deck.*" As the spectator counts the cards in her packet, you count one card from the top of the deck for each of her cards. You now have two equal packets of cards, but this fact is actually irrelevant to the working of the trick. The sole purpose of counting the cards to the table was to reverse the order of the spectator's cards, bringing the force card second from the top of her packet.

Place the balance of the deck aside and pick up your packet from the table. Say, "*Is there any way for me to know what cards you have or for you to know what cards I have?*" The spectator responds in the negative. "*Just to be sure, take the top card of your packet and push it into the center of your cards.*"

Here you use your packet to demonstrate what she is to do, taking the top card and burying it in the center of your packet. "*Now do the same with the bottom card of your packet.*"

Again, you demonstrate by taking the bottom card and burying it in the center of your packet while the spectator does the same with the bottom card of her packet. This, of course, brings the force card to the top of the spectator's packet.

"*Perfect! Now just take a peek at the top card of your packet and memorize it. I will do the same with my top card.*" Here you pretend to look at and memorize the top card of your packet—there is no need to actually remember the card. "*And then give your cards a good shuffle.*" Suit your actions to your words, shuffling your packet while the spectator shuffles her cards.

"*Great, now let's trade packets.*"

Exchange packet with the spectator. "*I want you to look at my cards and see if there is any way you can tell what card I chose.*"

As you speak, fan the spectator's original packet so the faces are towards you. Casually glance the cards and quickly determine how many cards are above the force card. This must take only a moment—it's one reason why you want to work with a fairly small number of cards—and should appear as if you are simply demonstrating what you want the spectator to do. Let's assume the force card is fifth from the top of the packet.

The spectator will admit she has no idea what card you looked at. Say *"Just like you have no idea what card I chose, I have no idea what card you chose."*

Have the spectator replace your original packet in the deck. Leave her packet face down on the table.

Ribbon spread the deck face up across the table. Take the spectator's wrist—this is the moment Sol lived for—and have her point her first finger towards the indices of the cards. Slowly move her hand back and forth over the cards. You will now gently lower her finger, one at a time, onto three different cards.

The first card is the same suit as the force card, the second card is the same value as the force card, and the third card is equal to the number of cards above the force card in the spectator's packet.

Sol has the spectator find all three cards without revealing their function. He then lets go of the spectator's hand and points to each card in turn, stating, for example, that the first card indicates that the selection was a spade, the second card indicates that it had a value of seven, and the third card indicates that it is five cards down from the top of the packet. The spectator confirms that her card was the seven of spades. Have her count down five cards in the packet to find the selection.

Sometimes, Sol would involve a second spectator in the selection process and only use the girl for the final three-card revelation. Done properly, this simple effect not only seems completely impossible, but nicely involves the spectator in the "magical moment." Of course, the audience "knows" that you are really responsible, but they appreciate your willingness to "share" your power.

THE POWER of ESP

This is another effect from Sol's teen years in which he enlisted the aid of a female spectator. Before his performance, he would invite a pretty girl aside and ask for her help in a magic trick. All she had to do was to memorize the following simple exchange:

Sol: "*You have the power.*"
Girl: "*What power?*"
Sol: "*The power of ESP.*"
Girl: "*Who me?*"
Sol: "*Let's see.*"

When it came time to perform, Sol would talk for a few minutes about ESP and would then look around the room as if searching for a potential subject. He would fix his attention on the girl, approach her, and initiate the dialogue outlined above.

Having spoken their lines, Sol would have three different spectators each select a card. The three cards would be returned to different parts of the deck and controlled to the bottom. Sol originally developed his own unique method of controlling the selected cards to the bottom of the deck, but he admits that his handling has been superseded by modern techniques. He now uses Vernon's Simple Shift to bring the selections to the bottom with a single cut. After the cards have been controlled to the bottom, you can give the deck a casual false shuffle, keeping the selections in place.

Spread the deck between your hands, get a left fourth finger break above the three selections, and close the spread. Turn to the female and ask her, as you slowly spread through the face-down deck to touch any three cards. As each card is touched it is outjogged from the spread for half its length. Close the spread into the left hand, leaving the three cards outjogged and maintaining the left fourth finger break.

Now comes a move that by today's standards may seem "old hat." Remember, however, that Sol developed this in the late 30's—it really was "ahead of its time." The left hand momentarily holds all the cards while the right hand regrips the deck in Hindu Shuffle position, thumb at the inner left corner, first and second fingers at the inner right corner.

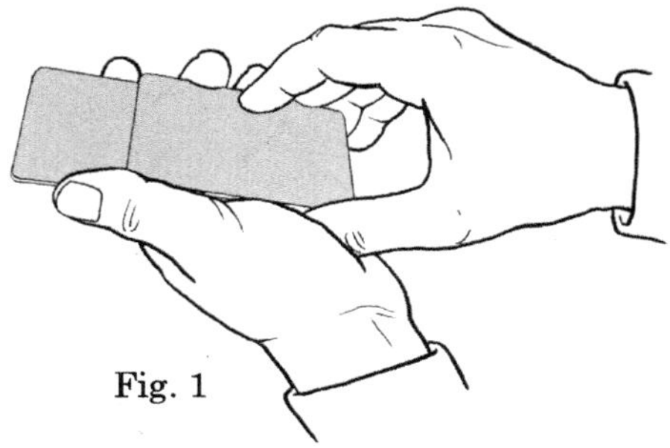
Fig. 1

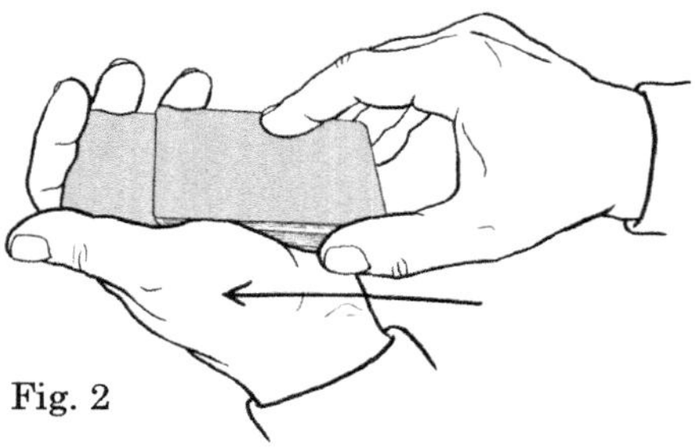
Fig. 2

The right hand holds the deck in position as the left hand moves forward, secretly carrying the three cards beneath the break flush with the outjogged cards.

The outjogged cards are stripped from the deck with the left hand and the three selections are secretly loaded beneath them. The left fourth finger maintains a break between the selections and indifferent cards.

Fig. 3
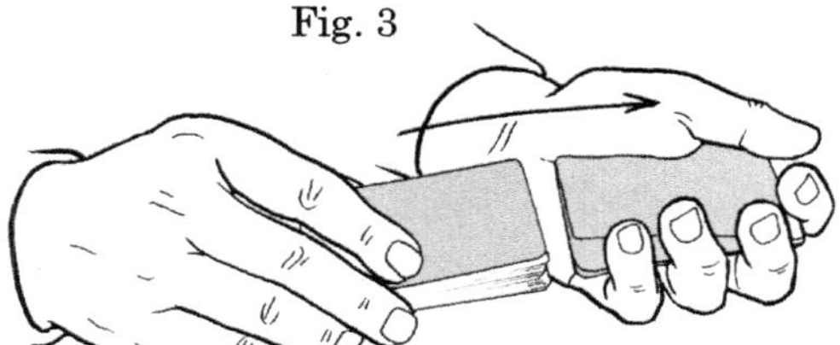

So far the action has been similar to the Vernon Strip-Out Addition. The question now becomes what to do with the three extra cards?

Here is Sol's solution. As soon as the cards have been stripped clear, the right hand rotates the deck until it is perpendicular to the cards in the left hand. The outer end of the deck is then tapped twice against the inner end of the left-hand cards, squaring them.

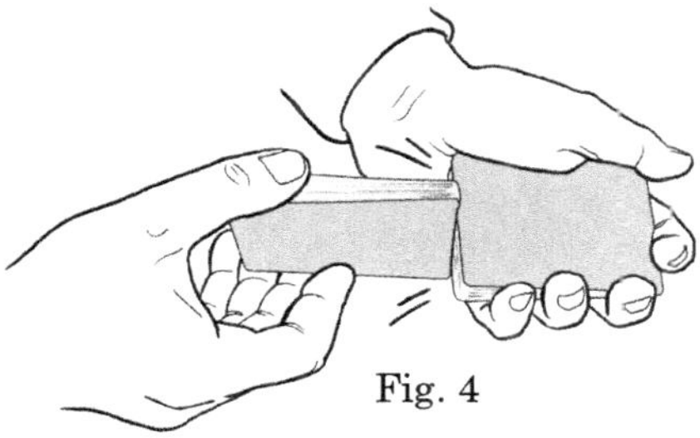

Fig. 4

The left fourth finger break is maintained as this is done.

Fig. 5

In a continuing action, the left hand moves directly underneath the deck. Without pausing, the three indifferent cards above the break are unloaded onto the bottom of the deck.

The left hand then moves out from beneath the deck and the end-squaring action is immediately repeated. Done properly, the unloading action blends into invisibility. Even done poorly, it looks as if you were going to place the cards onto the bottom of the deck and then simply changed your mind.

Set the deck aside and spread the three cards in your left hand. Ask the spectators to name their selections and one-by-one you reveal that your assistant was able to find them through "the power of her mind alone."

WHAT IT TAKES TO MAKE IT TO THE TOP

This is Sol's elegant and straight-forward **Ambitious Card** routine. It has only three phases and is performed to a simple story. Sol normally performs the effect impromptu, but a gaffed variation is outlined below.

Start by saying, "*When you are second in command of a small family business. . .*" Turn the top card of the deck face up in a manner duplicating that of your double lift. Display the card, turn it face down, and then openly place it second from the top of the deck. ". . . *it's relatively easy to get to the top.*" Execute a double lift, turning the two cards over as one, showing that the card has returned to the top. Flip the double face down.

Continue, "*When you are a middle manager in a large national corporation, it takes time, talent, and a little bit of luck to make it to the top.*" Take the top card, apparently the selection, and place it, still face down, in the middle of the deck. Square the cards, pause a few moments, and then turn the top card face up to reveal that the selection has again traveled to the top.

"*But if you begin on the bottom of huge multi-national corporation. . .*" Take the face-up selection and place it, still face up, on the bottom of the deck. As you speak, side steal the face-up selection into right-hand classic palm. Wave your right hand over the deck, secretly depositing the face-up selection on top of the deck causing the selection to appear in the traditional color-change fashion. ". . . *it takes time, talent, luck, and even magic to make it to the top.*"

That's it, short, simple, and to the point. Sol often asks card workers to "show him their favorite **Ambitious Card** routine." His biggest complaint is that most of the routines he sees are too long, overly repetitious, and lack motivation. Not wanting to fall into this same trap, he devised this very direct routine.

The gaffed handling makes use of a double-backed card and is probably familiar to those who have studied the works of Dai Vernon and S. Leo Horowitz. The double-backed card begins second from the top of the deck.

The top card is turned face up, displayed, and then openly inserted face down second from the top. A double turnover is executed to show that the selection has returned to the top of the deck. Thanks to the double-backer, the selection can immediately be pushed off the deck and taken in the right hand, where it is clearly seen to be a single card. The selection is placed face up on the deck, a double turnover is performed and the selection (really the double backer) is apparently placed into the center of the deck. The top card is then turned face up to reveal the selection back on top of the deck.

The final phase—utilizing the side steal—is identical to that described above.

ANOTHER MAN'S GAME

This is a four-phase, "**Three Card Monte**" effect. The routine is done completely "in the hands"—there is no Monte Toss. The first phase is a "fake" that sets up the action of the subsequent phases. The second phase uses a unique and deceptive move developed by Trevor Lewis. The third phase uses an improvement on that move devised by Ken Krenzel. The final phase employs Sol's own variation of the Lewis move. Sol developed this after World War II. Before 1940, Sol performed a more standard "**Three Card Monte**" routine.

You will need three cards of the traditional Monte pattern—two black aces and a red queen, for example. The cards are not bent or crimped in any way. You will also need a standard, trombone-style paper clip. Sol's patter for the routine revolves around a cheater's advice to his son about the perils of gambling. You can use this as a starting point or devise your own presentation.

First Phase: The red queen is between the two black aces. Hold the three cards face up in your right hand, spread to the right. With the left hand, grasp the two lowermost cards of the spread, fingers above and thumb below. Separate the hands for about an inch, the right hand taking the uppermost ace of the spread and the left hand taking the queen and lowermost ace. In a smooth, continuing action both hands turn their respective cards face down.

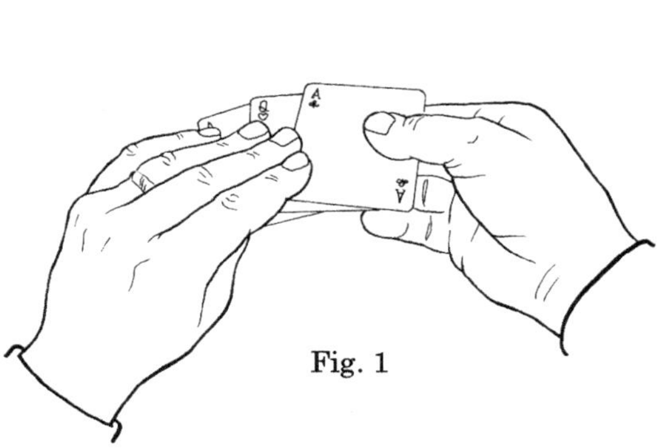

Fig. 1

The left-hand cards rotate away from you and the right-hand card rotates toward you. As soon as the cards are face down, place the right-hand card beneath the left-hand cards, creating a three-card spread.

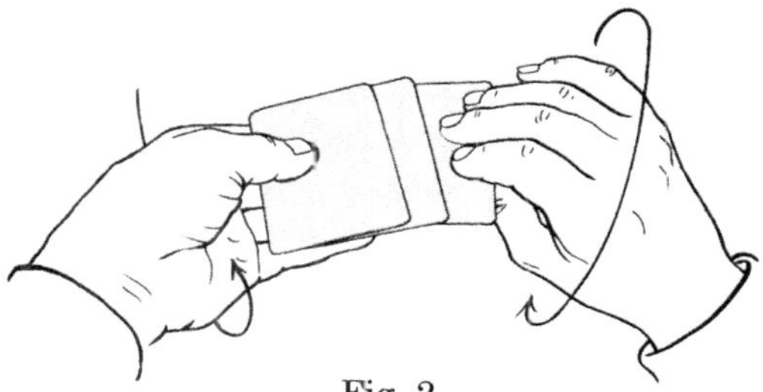
Fig. 2

You have simply turned the cards face down and it should be clear to the audience that the queen is still in the center of the spread.

Re-grasp the spread with the right hand and reverse count the cards into the left hand, keeping them in a fanned condition. This of course, keeps the queen between the two aces. Remove the center card with your right hand and turn it face up to reveal the queen. This is the "come on" in which you establish the action and in which the potential victim is led to believe he can win. Replace the queen face-down between the aces.

Second Phase : Square the spread and flip it face up in the left hand. Spread the cards to the right and take them in the right hand. The left hand grasps the lower two cards, fingers above and thumb below, as before (see Figure 3).

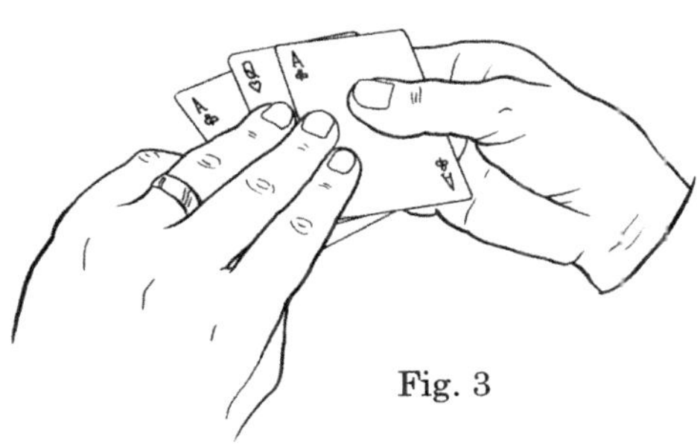
Fig. 3

Separate the hands and turn the cards face down. This time, however, as the left-hand cards are turned over, the left thumb pushes the card it is touching (an ace) to the right as the fingers pull the card they are touching (the queen) to the left. The smaller action of the thumb and fingers is completely hidden by the larger action of the hand as it turns the cards over.

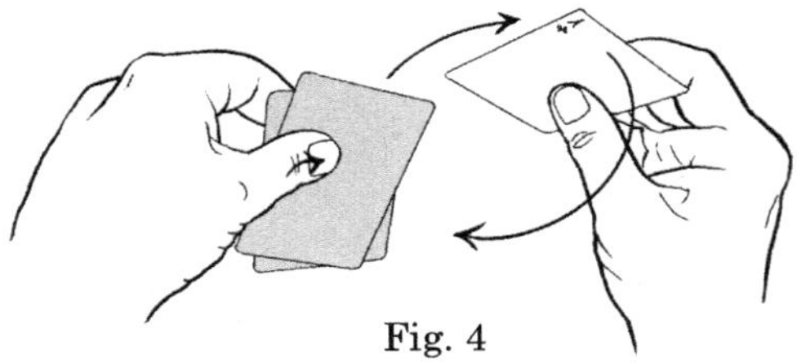

Fig. 4

In a continuing action, replace the right-hand card ***on top of*** the left-hand cards, stepped to the right. Although this sequence appears identical to the first phase, the queen is now the lowermost card of the spread. This is the **Trevor Lewis Twist Turn** move and is unbelievably deceptive when done smoothly.

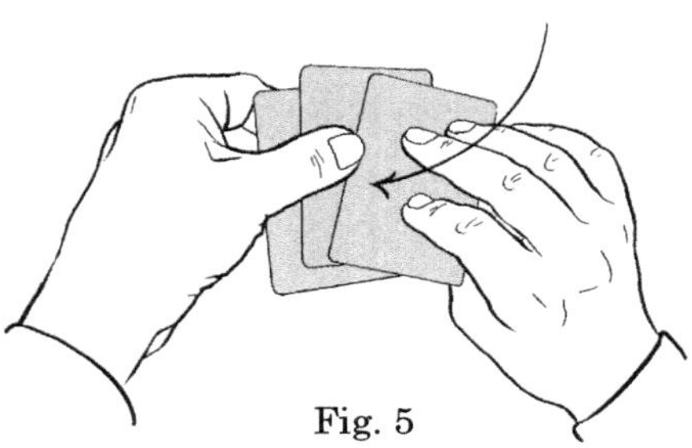

Fig. 5

The audience should still believe that the queen is the center card of the three. Slowly remove the center card and turn it face up to reveal a black ace. Sol, speaking as the gambler talking to his son, says, "*Never gamble with strangers.*" Turn the black ace face down and place it beneath the other two cards (this returns the queen to the center of the packet). Close the spread into your left hand.

Third Phase: Flip the cards face up in the left hand, spread them, and take them in the right hand. Openly outjog the queen for half its length.

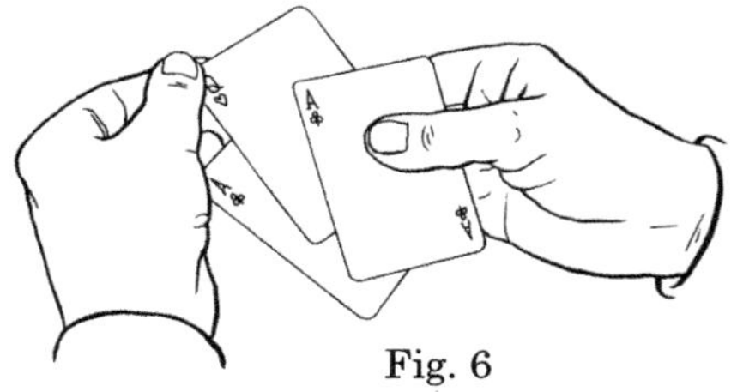

Fig. 6

You will now do the **Twist Turn** move exactly as described above, except that the queen is outjogged. Grasp the two lowermost cards with the left hand, fingers above and thumb below. Separate the hands and turn the cards face down. As you do so, the left fingers pull the queen to the left and the left thumb pushes the ace to the right. This switches the cards, leaving the face-down ace diagonally outjogged off the outer right corner of the face-down queen.

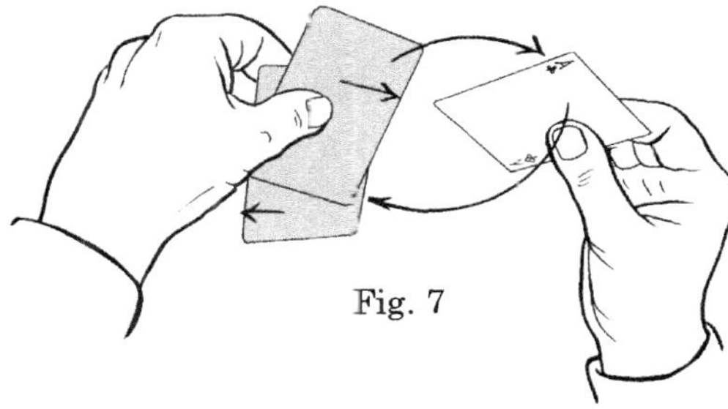

Fig. 7

Replace the right-hand card onto the spread, leaving the center card outjogged. Although there is a discrepancy in this action, the optical illusion created by the outjogged card is incredible. There seems to be no possibility of losing track of the outjogged queen.

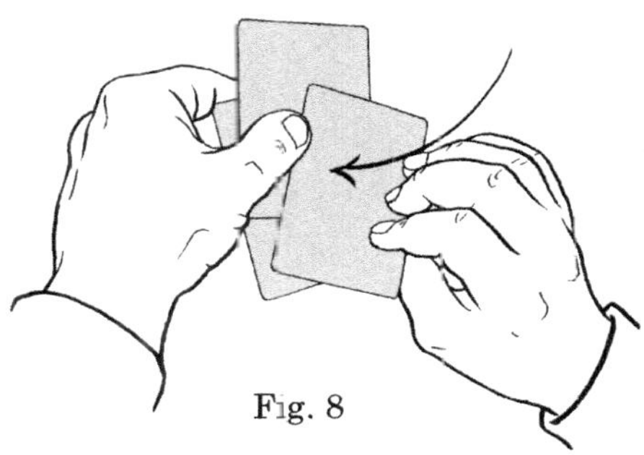

Fig. 8

Remove the outjogged card and turn it face up to reveal a black ace. Sol says, "*Never try to beat a man at his own game.*" Flip the black ace face down and drop it onto the left-hand cards. Square the packet in your left hand.

Phase Four: Flip the cards face up in the left hand and spread them. This time the queen will be the uppermost card of the spread

Pick up the paper clip with the right hand and slide it onto the center of the right long side of the queen. The smaller loop of the clip should be facing you. Don't push the clip flush, leave it sticking out for about half its length.

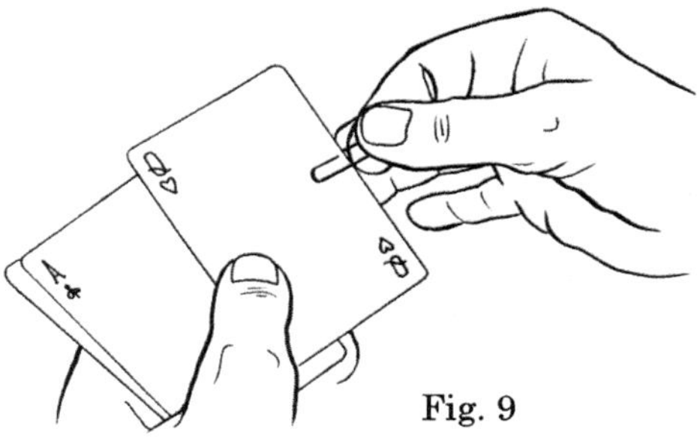

Fig. 9

Slide the center card, Ace of Clubs, to the right, its right long side just slipping between the queen and the clip – (Figure 10 is an exposed view.).

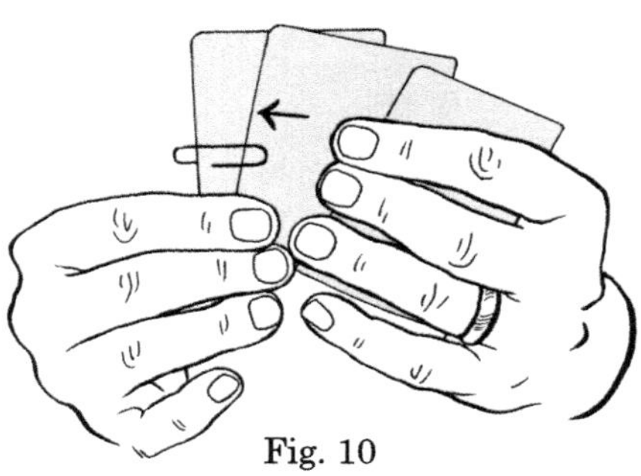

Fig. 10

Remove the lowermost Ace and transfer it sidejogged to the right on top so that it covers the clip. (Figure 11 is an X-Ray view.)

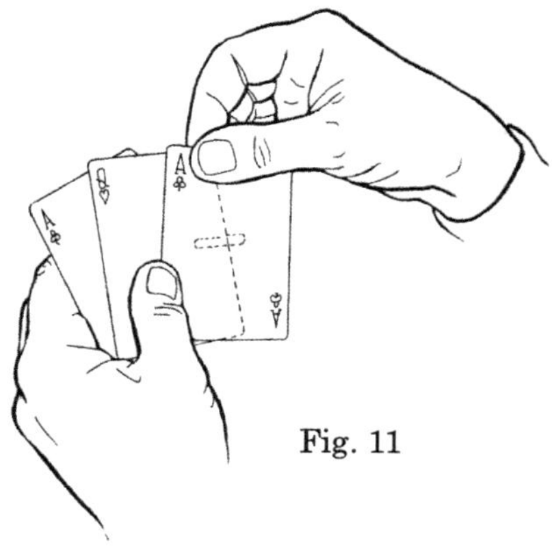

Fig. 11

Grasp the spread in the right hand. Now do the Twist Turn move exactly as described in phase two. The paper clip will be automatically transferred to the ace as you do the move. Moreover, as the backs of the cards come into view, the audience sees the clip—which has already been transferred to the indifferent card!

Fig. 12

Reverse count the cards as before, bringing the clip clearly into view. Place the cards in a row on the table or spread them widely between your hands. Have the spectator take the clipped card and turn it face up to reveal that once again the "sure winner" is a loser. To conclude, Sol says, "*Never trust anyone—not even your own father.*"

If the paper clip does not slide smoothly from one card to the other, try separating the loops of the clip slightly. You should be able to execute the **Twist Turn** move while the clip is on the cards with no extra effort or motion.

SS Cards to Pocket

Sol developed this very early in his magical career after being given a copy of T. Nelson Downs' ***The Art of Magic*** in 1940. Downs' "**Ten Cards to Pocket**" effect was the starting point for Sol's routine. Over time, Sol slowly modified the effect, changing some of the palms, adding ideas from Tommy Martin, and incorporating his own **Soft False Count** (described at the end of the routine). Even though this effect is no longer in his active repertoire, Sol still executes it with an amazing lightness of touch.

Before beginning, secretly place three cards in your right trouser pocket. At the start of the routine, Sol generally showed this pocket to be "empty" using the "top-of-the-pocket" dodge familiar to, if rarely used by, most magicians. Pick up the deck in the left hand and apparently count off ten cards into the right hand. In reality, execute the **Soft False Count**, holding back the third, fifth, and seventh cards. This leaves you with seven cards (apparently ten) in the right hand. Set the deck aside.

Fig. 1

Say, "*Each time I snap these cards, one card travels up my arm, across my chest, and down into my pocket. Watch.*" As you speak, trace the imaginary path of the card with your right hand. The cards are in your left hand. Snap the packet with your left thumb, follow the imaginary path of the card with your eyes, and then reach into your right trouser pocket and remove one card. Display the card and drop it to the table.

"If I snap the cards twice, two cards jump to my pocket." Snap the packet a two times, reach into your pocket, and remove the second and third cards one at a time. "*Three from ten leaves seven cards.*" Slowly count the cards one at a time from the left to the right hand. Here you are mimicking the actions of the **Soft False Count**, but because you actually have seven cards, the count looks exceedingly fair.

As the cards are counted into the right hand, secretly injog the third card from the top of the packet. You will now Top Palm the three cards marked off by the injog into the right hand. Obviously, there are a lot of methods for accomplishing this. Here is the method Sol devised during the early 1940s...

The cards are being held loosely in the left hand. As the right hand reaches over from above to square them, the right thumb lifts up on the injogged card. The inner ends of the three top cards are raised about half an inch (the outer ends remain flush with the packet) and the right hand grips all the cards in what today we refer to as Biddle Grip. The right fingers are at the outer end of the packet and the right thumb is at the inner end. The thumb is holding the break between the top three cards and the balance of the packet.

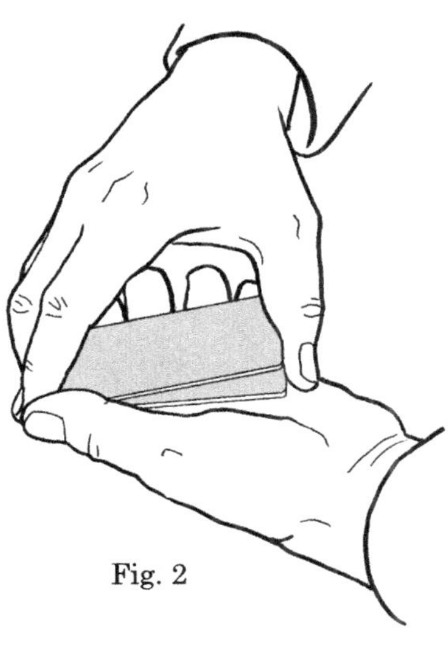

Fig. 2

This allows the left hand to move to a new position. The left hand slides inward and regrips the packet so that the left thumb rests on the left side of the cards near the inner corner. The left first second and third fingers are on the right side of the packet with the third finger resting near the inner corner.

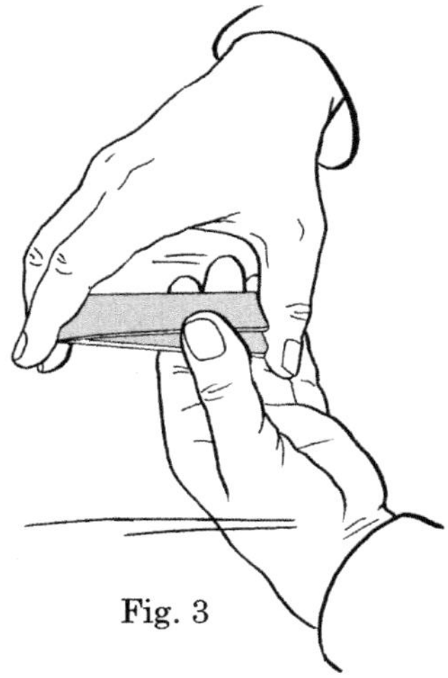
Fig. 3

The tips of the left thumb and fingers should be touching the edges of the top three cards. The palm of the left hand is not touching the face of the packet.

To palm the cards, the right hand lowers the bulk of the packet onto the left palm. At the same time, the left fingers and thumb push the top three cards upward, the left hand moving slightly forward as this takes place. Almost automatically, the cards pop up into right-hand Full Palm.

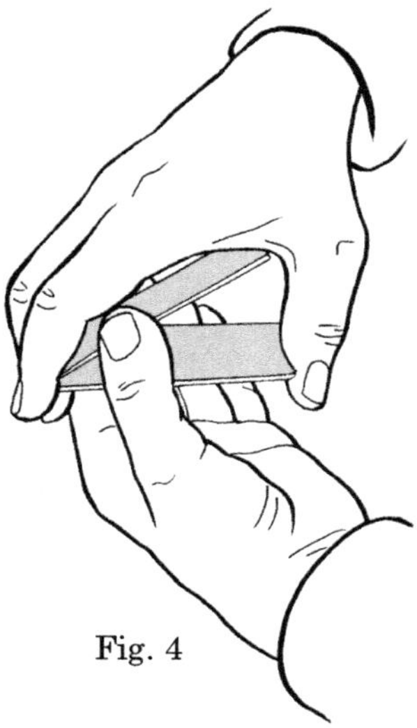
Fig. 4

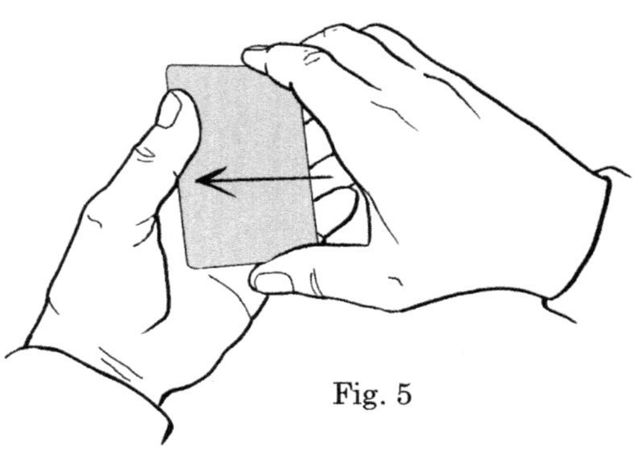
Fig. 5

The left hand pulls the lower packet to the left.

As he palms the cards, Sol makes a slight turn to his left. The packet (minus the three palmed cards) is taken into the left hand and given a snap. The right hand reaches into the pocket, leaves two of the cards behind, removes a single card, and tosses it to the table. The packet is given another snap and the (clearly empty) right hand removes another card from the pocket.

There are now four cards left in the packet. If you are working directly with a spectator, say, "*Five cards from ten leaves five cards to go.*" You might even do a casual **Soft False Count**, miscounting the four cards as five.

Hand the packet to the spectator and ask her to wave it toward your pocket. Reach in, remove the card, and toss it to the table. Finally, have the spectator count the four remaining cards into your hand. If a spectator is not within easy reach, simply snap the packet and remove the card from your pocket.

There are now four cards remaining. Take these in your right hand and fan them so that the faces are toward the audience. "*Four cards left.*" (Name the cards.) "*Please tell me your favorite card.*"

Whichever card is named, you casually transfer to the face of the fan. Square the fan, still face up, in your right hand. As you transfer the packet to your left hand, the named card is secretly stolen into the right hand using the **Lowey Palm**. This palm is probably best known to magicians from its appearance (although uncredited) in Dai Vernon's "**Travelers**" routine which appeared in the ***Stars of Magic***.

Here is a rather abbreviated description of the move in this context -- The packet is squared so that it is considerably forward in the right hand. The right inner corner of the packet should be resting on the base of the right thumb. This is the pivot point, the point at which the card will rotate. When the card is in Full Palm, the position of this corner will not have changed. The right thumb lies across the top of the packet.

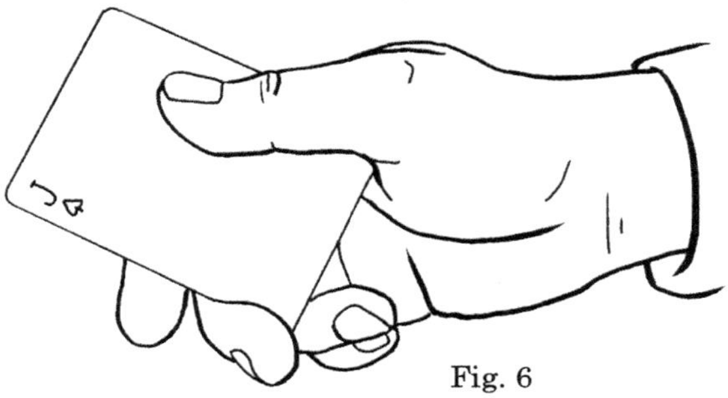

Fig. 6

As the body makes a small turn to the left, the cards are transferred from the right to the left hand. At the same time, the right thumb pivots the named card into Full Palm.

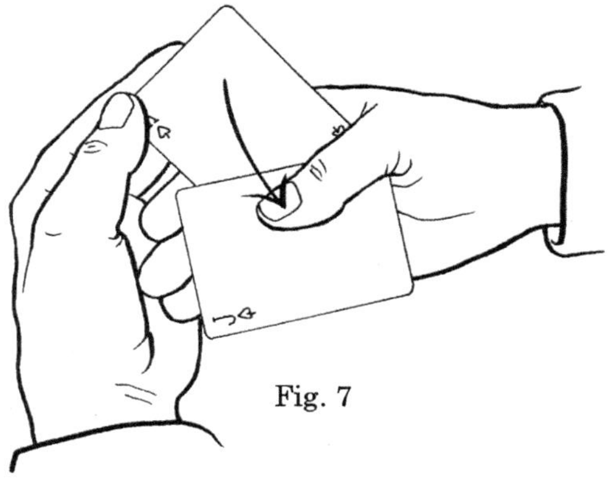

Fig. 7

Any motion caused by this action is screened by the back of the left fingers as they take the packet.

Fig. 8

Fig. 9

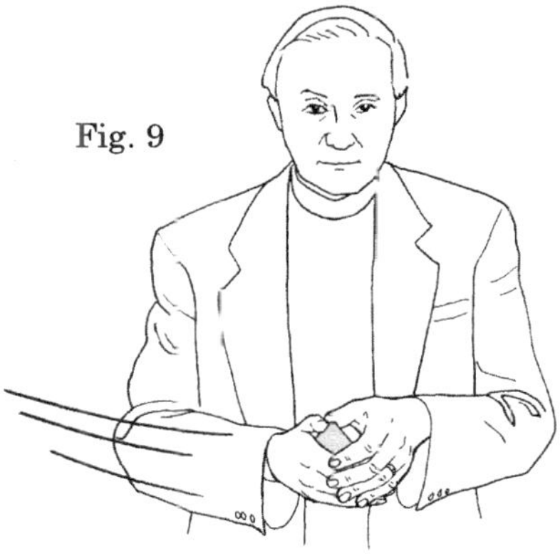

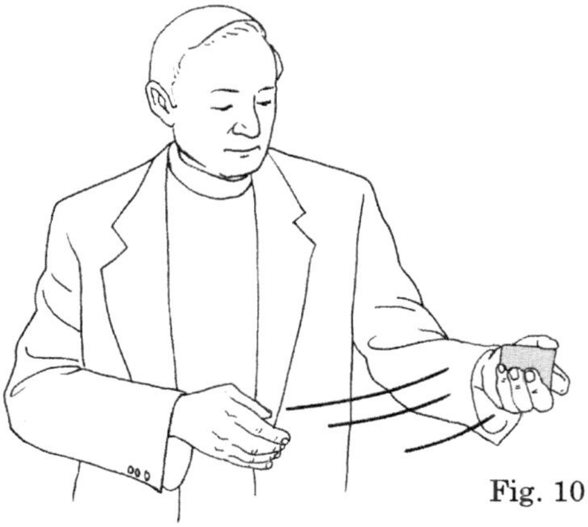

Fig. 10

Also, it is important to tilt the outer end of the packet slightly upwards, moving the named card out of the audience's line-of-sight.

The right hand immediately drops to your side—your attention must be focused on the left-hand packet. Give the packet a snap (still keeping its face away from the audience) and then reach into your pocket and remove the named card. As this card is being displayed, casually turn the cards in the left hand face down. Drop the named card to the table.

Transfer the three cards to the right hand and immediately back palm them. You now vanish these cards using the classic card manipulator's Back Palm.

This move is so well known that I'm not going to describe it.

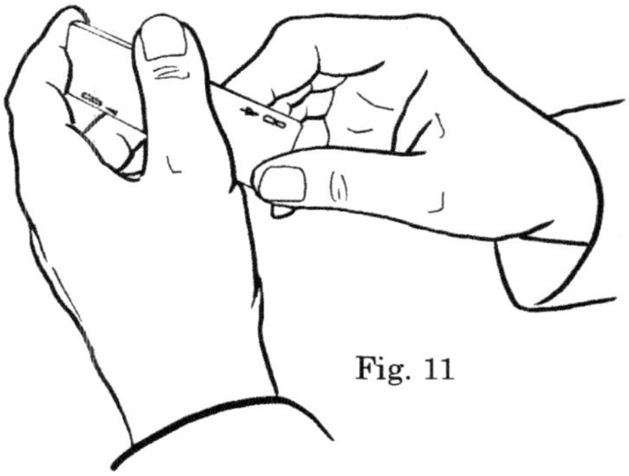

Fig. 11

Sol uses his left hand to screen the action of the Back Palm-- it appears as if he simply presses the cards between his hands—and under the cover of this action the three cards are Back Palmed.

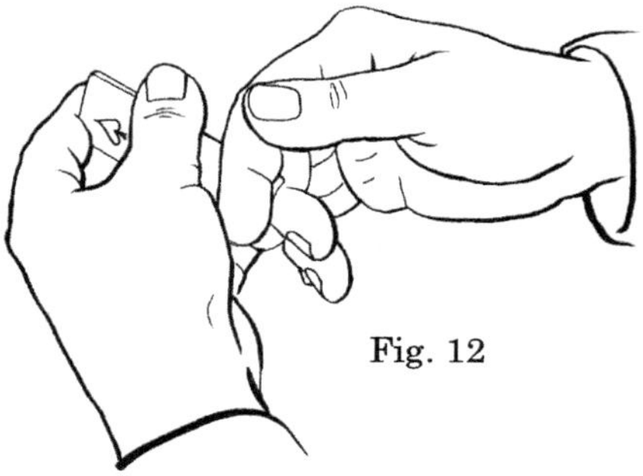

Fig. 12

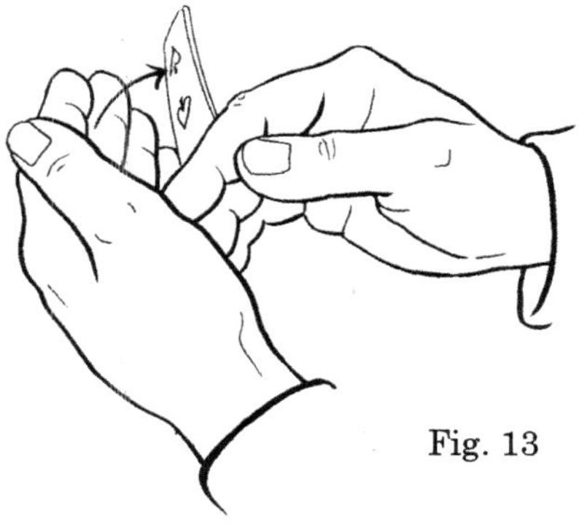

Fig. 13

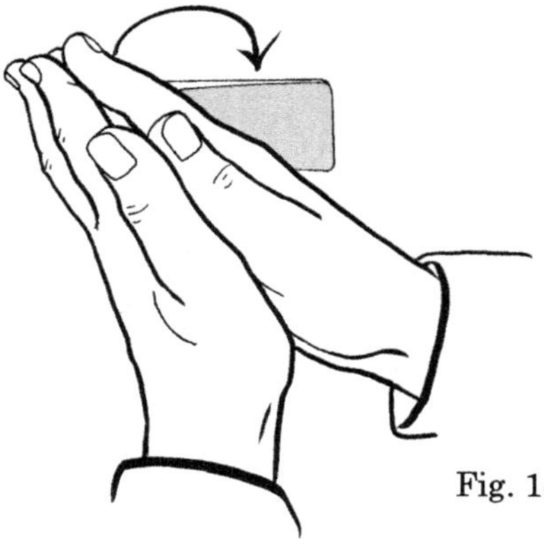

Fig. 14

This is followed immediately with an upwards tossing gesture during which the palms of both hands are seen empty.

Fig. 15

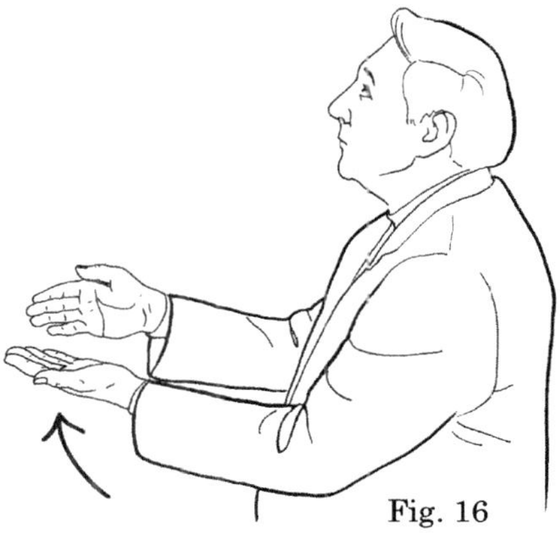

Fig. 16

Pause for a beat, then reach down behind your right leg with your right hand and produce the three cards in a small fan.

Fig. 17

The three cards are now apparently transferred to the left hand, from where they vanish. The right hand then reaches into the pocket and removes the three cards. Again, a card manipulation sequence is responsible for the vanish.

The cards are held in a fan at the right fingertips. Curl the right hand inward at the wrist so that the outer edges of the cards point toward the body. Bring the fingers of the left hand against the lower edge of the lowermost card of the fan.

Fig. 18

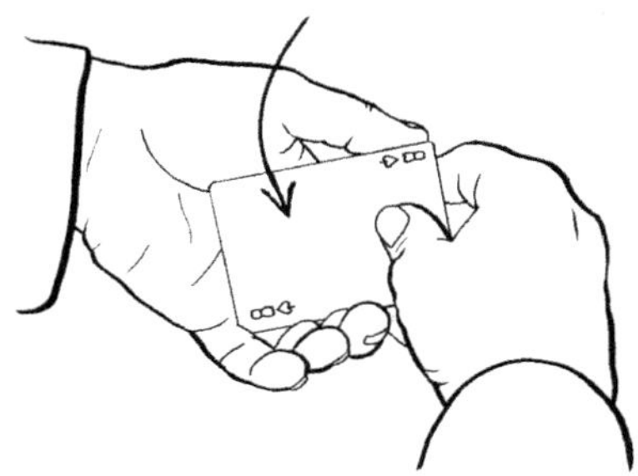

Fig. 19

Square the fan against the left fingers and then allow the packet to fall flat against the left palm.

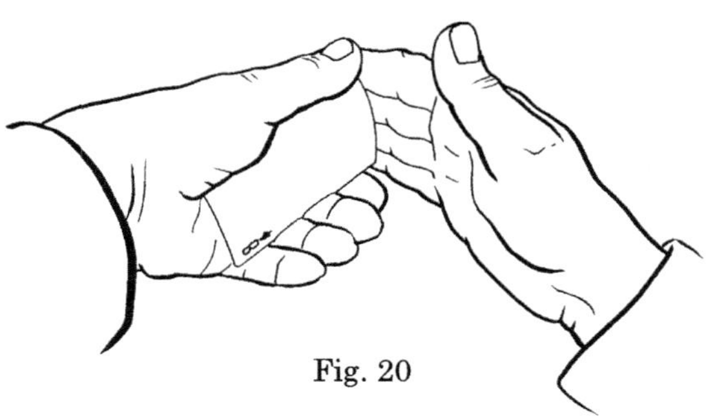

Fig. 20

As the cards fall flat, the right fingers move in front of the packets outer edge, screening it momentarily from view.

At that precise instant, the right fingers push down on the outer end of the packet, snapping it up into right Full Palm.

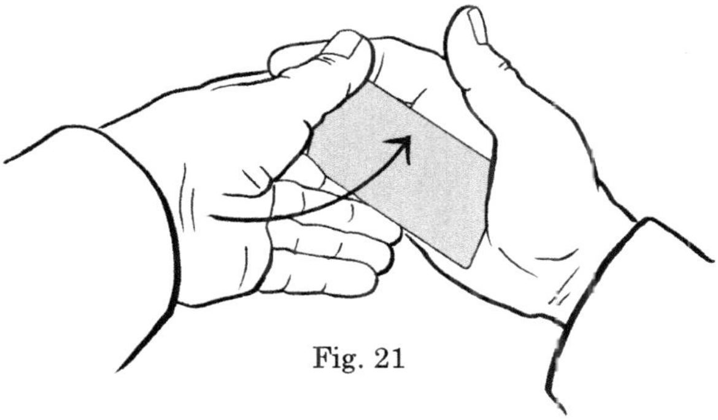

Fig. 21

Audience views -- Figures 22, 23

Fig. 22

The left hand immediately turns palm down and moves away as if holding the cards in a cramped palm.

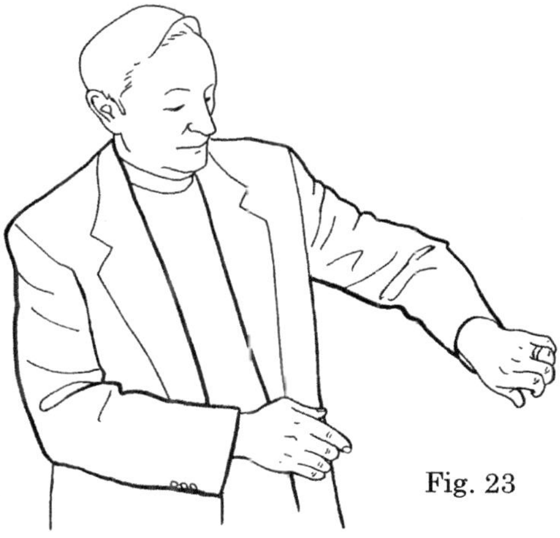

Fig. 23

The right hand falls naturally to the side. Crumple the left fingers and make a tossing motion—the cards have vanished. Reach into the pocket with the right hand and remove the cards, one at a time, to conclude.

The Soft False Count: Sol does not claim originality for this false count, its just the way he's been doing it for years. As you will see, it is really a very simple idea—I would not be surprised at all if others have devised similar or identical techniques. In Sol's hands, this false count looks clean and natural.

Let's assume that you intend to count ten cards off the top of the deck, really taking only seven cards. Begin with the deck in the left hand. The left first, second and third fingers are along the right side of the deck, the fourth finger rests at the deck's inner end. The face of the deck is tilted towards the audience at roughly a forty-five degree angle, the cards held at roughly chest level. The bulk of the weight of the deck is supported by the left fourth finger.

Fig. 24

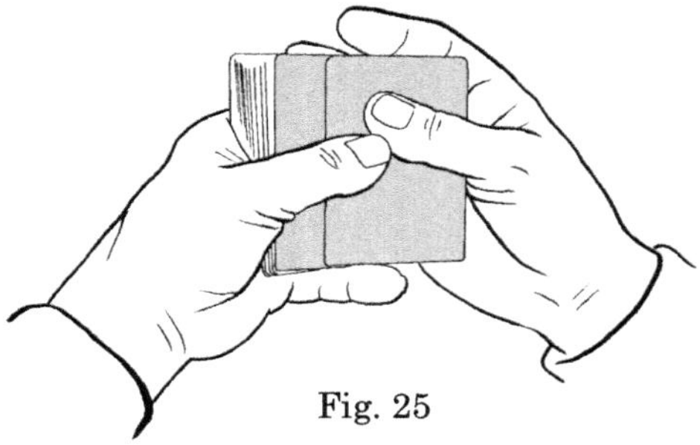

Fig. 25

The first card is of course taken legitimately. The left thumb pushes the top card of the deck to the right.

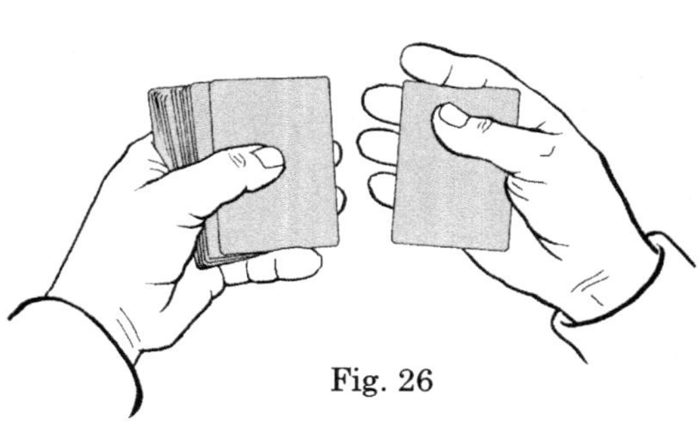

Fig. 26

The right hand comes over and takes this card so that the right first finger is at the card's outer end and the right second, third, and fourth fingers rest along its left side.

As each subsequent card is taken, the left thumb again pushes the top card of the deck to the right. The packet in the right hand travels ***underneath the left-hand fingers***.

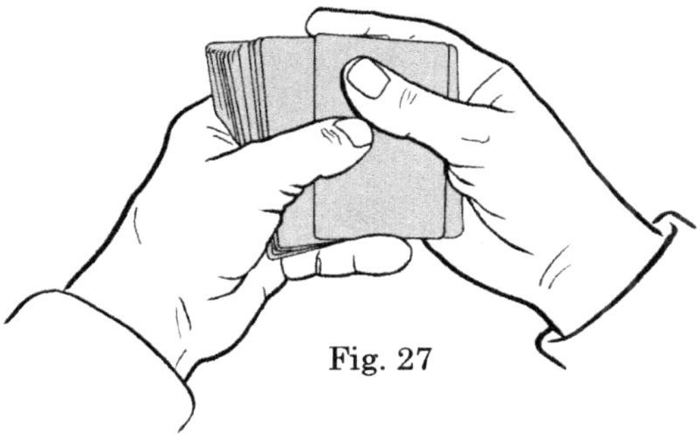

Fig. 27

The right thumb pulls it onto its packet and then moves away to the right. Of critical importance here is the sound made by the cards scraping across each other and by the back of the right-hand packet scraping across the nails of the left hand.

When you want to execute a false take, the left thumb pushes the top card of the deck to the right. The right hand and packet move over into exactly the same position as before. This time, however, as the right hand moves away, the left hand pulls the card back on top of the deck. This action is completely screened from view due to the angle at which the cards are held (remember, the faces of the cards are pointing toward the audience). Moreover, the sound of a legitimate take is created by the back of the right-hand packet sliding over the nails of the left hand.

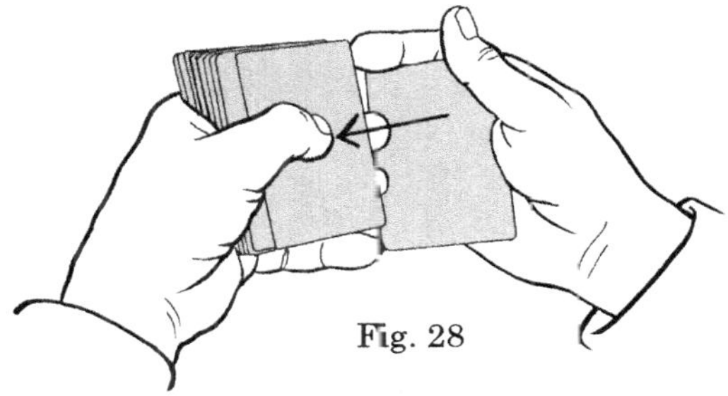

Fig. 28

As a general rule, each false take should be preceded and followed by a legitimate take. So, if you want to perform a seven-as-ten false count, you would execute the false takes on counts three, five, and seven. Finally, the most important aspect of this, or any, false count is to maintain a smooth and uniform action. Done properly, there should be absolutely no difference in action between the real and the false take. Practice this for even a little while and you will soon see how deceptive it can be.

Basic Coin Sleights The Sol Stone Way

Everyone who watches Sol perform raves about his "soft touch" and I have already discussed how difficult it is to capture this aspect of Sol's "style" on paper. There is another aspect of Sol's coin work, however, that is more readily described—the very open manner in which he handles the coins.

As I began to dissect Sol's coin effects, I realized that they were structured around a series of related sleights. These sleights, in turn, were based on the simple idea of always holding the coins at the fingertips while (generally) keeping the palms upward and the hands open. As you work your way through the following sleights, you will see how Sol relies on this basic display position to perform vanishes, changes, switches, and transformations. Because all his sleights are based on the same basic starting grip, they look consistent and natural.

FINGERTIP PINCH GRIP

While I do not want to bog down the following descriptions with a lot of excess terminology, our lives will be a little easier if I first define a basic method of holding a coin that recurs again and again in the following sleights and routines. This grip lies at the heart of Sol's coin technique.

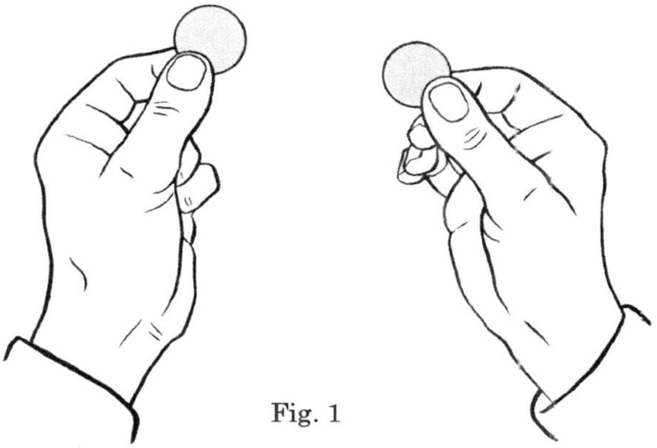

Fig. 1

Fingertip Pinch Grip (or just Pinch Grip) simply means holding a coin at the fingertips between the thumb and first finger. The coin is held by its extreme edge, so that the bulk of both sides are visible. Figure 1 shows a coin being held in Pinch Grip in both the right and left hand. Note that the fingertips do not point straight up, but are held in a loose and relaxed manner. If a coin is in right-hand **Fingertip Pinch Grip**, the tips of the fingers point to the left at about a forty-five degree angle. Also, Pinch Grip does not have to be static—Sol often revolves a coin around so that the audience can see both faces. Finally, do not keep the hands rigidly fixed in space while displaying a coin in Pinch Grip—the hands should move and sway naturally.

Fingertip Pinch Grip is Sol's basic display position. Not only does it show the coin in an easy-to-see manner, but it allows the same hand to naturally conceal a coin in Finger Palm via the **Ramsay Subtlety** (see next sub-section).

Moreover, **Fingertip Pinch Grip** is the starting position for many of Sol's basic coin sleights, including: the **Pivot Vanish**, the **Pivot Transformation**, the **"No Table" Pivot Vanish**, the **Simplified Spider Vanish**, and the **Brush Change**.

Finger Palm and Ramsay Subtlety

Sol relies extensively on the Finger Palm in his coin work. He also, of course, employs the Classic Palm, but Sol believes that the Finger Palm is more generally useful—primarily because Finger Palm permits you to employ the "**Ramsay Subtlety**." The **Ramsay Subtlety** allows you to casually and almost openly show your hand to be empty, while in fact you are concealing a coin (or coins) in Finger Palm. It is an interesting fact that virtually every advanced coin worker that I have seen relies heavily on the **Ramsay Subtlety**.

First, let me describe the basic Finger Palm, which I am sure is familiar to most readers. Place a coin (Sol usually uses American fifty-cent pieces or coins of similar size) at the base of your right second and third fingers.

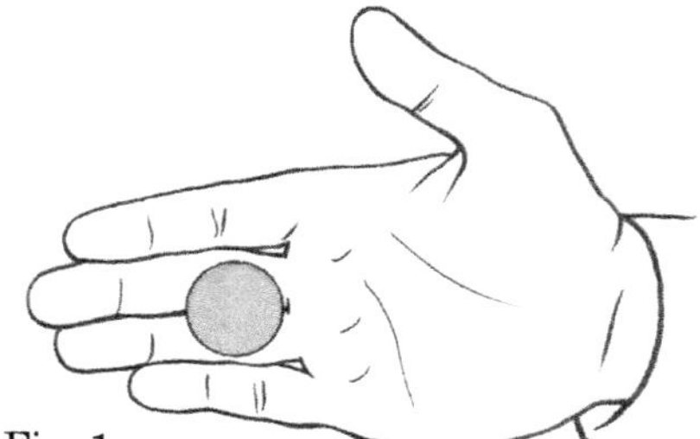

Fig. 1

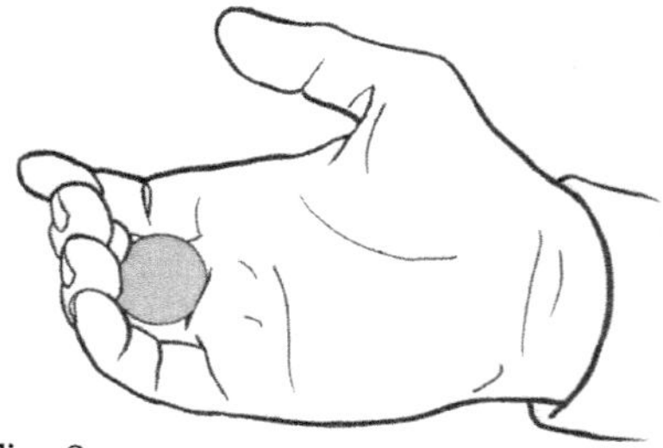

Fig. 2

Gently curl your fingers inward, lightly gripping the coin by opposite edges between the middle joints of the second and third fingers and the base of the same fingers. Turn your hand palm down.

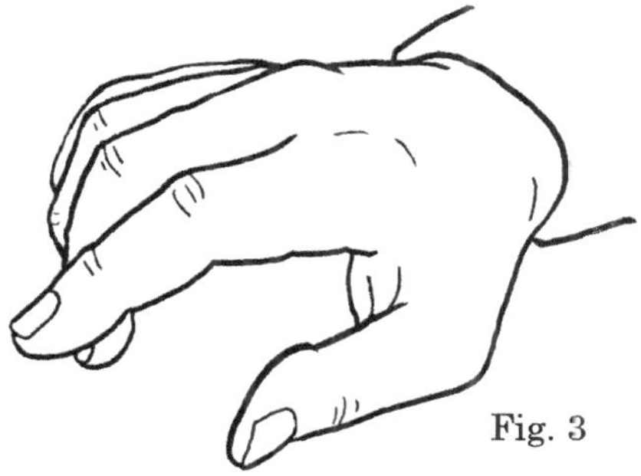

Fig. 3

From the audience's point of view the coin is now concealed by the back of the fingers. Be sure to keep the fingers loosely pressed together, or the coin will flash—this is particularly true if you have thin or bony fingers. You must become completely comfortable Finger Palming a coin in either the right or the left hand.

Ramsay Subtlety is simply a way of letting the audience look into the palm of the hand while concealing a coin in Finger Palm. There are two basic approaches -- palm up or palm down. In either case, it is also possible to display something at the fingertips—i.e., to hold an object between the thumb and fingers. Indeed, this often provides a natural excuse for holding the hand in "display mode."

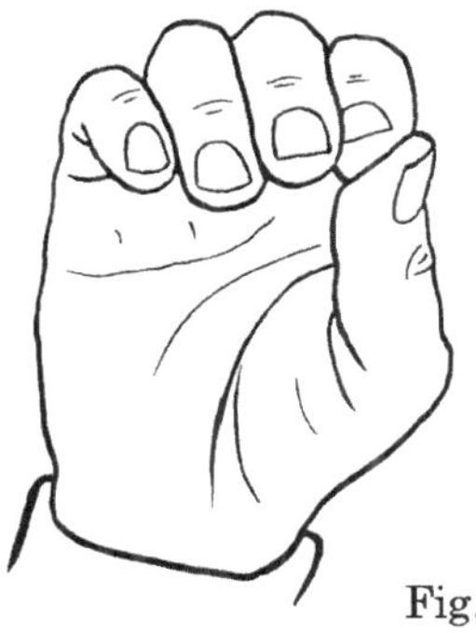

Fig. 4

Palm-down Ramsay Subtlety: The hand is palm down at chest level or a little lower with a coin in Finger Palm. Slowly begin to raise the hand at the wrist, bringing the palm toward the audience and the knuckles toward your body. The fingers remain curled and the ***fingertips should be pointing toward the floor.***

In this position, the audience is looking directly into the right palm, but the coin is concealed behind the curled fingers. You may keep the thumb either lightly pressed against the fingertips or in a relaxed position just below the fingertips.

Palm-up Ramsay Subtlety: The hand is palm up at about waist level or a little higher with a coin in Finger Palm. Slowly lower the hand at the wrist, bring the palm slightly toward the audience. The backs of the curled right fingers point toward the audience and the fingertips point upward. Again, the coin is concealed from view by the curled fingers.

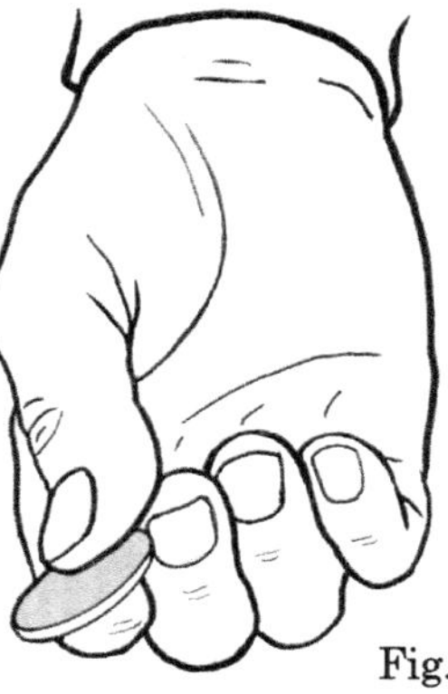

Fig. 5

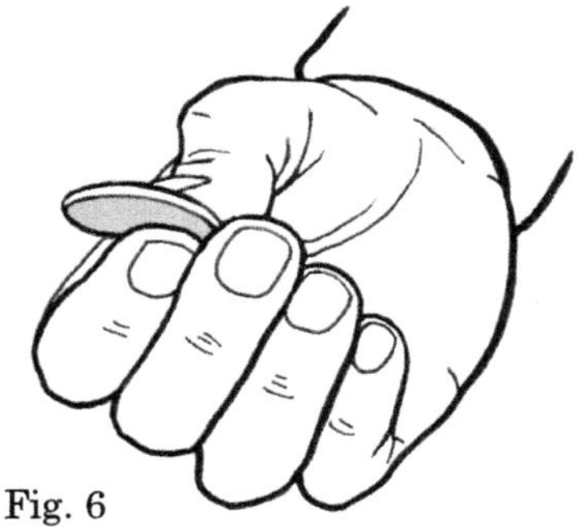

Fig. 6

This is a very natural and disarming position, because it appears to the spectators that they are looking directly into your hand. **Palm-up Ramsay Subtlety** is used continuously by Sol in virtually all of his coin routines.

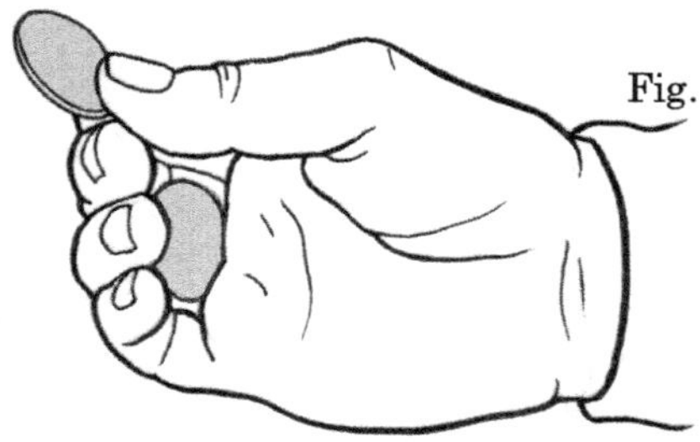

Fig. 7

Experiment in front of a mirror until you know exactly how far you can raise or lower your hand without exposing the coin. You should be able to assume the correct position instantly. In addition, you should become comfortable displaying a coin in Pinch Grip while concealing a coin in Finger Palm.

The Basic Pivot Vanish

This is the basic coin vanish that Sol almost always employs. It is a variation of John Ramsay's **Pivot Vanish**. Ramsay had very small hands and Sol found Ramsay's technique to be overly confining. Sol therefore modified the mechanics of the sleight to allow for a more open handling and to incorporate a "retention of vision" element.

Before outlining the actual mechanics of the move, let me digress briefly and discuss Sol's thinking as regards coin "vanishes" in general. Small object vanishes can be divided into three categories: false takes, false puts, and combination false puts and takes. The most deceptive, natural, and practical are, Sol believes, "false-take" vanishes. Here, the hand holding the object remains stationary while the other hand apparently takes the object and moves away with it. Not only does this closely mimic the way an object is naturally transferred from hand to hand, but the movement of the "taking" hand naturally misdirects away from the object left behind in the "stationary" hand. By contrast, during a "false-put" vanish the taking hand remains stationary while the other hand apparently places the object into it and then moves away. This means that the moving hand is also concealing the coin—which naturally draws attention to itself. Thus, in Sol's words, with a false-put vanish your timing must be "split-second and precise" if you are to deceive, while a false-take vanish is "very forgiving."

Sol's **Basic Pivot Vanish** is a false-take vanish. The coin is held by the right hand and apparently taken by the left hand. The coin begins pinched lightly between the right thumb and first finger. The coin is held by its extreme edge, so that virtually all of the face of the coin on both sides is visible. (This is essentially **Fingertip Pinch Grip**, except that you must be sure to hold the coin by its extreme edge.)

Casually display the coin, with the fingertips pointing upward and the back of the hand toward the audience.

Fig. 1

The left hand now moves to take the coin, fingers pointing toward the right and the back of the hand toward the audience. The fingers are not pressed tightly together, but instead are held loosely open. The fingers move in front of the coin and the thumb passes behind the coin.

Fig. 2

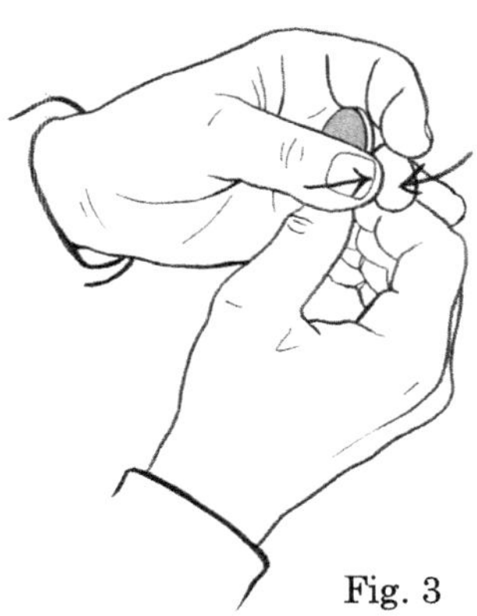

Fig. 3

Now comes the crucial action. The tip of the thumb and second finger are pressed together, ***beyond the right side of the coin.***

The left hand now moves directly to the left and the following actions take place in roughly the following order:

(1) the thumb and second finger contact the right edge of the coin at midpoint. (2) The left fingers press lightly together, closing the "windows" between the fingers. (3) As the left hand continues to move to the left, pressure from the left thumb and second finger causes the coin to rotate or pivot downward, out of sight behind the right fingers.

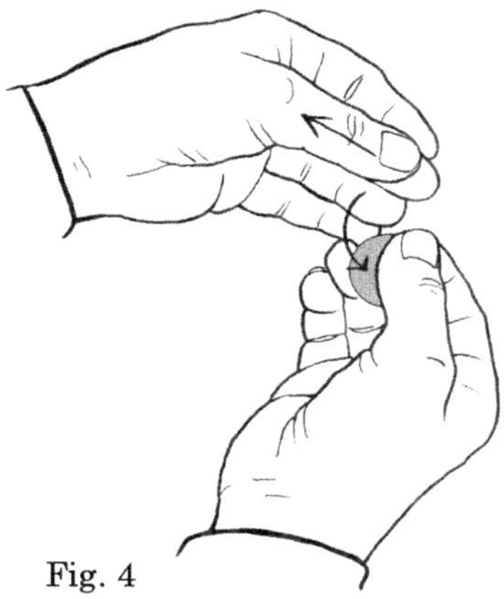

Fig. 4

The reason for holding the coin at its extreme edge now becomes clear: if the coin is not held in this fashion, then its lower edge may come into view as the bulk of the coin rotates downward behind the fingers. Also, the timing of the above actions is crucial. Done properly, the audience should see a flash of silver between the fingers as the left hand closes around the coin. This creates the retention of vision illusion that will make a spectator swear that the coin was taken by the left hand.

Once the coin has rotated out of sight, the right thumb releases pressure and the coin slides directly into Finger Palm. In practice, there should be virtually no pause between the coin's rotating and its dropping into Finger Palm. Also, there should be no visible tightening or clenching of the right hand as the coin is Finger Palmed.

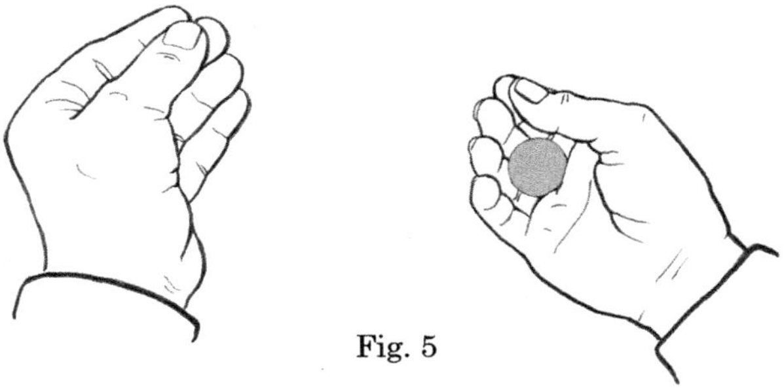

Fig. 5

After a moment, the right hand falls naturally to waist level. The coin is concealed by the Ramsay Subtlety, allowing the audience to apparently see into the "empty" right hand.

Meanwhile, the left hand moves away, the left thumb pressed against the fingers (which now point slightly upward, as if holding a coin against them). The right hand curls into a loose fist and the coin is vanished in the manner called for by the routine.

Pivot Transformation

One of the advantages of the **Basic Pivot Vanish** is that it allows for this almost automatic switch of two coins. Let's say that you have a copper coin secretly concealed in left-hand Classic Palm. You are displaying a silver coin at the right fingertips in preparation for the Pivot Vanish. All that is necessary is to execute the Pivot Vanish—apparently taking the silver coin in the left hand—while being sure to keep the back of the left hand toward the audience. Close your left hand into a loose fist, gently massage the coin, and open the hand to reveal that the silver coin has transformed itself into a copper coin.

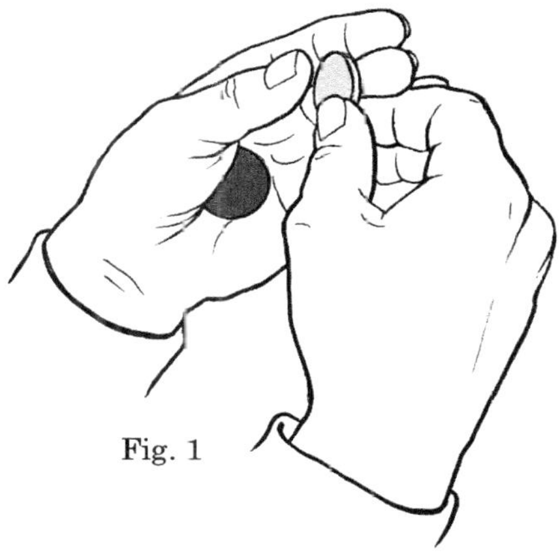

Fig. 1

"No Table" Pivot Vanish

In this Pivot Vanish variation a coin is held at the left fingertips while the right hand apparently places a second coin into the left hand. The second coin then disappears. It is a very natural solution to a situation that occurs during many routines—would a real magician have to place one coin aside just to vanish another coin?

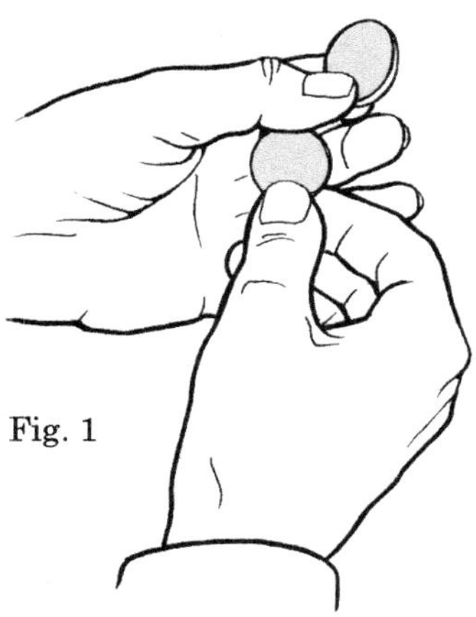

Fig. 1

Start with a coin in each hand, both held in **Fingertip Pinch Grip**. The left-hand coin is held between the thumb and first finger as the remaining three fingers open up to take the right-hand coin.

The right-hand coin is apparently taken by the left hand and the Pivot Vanish executed. The secret to obtaining a true "retention of vision" illusion with this vanish is to flash the coin between the left first and second fingers. The coin is placed directly behind the base of the left first and second fingers, so that about a third of the coin is visible from the audience's perspective.

Fig. 2

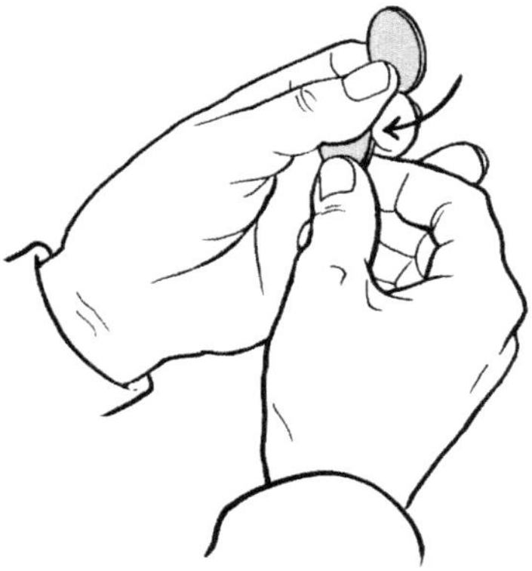

Fig. 3

The left second finger then curls inward, until it touches the tip of the left thumb.

The left hand now moves directly to the left, contacting the right edge of the coin and causing it to pivot into right-hand Finger Palm.

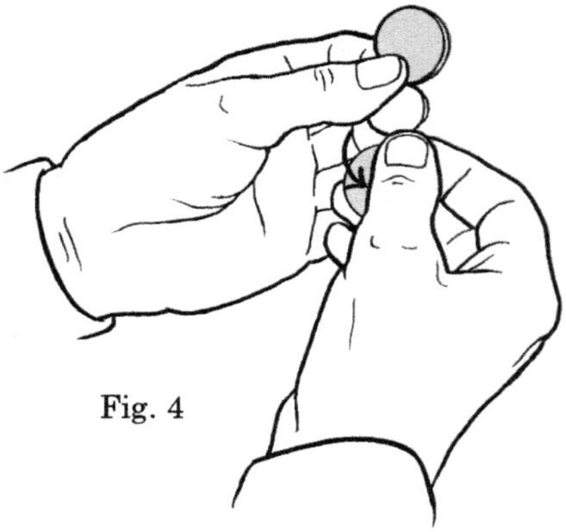

Fig. 4

The left second, third and fourth fingers apparently close around the coin.

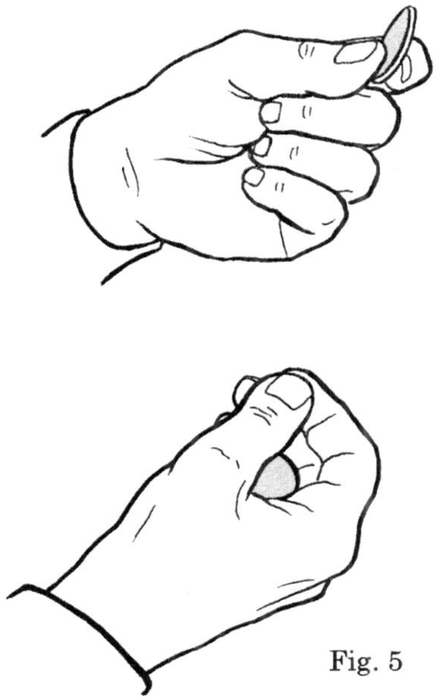

Fig. 5

Because the left first finger is holding the other coin, it cannot participate in the pivoting action which is accomplished entirely by the thumb and curled second finger.

Where you proceed from here depends on the specific routine you are doing. Very often, however, Sol immediately transfers the coin pinched between the left thumb and first finger to right-hand **Fingertip Pinch Grip**. This coin is then waved over the left hand which opens to reveal that the other coin has vanished. The entire sequence—display, false take, open transfer, and vanish—should flow smoothly together.

Sometimes Sol will do this move with an extra coin concealed in left-hand Classic Palm. The move then becomes a combination of the **Pivot Transformation** and the "**No Table" Pivot Vanish**. When necessary, this will be referred to as the "**No Table" Pivot Transformation**.

Pivot Click Pass

This natural and deceptive move is not a Click Pass in the traditional sense (in which only one coin disappears). Rather, it is a double vanish. Two coins are apparently placed in the left hand—the audience hears them "clink" together—the hand opens and both coins are gone.

The move begins with the **"No Table" Pivot Vanish** exactly as described above. Two coins are displayed, one in each hand. Both coins are in **Fingertip Pinch Grip**. You apparently take the coin at the right fingertips with the left hand (actually executing the Pivot Vanish). In a smooth, continuous action, openly take the coin at the left fingertips between the right thumb and first finger.

The right hand now moves a few inches above the closed left fist. You will apparently drop the right-hand coin into the left hand. Here's what really happens: As the left fingers open momentarily, the right hand drops sharply downward at the same time allowing the coin in Pinch Grip to fall onto the coin in right-hand Finger Palm, causing a loud "clink." The backs of the right hand fingers actually brush the palm of the left hand at this moment.

It is important that the left hand is tilted slightly towards your body, preventing the audience from getting a good look inside the hand. The right hand continues downwards, until it is a few inches below the left hand. At the same time, the left hand fingers rapidly close into a fist.

What makes this moment especially deceptive is that the right hand is now palm up. The two coins in Finger Palm are concealed in **Ramsay Subtlety**. The audience gets a glimpse of your "empty" right hand. The right hand turns palm down and falls to your side as you focus attention on the left hand. Massage the imaginary coins together and then slowly open your left hand to show that the two coins have disappeared.

The Simplified Spider Vanish

This is Sol's simplified handling of **Walter Gibson's Spider Vanish (Sphinx, 1910)**.The essence of the Spider Vanish is that you really do take the coin and only mimic vanishing it. The "sophisticated" spectators believe that the coin has been left behind in the other hand, which is then casually shown to be empty—catching them completely off-guard.

Begin with a coin held in Pinch Grip at the left fingertips. The right fingers move in front of, and the right thumb moves behind, the coin. You now mimic the action of the Pivot Vanish, but in reality the coin is placed directly into right-hand Thumb Palm.

Fig. 1

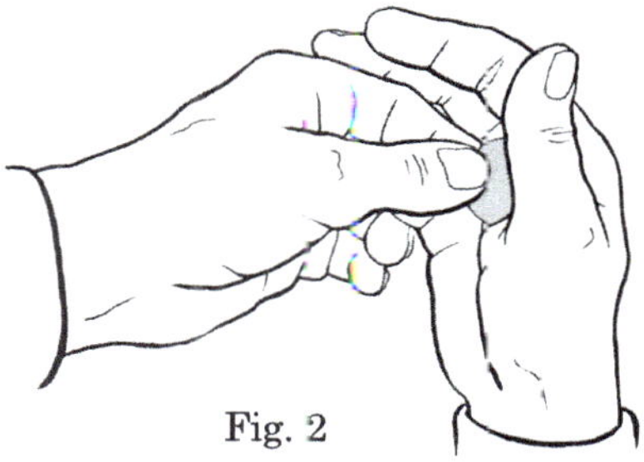

Fig. 2

The right hand moves away, fingers closing slightly, apparently holding the coin behind the right fingertips. At the same time, the left hand closes into a loose, rather suspicious, fist.

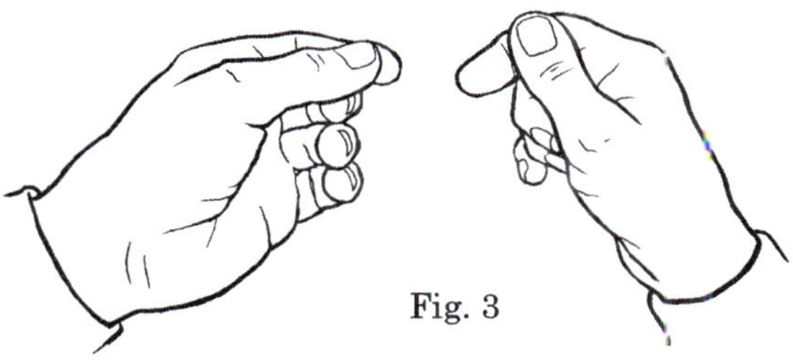

Fig. 3

Make a downwards tossing action with the right hand, as if vanishing the coin. The right fingers should open wide, so that it is clear that the coin is not in Finger Palm. Also, the back of the hand should be quite flat, dispelling any notion that the coin is Classic Palmed. The coin, of course, is secretly retained in Thumb Palm.

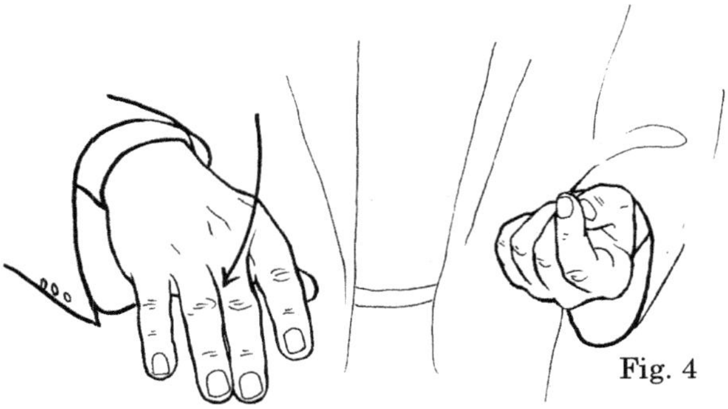

Fig. 4

Pause a beat and then look at your left hand as if suddenly realizing that the audience suspects that the coin is hidden there. Casually open the palm-up left hand to reveal that it is empty.

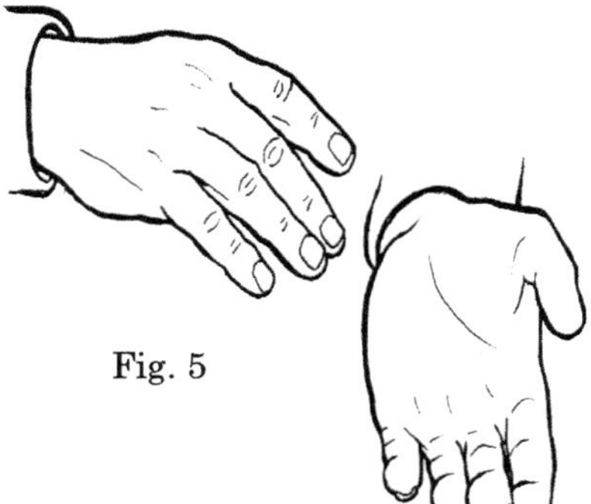

Fig. 5

Do not do this with a "Ha! You're wrong!" attitude, but with an innocent "I wouldn't cheat you for the world!" shrug. From here, Sol almost always proceeds directly into the **Townsend Acquitment Sequence**, described next. Prepare by reversing the position of your hands, retracting the right hand and extending the left.

THE TOWNSEND ACQUITMENT SEQUENCE

Sol often follows the Spider Vanish with the following acquitment sequence to casually show that both hands are empty. While in general Sol disapproves of excessive "hand-washing" this technique does not seem to arouse suspicion—primarily because both hands are palm up at the end of the sequence. The basic handling was developed by Jonathan Townsend — Sol has modified it only slightly.

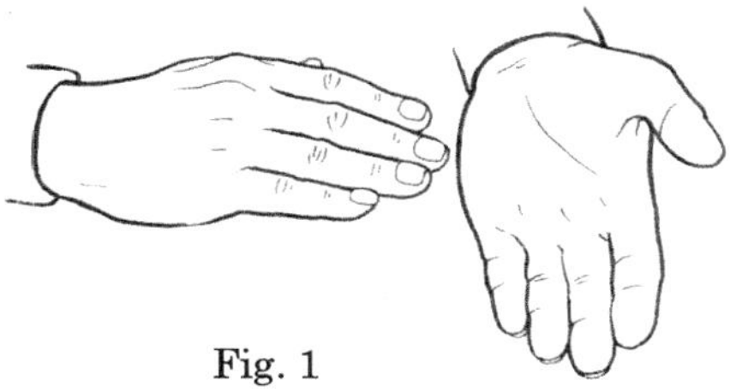

Fig. 1

At the conclusion of the Spider Vanish the right hand is palm down with the coin concealed in Thumb Palm and the empty left hand is palm up. The palm-down right hand now brushes across the top of the palm-up left hand.

The hands are perpendicular to each other. The right hand begins behind the left wrist and moves toward the left fingertips until the edge of the coin opposite the right thumb contacts the base of the left second and third fingers.

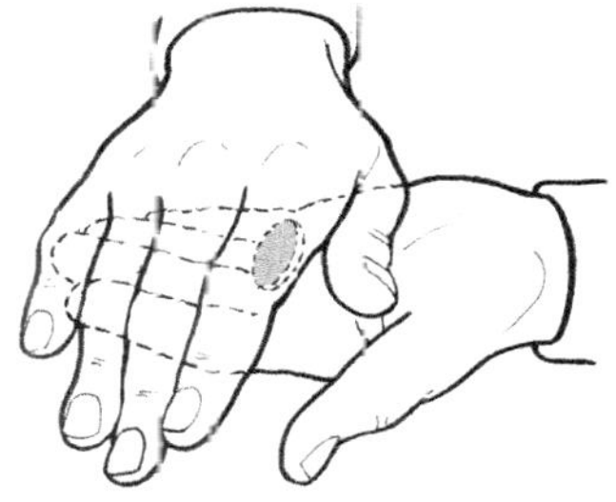

Fig. 2

As the right hand apparently continues its forward action, the coin will be transferred from right-hand Thumb Palm to left-hand Finger Palm. The edge of the coin opposite the thumb must press lightly but firmly against the base of the left second and third fingers. Pressure from the right thumb as the right hand continues to move forward will automatically cause the coin to flop over end for end, allowing the coin to pop free from Thumb Palm and to fall onto the base of the left second and third fingers.

Once the coin has fallen onto the left second and third fingers, the same fingers curl inward, taking the coin securely into Finger Palm. The left fingers actually curl around the right thumb for a brief moment (the thumb can help to push the coin securely into Finger Palm, if necessary). The right fingers move past the tips of the left fingers in order to accommodate this action.

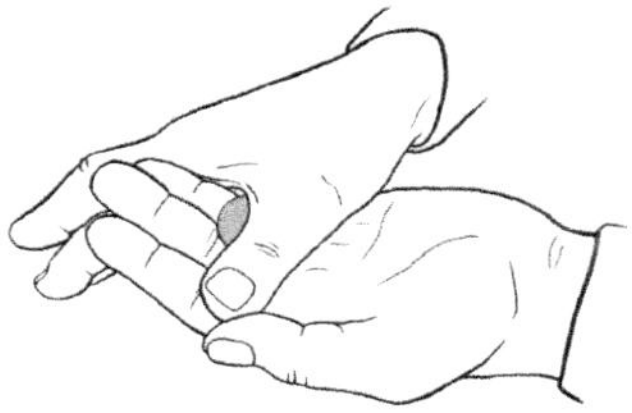

Fig. 3

Fig. 4

As soon as the coin is in Finger Palm, the left hand begins to rotate palm down and the right hand begins to rotate palm up. In a continuing action (it must be a continuing action otherwise the right thumb will prevent the left hand from turning completely palm down) the palm-down left hand slides down the right thumb, across the palm-up right hand, and past the right fingertips—all the while keeping the coin concealed in Finger Palm.

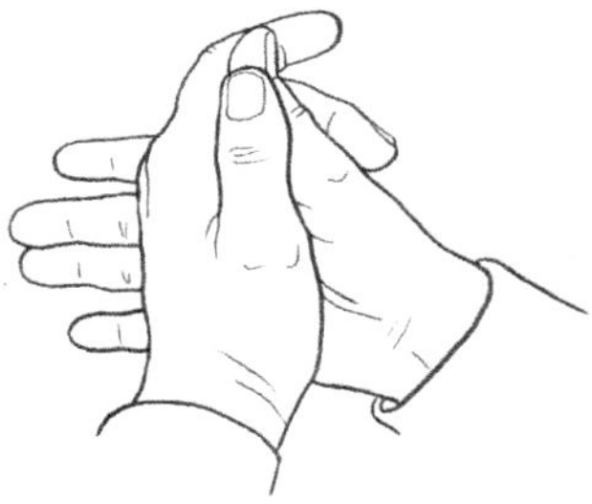

Fig. 5

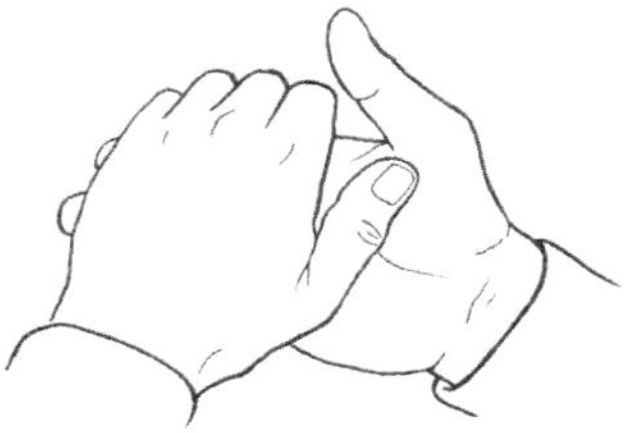

Fig. 6

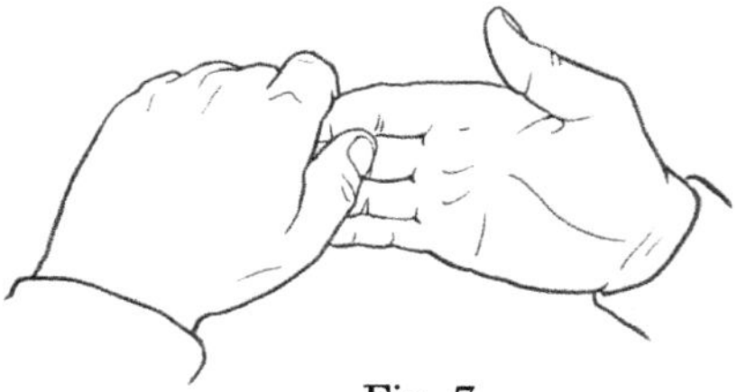

Fig. 7

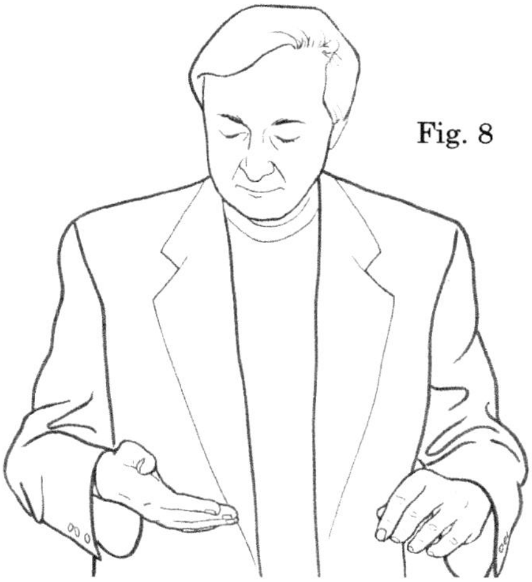
Fig. 8

Finally, the left hand rotates palm up allowing the audience to apparently see the empty palms (the coin is safely concealed in **Ramsay Subtlety**) as you give a small shrug of puzzlement as to the whereabouts of the coin. To be effective, the entire sequence must be executed in a smooth and flowing manner.

In addition, your attitude is crucial. You must ***not*** convey the impression that you are saying "Look how well I can conceal a coin!" Rather, you are simply dusting the invisible remnants of the coin from your hands in a casual and non-contrived manner.

Fig. 9

Done properly, this acquitment will leave even knowledgeable magicians confused as to the location of the coin.

Sol sometimes does the Spider Vanish and Acquitment sequence with two coins simultaneously. The two coins are held in an overlapping spread in left-hand Pinch Grip. The coins are aligned as they are taken into right hand Thumb Palm. From this position you will find that the Acquitment Sequence can be performed without the coins talking—they are "locked up" throughout the entire action and end up, still locked together, in left-hand Finger Palm. Just treat the two coins as a single coin and perform the sequence exactly as described.

ONE-HAND THUMB PALM TURNOVER SWITCH

This is a utility move that Sol has been using for over thirty years. It can be used as an almost visible transformation or as a secret switch. Let's assume that there is a copper-silver coin on the table, silver side up. You have a silver coin in right-hand Finger Palm. In the act of casually turning the tabled coin over with one hand, you will switch the regular coin for the gaffed coin.

The palm-down right hand moves over the tabled coin. The right thumb presses down on the coin's inner edge, levering its outer edge upward. This allows you to slide your right first and second finger under the coin. By pressing the tips of the first finger and thumb together, the coin will be levered into a vertical position—its inner face basically flat against the thumb.

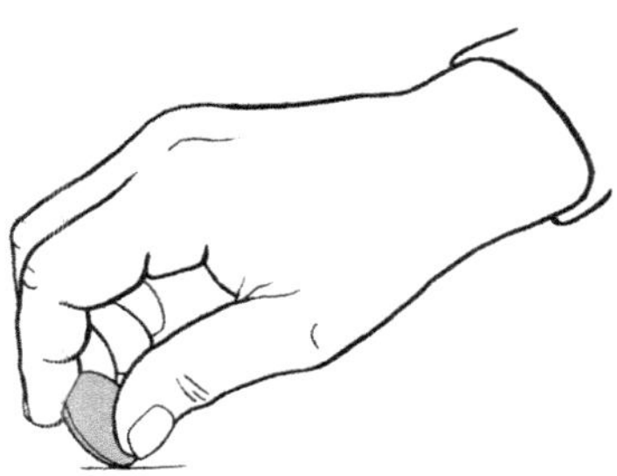

Fig. 1

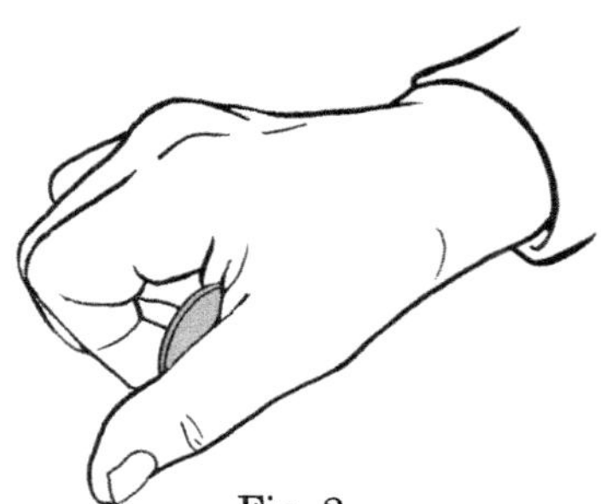

Fig. 2

From this position, slide the first and second finger inward, pushing the coin into Thumb Palm.

At the same time, the hand is beginning to move up and slightly outward.

Fig. 3

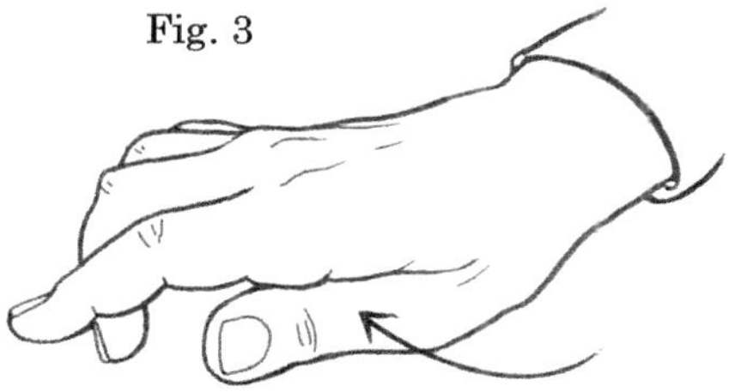

As soon as the coin is securely in Thumb Palm, the fingers of the hand open and the coin in Finger Palm is gently slapped onto the table.

Fig. 4

Although I have described the move as being done from the table, it can also be done from a coin resting on your left palm. On occasion Sol even does the move off a spectator's palm-up hand.

THE HOT POTATO SHUTTLE PASS

This is an easy-to-do Shuttle Pass that Sol uses in a several routines. It is almost always done on the off-beat and looks casual and natural. Begin with a coin concealed in Thumb Palm in the palm-down right hand. A duplicate coin is displayed on the palm-up left hand in position to be Classic Palmed.

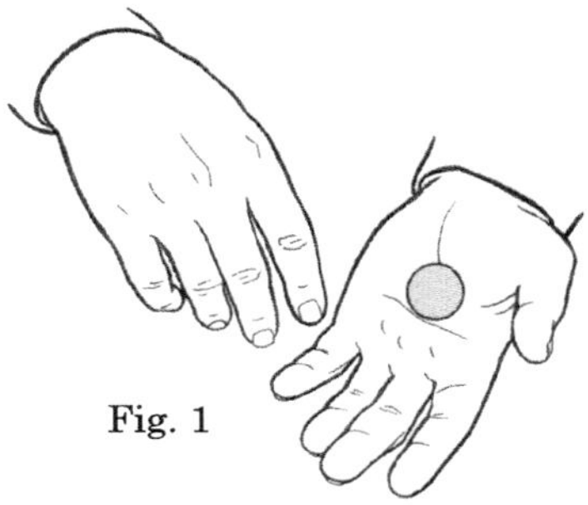

Fig. 1

You begin by apparently tossing the left-hand coin onto the right fingers. The left hand turns palm down, Classic Palming its coin as it does so. At the same time, the right hand turns palm up, releasing the Thumb Palmed coin so that it lands on the right fingers. Timed properly, the audience should see the right-hand coin actually fall onto the fingers.

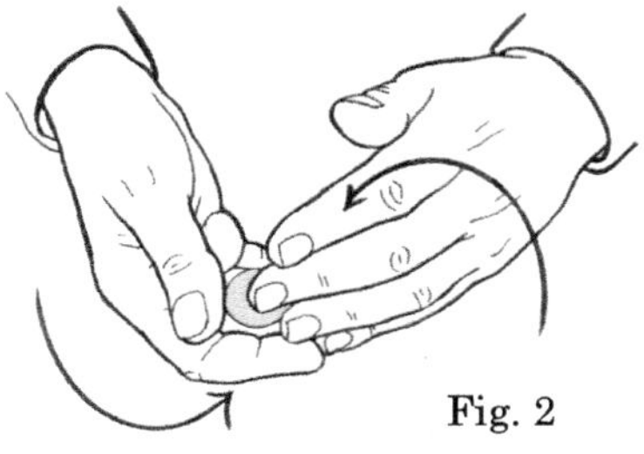

Fig. 2

Do not pause, but proceed immediately to toss the coin from hand to hand. The right hand turns palm down, tossing the coin onto the left fingers, near the tips. The left hand has, of course, turned palm up to receive the coin. However, the left hand does not turn completely palm up or the extra coin in Classic Palm would be exposed. Instead, the left hand turns only part way up and the Classic Palmed coin is concealed from the audience's view by the base of the left thumb. This is the **Malini Subtlety.**

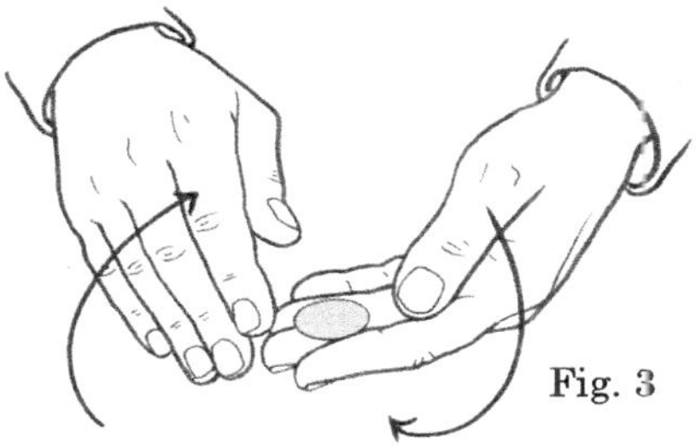

Fig. 3

The left hand immediately turns palm down, tossing the coin back onto the right fingers. The Shuttle Pass ends here and the coin can either be tabled, passed to a spectator, or pocketed as the left hand (with the Classic Palmed coin) falls casually to your side.

The tossing of the coin back and forth is done fairly rapidly—treat the coin as if it were a "hot potato" that cannot be handled for more than a moment or two. The action should appear natural and open.

Sol's "Spellbound" Sequence

This is Sol's basic handling for transforming a silver coin into a copper coin and back again. It is based on Edward Victor's "**The Changing Coin**" from the book ***The Magic of the Hands***, which in turn was popularized by Dai Vernon as "**Spellbound**" and was described in the ***Stars of Magic***. The Victor routine was actually a refined handling of an earlier routine by Ellis Stanyon, called "**Florin vs. Penny**", which had been published in the March 1899 issue of ***Mahatma*** magazine.

Sol's sequence is divided into two distinct phases. As a rule, Sol believes that if you have changed, say, a silver coin into a copper coin, you should conclude by changing the copper coin back into a silver coin. Thus, if he is doing a simple, direct transformation, Sol performs both Phase One (silver to copper) and Phase Two (copper to silver). However, in some of Sol's longer routines—for example, "**Two-Timing Transpo**"—only Phase One is used.

Phase One: Begin with a copper coin in right-hand Finger Palm and a silver coin displayed in right-hand Pinch Grip. Casually rotate both hands palm down and then palm up—displaying both sides of the coin and apparently showing the hands to be empty (the copper coin is, of course, concealed **Ramsay Subtlety**).

Transfer the silver coin to the left hand so that it is held by opposite edges between the left thumb and first finger. The silver coin is held so that its face is parallel with the length of the fingers (not perpendicular to the fingers, as is more traditional).

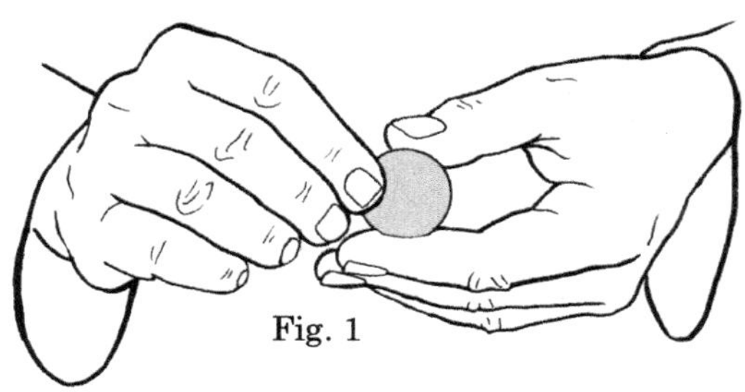

Fig. 1

With the tip of the right first finger, rotate the silver coin around its vertical axis by pressing the right edge of the coin inward and then to the left.

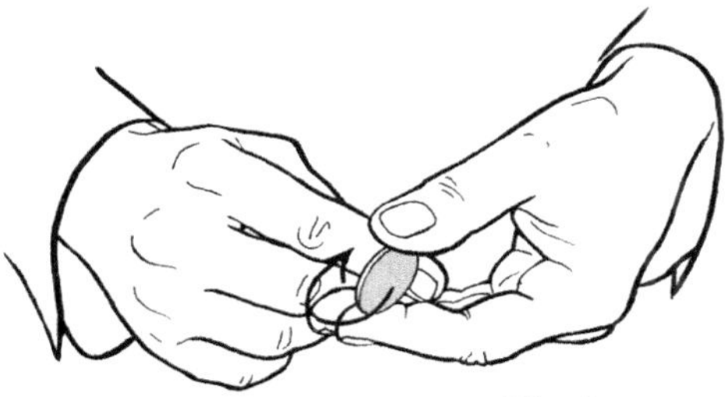

Fig. 2

This allows the audience to see both sides of the coin and also brings the right hand behind the coin.

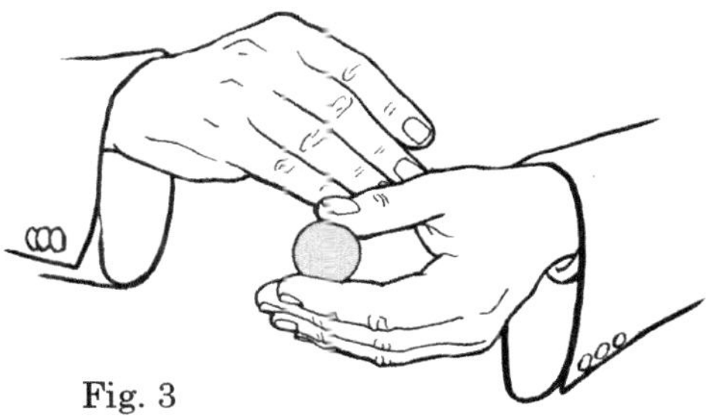

Fig. 3

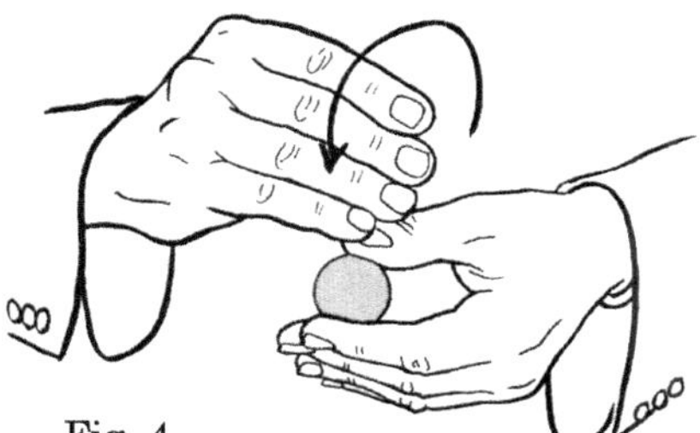

Fig. 4

The right hand moves *up and over* the left thumb and down in front of the silver coin.

As this occurs, the right fingers straighten and the right thumb presses the finger-palmed copper coin against the base of the left second and third fingers.

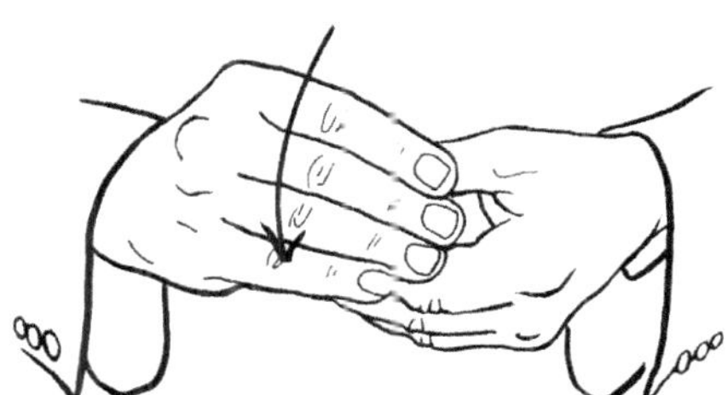

Fig. 5

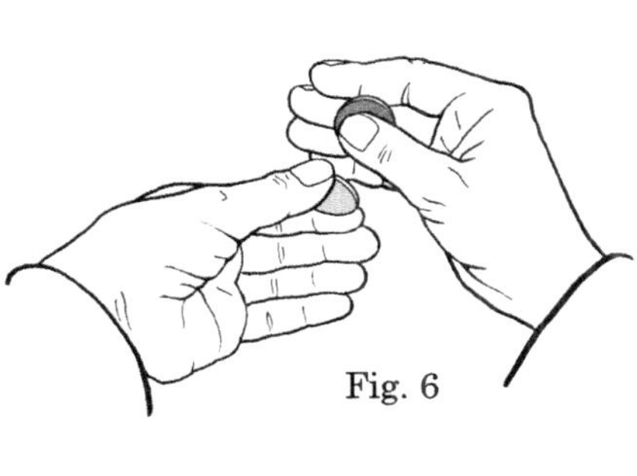

Fig. 6

At this point, the back of the right thumb traditionally knocks the silver coin from between the left thumb and first finger and onto the base of the left second, third, and fourth fingers. Instead of doing this, Sol prefers to raise the left thumb slightly—just enough to allow the silver coin to fall backwards into the same position. Sol believes that this results in a smoother, more natural transformation.

Without pausing, the copper coin is placed between the left thumb and first finger—in exactly the same position previously occupied by the silver coin.

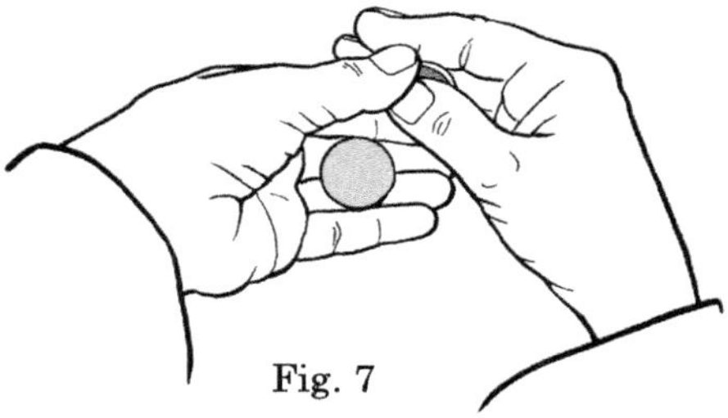
Fig. 7

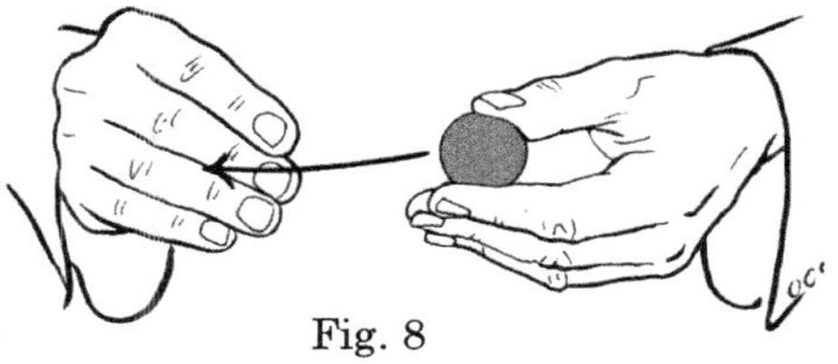
Fig. 8

Once the copper coin has replaced the silver one, the right hand moves to the right. The second and third fingers brush across the face of the coin to reveal the transformation.

The right hand now makes a gentle tossing motion towards the floor as though it was disposing of an invisible coin. The right hand is seen to be empty. At the same time, the copper coin is snapped into Pinch Grip as described in the next paragraph.

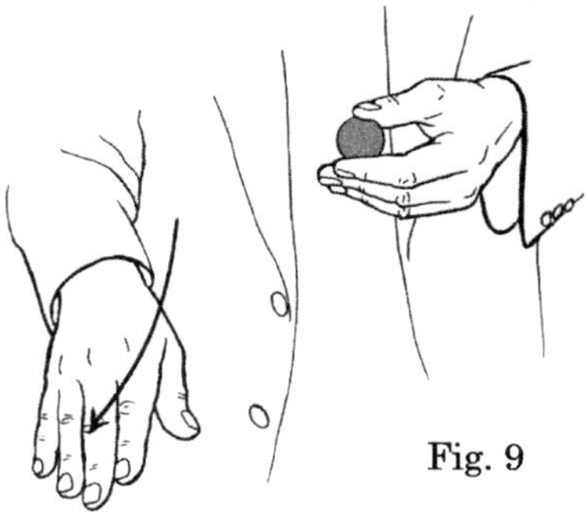
Fig. 9

The copper coin is in Spellbound Position, while the silver coin is simply resting on the open left fingers, hidden from view by the angle of the left hand. The left thumb and first finger squeeze or pinch together, causing the edge of the copper coin that contacts the first finger to snap free.

The coin ends up pinched between the thumb and first finger. This subtly displays the opposite face of the copper coin. As this action takes place, the left hand rotates slightly inwards.

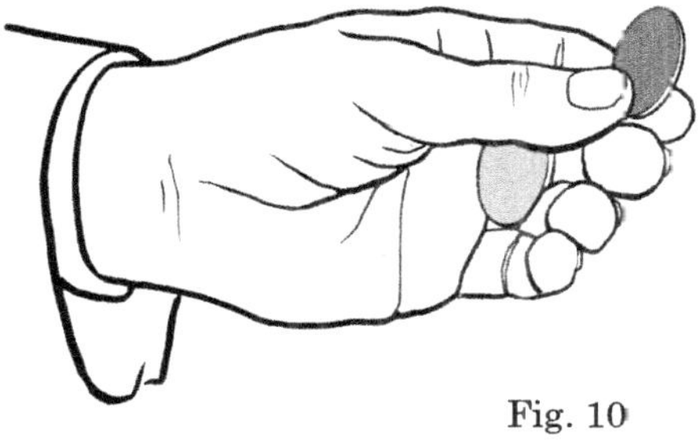

Fig. 10

At the same time, the left second, third, and fourth fingers curl inward securing the silver coin in Finger Palm.

Naturally, angles are critical when performing this sequence. The spectators must not be looking directly down at the palm of the left hand or they will see the "concealed" coin after the change. To ensure this, keep the following rules in mind:

(1) The spectators should be standing at least two to three feet in front of you, not directly on top of you.

(2) Point the face of the visible coin directly toward the eyes of the spectators. This will automatically tilt the concealed coin out of the audience's direct line-of-sight.

(3) Do not perform the move if you are sitting and the spectators are standing. The move is virtually angle-proof if these simple rules are kept in mind.

Phase Two: This is virtually identical to Phase One, except that the action takes place in the right hand. Openly transfer the copper coin from left-hand Pinch Grip to right-hand Spellbound Grip (exactly the same grip described above, except in the right hand).

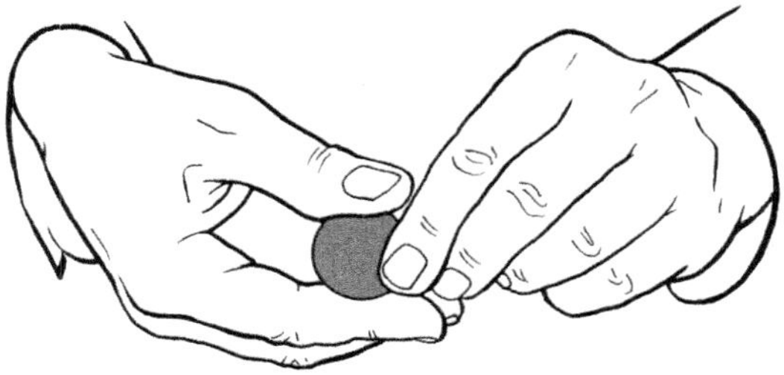

Fig. 11

Now, instead of using the left first finger to rotate the copper coin, simply turn the right hand palm down, rotating it at the wrist, to display the opposite face of the coin. Then return the right hand to its palm-up position.

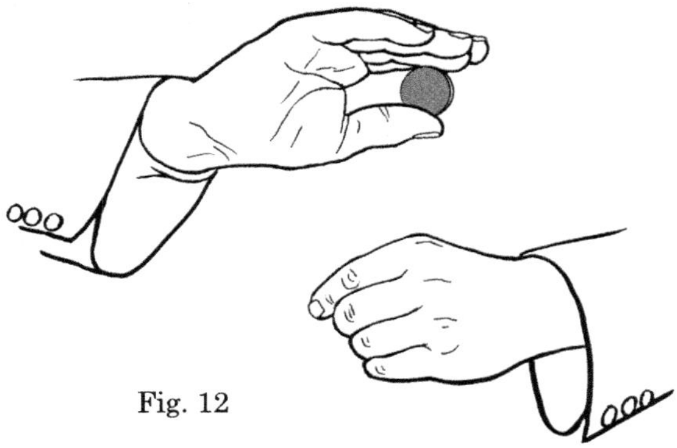

Fig. 12

As this is taking place, the left thumb secretly moves onto the silver coin in Finger Palm, slides it slightly forward, and holds it in position against the left fingers.

As soon as the right hand has turned palm up, the left hand moves over the top of the silver coin and executes the Spellbound Change, allowing the copper coin to fall backwards onto the base of the right fingers and replacing it with the silver coin.

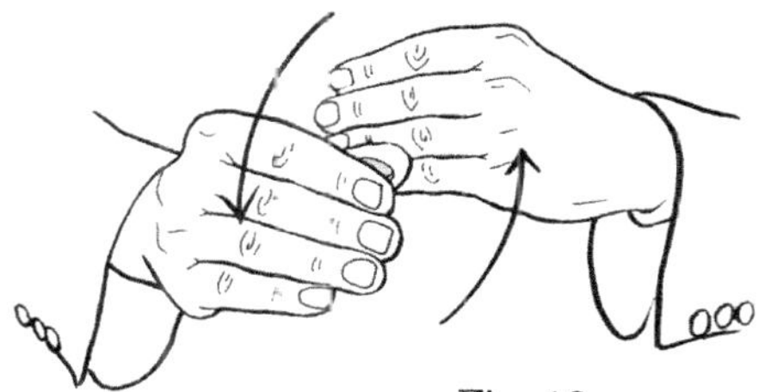

Fig. 13

With the left hand make the tossing gesture, disposing of the invisible coin as outlined in the first phase. Pause for a moment and then snap the silver coin into Pinch Grip as described above.

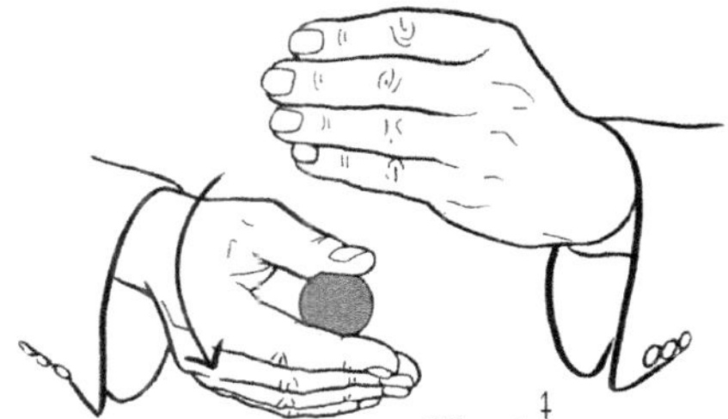

Fig. 14

Rotate both hands palm down and then palm up, concealing the copper coin in **Ramsay Subtlety** and displaying both sides of the silver coin. The two-phase change is complete—and, incidentally, you are back in your starting position.

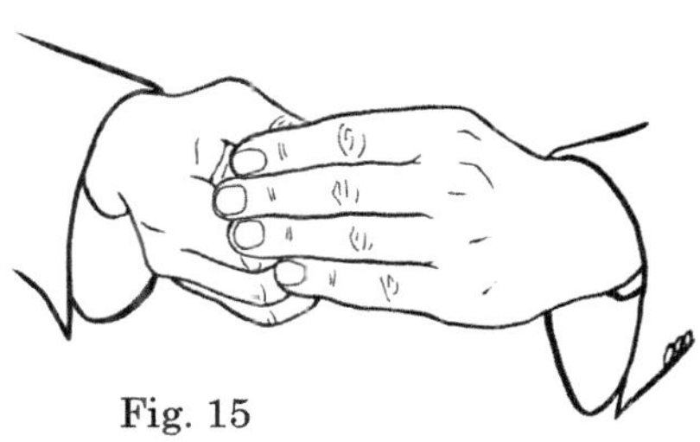

Fig. 15

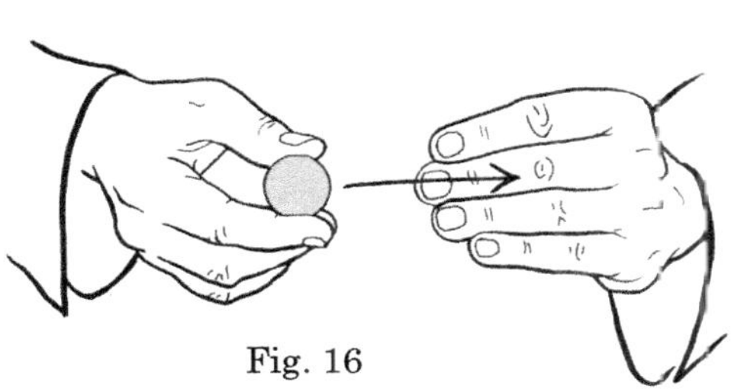

Fig. 16

The Brush Change

A.K.A. Tumble Switch/Change

Although this move was described in ***CoinMagic***, I have yet to see anyone else use it on a regular basis. Frankly, I think the description in ***CoinMagic*** made the sequence appear to be much more difficult than it really is. Part of the problem may be conceptual: the move was originally described as a "tumble" change and the emphasis was placed on turning the coin over; I view the action as involving more of a brushing motion, and have re-named the move accordingly. In any event, I hope you give this sleight the attention it deserves.

For teaching purposes, I am going to explain the **Brush Change** as a "**Spellbound**" sequence in which a silver coin is transformed into a copper coin which is then transformed back into a silver coin. Please remember, however, that the sequence has many potential uses and variations.

The copper coin begins in right-hand Finger Palm. Actually, Sol begins with the copper coin in a modified Finger Palm—the edge of the coin nearest the fourth finger is levered slightly away from the base of the fingers. Call this the "**Angled Finger Palm**." This position—halfway between Finger Palm and Curl Palm—allows you to easily and certainly grasp the edge of the coin at the proper moment. The silver coin begins in right-hand **Fingertip Pinch Grip**.

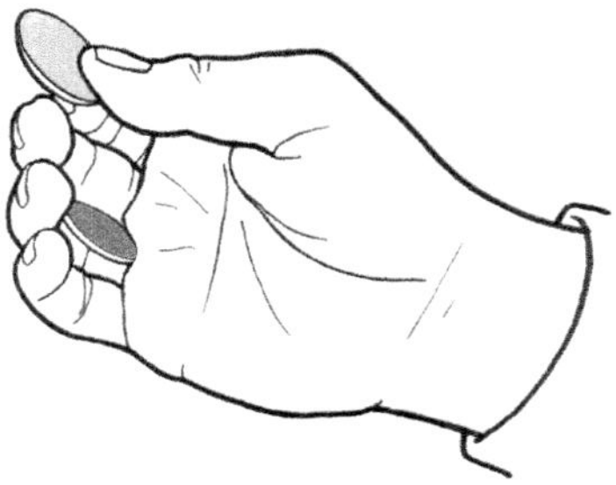

Fig. 1

Phase One: Begin by transferring the silver coin from right to left-hand Pinch Grip. As this is done, however, the coin is rotated 180 degrees, allowing the audience to see both faces.

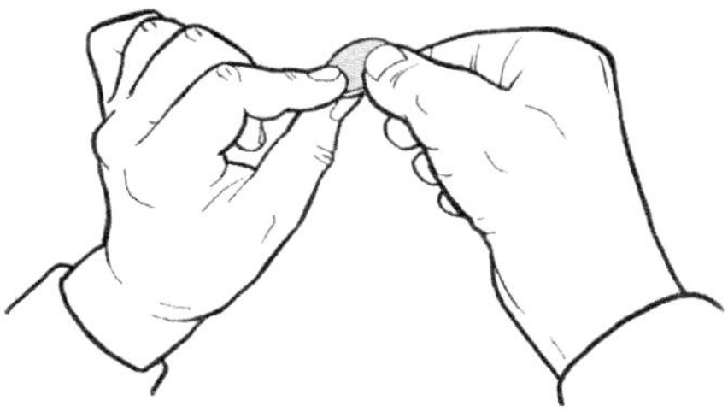

Fig. 2

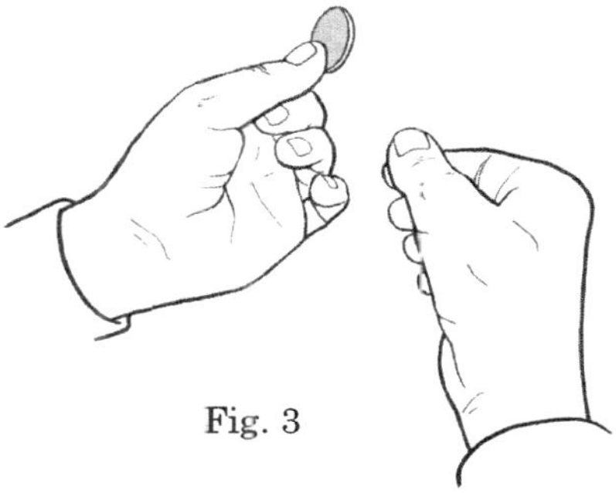

Fig. 3

This is very simple. The right hand holds the silver coin so that it points to the left; the right thumb is on the upper side of the coin, the right first finger on the under side of the coin. The left hand comes to take the silver coin, ***thumb on the under side and first finger on the upper side***. As the left hand moves away with the coin, it automatically turns palm up, displaying it.

After displaying the silver coin in left-hand Pinch Grip, the right hand comes over to apparently brush its fingers across the face of the coin. The back of the right hand is toward the audience, the fingers (with the copper coin in **Angled Finger Palm**) move in front of the silver coin while the thumb moves behind it. The right hand moves to the left until it can take the silver coin directly into right-hand Thumb Palm.

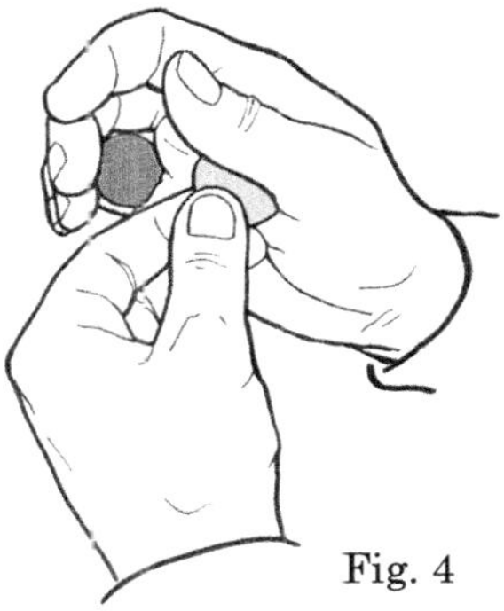

Fig. 4

As the silver coin is taken into thumb palm, the right thumb naturally presses inward to hold it gently in place.

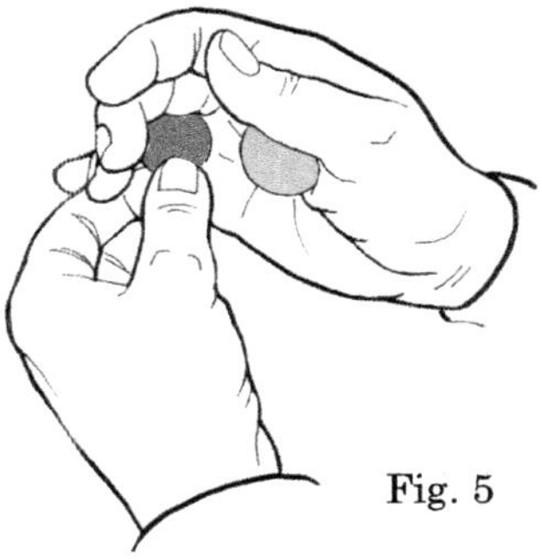

Fig. 5

The right hand then moves about half an inch toward the body, which removes the silver coin from the left fingertips and brings the copper coin (in **Angled Finger Palm**) directly over the left fingers in position to be taken directly into left-hand Pinch Grip. All this takes only a moment—the exchange of the copper for the silver coin must be almost instantaneous.

Without hesitation, the right hand begins to move to the right, retracing it's original path. The hands separate, the fingers of the right hand brushing across the face of the copper coin. The coin comes into view, having apparently been transformed from silver to copper.

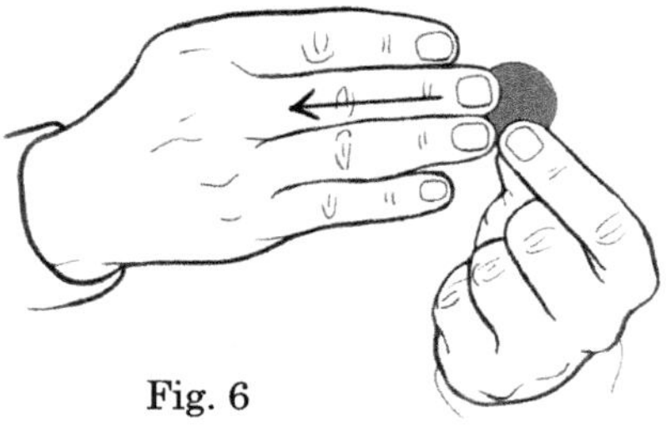

Fig. 6

Phase Two: Pause for a beat, and then lower the left hand at the wrist so that the opposite face of the copper coin comes into view—the left palm is pointing upward and the fingertips are pointing directly toward the spectators. You are dispelling any notion of a double-faced coin.

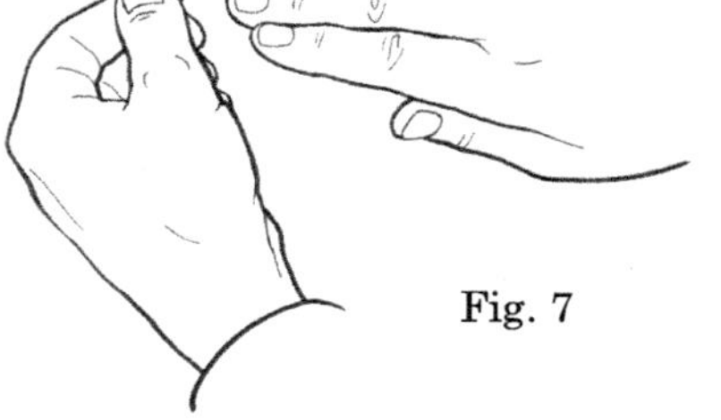

Fig. 7

The palm-down right hand (with the silver coin concealed in Thumb Palm) now moves over the copper coin. The right fingers are straight and point to the left. The right hand moves over the copper coin until the coin is directly below the base of the right second and third fingers. Now several things occur in close succession.

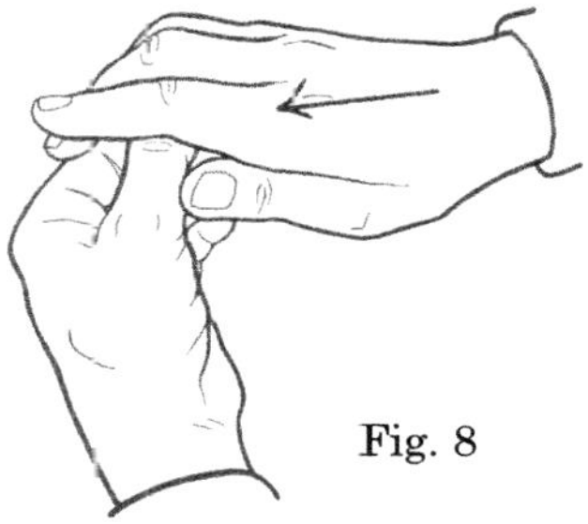

Fig. 8

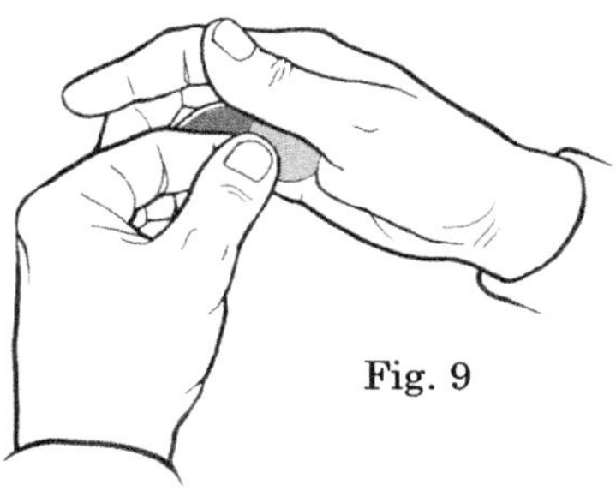

Fig. 9

First, the right fingers curl inward, taking the copper coin in Finger Palm.

Second, the right hand begins to turn palm up, which almost automatically brings the silver coin in position to be gripped at the left fingertips.

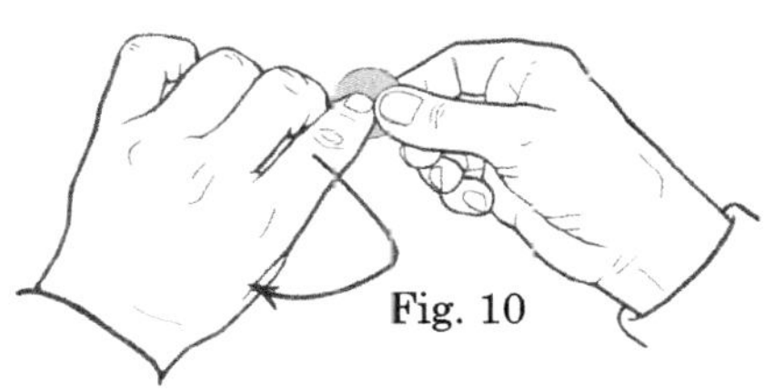

Fig. 10

Third, the right hand stops rotating with the back of the hand toward the audience (thus avoiding exposing the copper coin in Finger Palm). The left hand, holding the silver coin in Pinch Grip, moves to the left. ***As the left hand moves, it also rotates palm down***.

As soon as the silver coin has been brought back to the palm-up right fingertips, it is transferred to right **Fingertip Pinch Grip**. If you have done this properly, the right thumb will be grasping the coin on the face opposite the left thumb.

In a continuing action, the left hand releases the silver coin and turns palm up. Turn the right hand palm down and place the silver coin deep in the left thumb crotch. Draw the left hand away, brushing the left thumb across the coin.

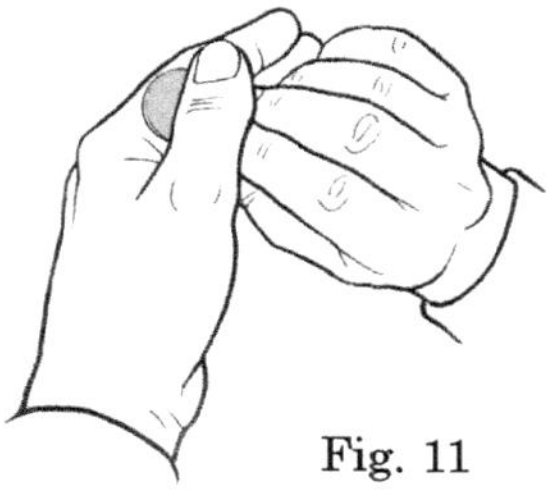

Fig. 11

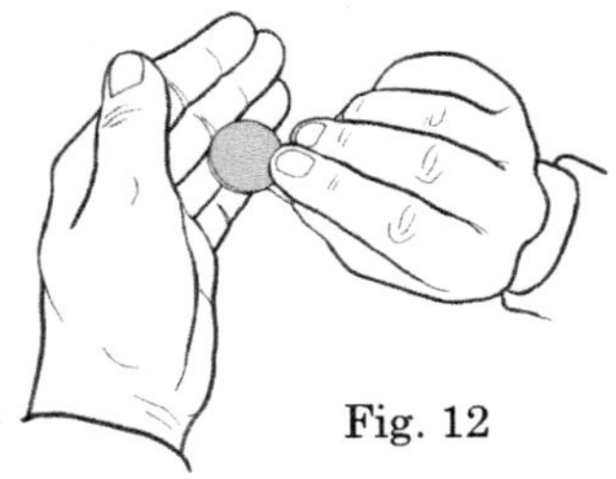

Fig. 12

Turn the right hand palm up and repeat this action, placing the silver coin in the left thumb crotch and drawing the left hand away in a "brushing" action.

Phase Three: Without pausing, transfer the silver coin to left hand Pinch Grip, rotating it 180 degrees as was done in Phase One. Immediately go into the change as described in the first phase, moving the right hand in front of the silver coin and secretly placing the silver coin in right-hand Thumb Palm.

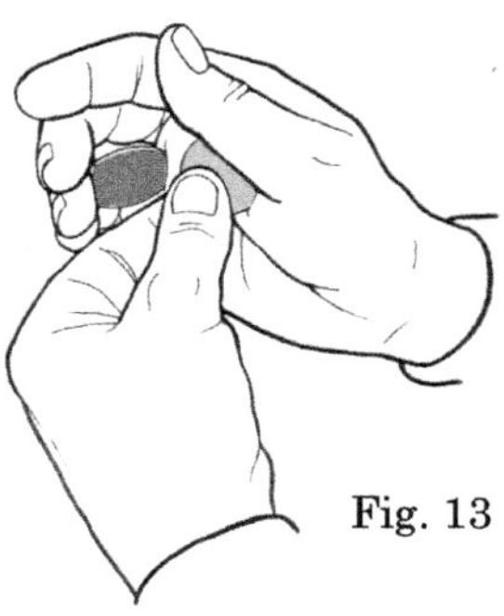

Fig. 13

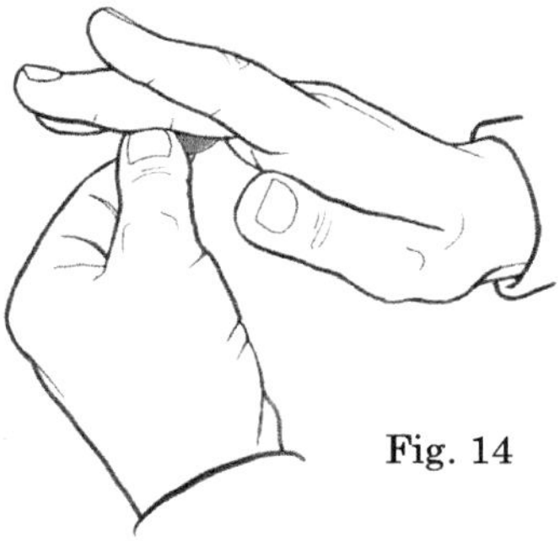

Fig. 14

Now the procedure changes very slightly. Instead of grasping the lower edge of the copper coin in left-hand pinch grip, rotate the right hand palm down and grasp the upper edge (now pointing toward you) in left hand Pinch Grip.

Brush the right fingers over the copper coin to reveal the transformation. The left hand should be palm up and the right hand palm down. Turn the left hand palm down and again brush the right fingers over the copper coin.

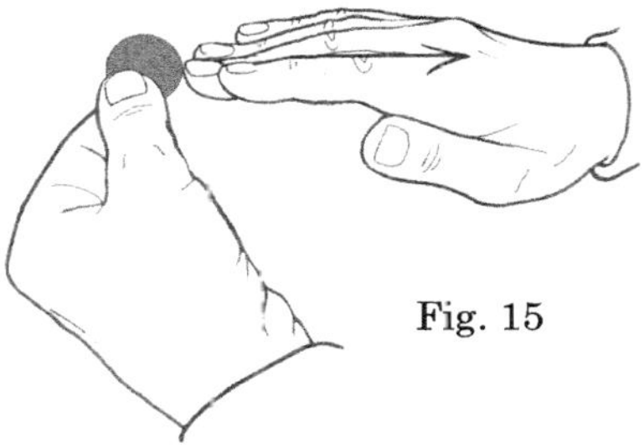

Fig. 15

Phase Four: Turn the left hand palm up again. You are now in position to repeat the change as described in Phase Two, with one slight difference. As soon as the copper coin is Finger Palmed and the left hand has transferred the Thumb Palmed silver coin to Fingertip Pinch Grip, the empty left hand makes a gentle tossing motion towards the floor. Turn both hands palm up and then palm down, the copper coin remaining concealed in **Ramsay Subtlety**.

Smile to indicate that the routine is over and acknowledge the well-deserved applause.

Amazing Penetrations

Sol believes that penetrations make for strong magic. They certainly make for a good introduction to his coin routines. The following effects are simple to do (one is virtually self-working); the only sleights required are the Pivot Vanish and the ability to casually and naturally conceal a coin in Ramsay Subtlety.

The Jarred Coin

This is a triple penetration. A coin is apparently passed twice through the bottom of a small glass jar. For the final penetration, the lid is screwed onto the jar—completely sealing it—but the coin still magically penetrates the glass.

During the adventures that ensued after he was shot down over Eastern Europe during the Second World War, Sol picked up a variety of "mementos." Among these were several Rumanian 100 lei coins which, experimentation proved, were magnetizable. This was before the days of steel-shim coins and the secret possession of a magnetizable coin was a powerful magical weapon. This routine—developed by Sol upon his return to the States—is as deceptive now as it was in 1945.

You will need two identical coins, at least one of which is magnetizable. The magnetizable coin can be a steel-shim half dollar or a foreign coin with magnetizable properties. Today Sol uses a Dutch coin that is slightly smaller than a half dollar. Rumanian 100 Lei, Italian 50 and 100 Lira, and some French, Belgian and Canadian coins are also magnetizable. A little research will soon turn up appropriate coins.

Also required is a small Maxim Instant Coffee jar (or similar) and a sheet of rubberized magnetic material. This material can be obtained from a scientific supply house, but is often found in flat kitchen magnets. Remove the label from the jar so that there is a clear view inside. Then carefully remove the cardboard circle from inside the lid of the jar. Cut a circle of similar size from the rubberized magnetic material. Glue the magnetic material into the lid of the jar and then glue the cardboard circle onto the magnet. The lid appears ordinary, but will securely hold the magnetizable coin. To set up, place one coin in the bottom of the jar and attach the magnetic coin to the inside of the lid. Screw the lid on the jar and you are set to perform.

Bring out the sealed jar—one coin is loose and clearly visible and the other secretly attached to the inside of the lid. Unscrew the lid with your right hand—being careful not to dislodge the concealed coin—and casually place it, mouth down, on the table. Dump the coin from the jar into the right hand and place the jar on the table so that it is resting on its side with the opening pointing to the right.

Casually display the coin in right-hand **Fingertip Pinch Grip**. Execute the **Basic Pivot Vanish** as you apparently take the coin into the left hand. The right hand, with the coin concealed in Finger Palm, drops to the table to pick up the jar.

The jar is grasped so that the crotch of the thumb circles the rim of the jar and the fingers are above the mouth of the jar.

Because the jar was placed on its side, with the opening to the right, this position is easily assumed.

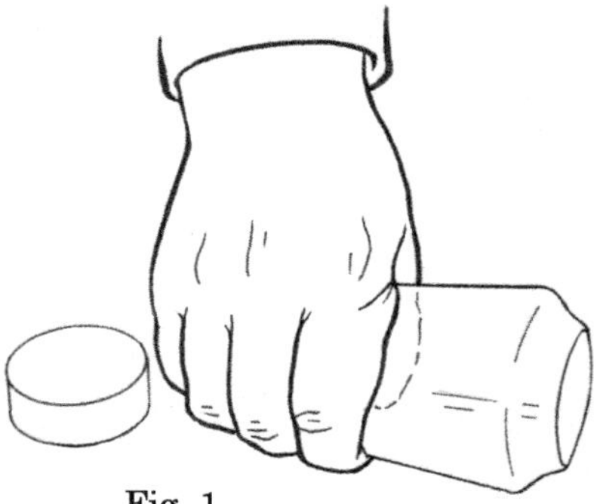

Fig. 1

Lift the jar from the table, keeping the bottom of the jar pointing to the left.

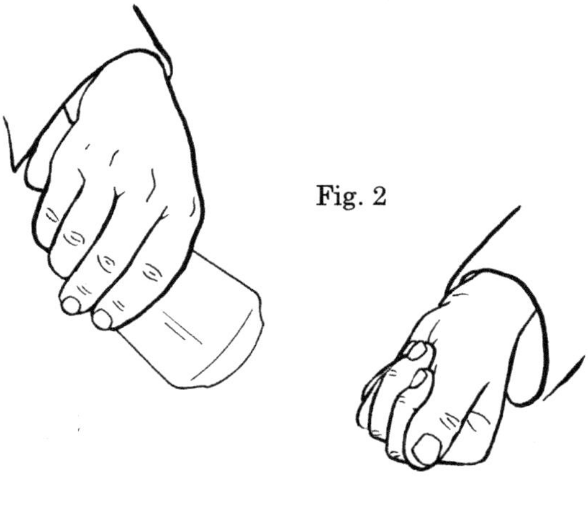

Fig. 2

The left hand is now sharply smacked against the bottom of the jar, the hand opening in the process. The impact of the left hand will cause the coin to fly out of right-hand Finger Palm and into the jar—appearing as if the coin has penetrated the bottom of the jar.

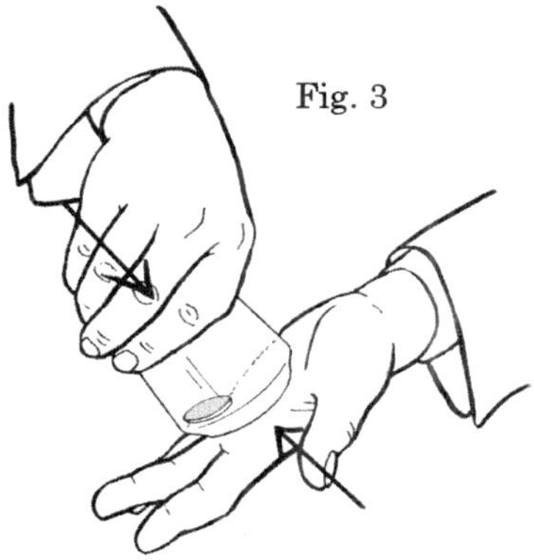

Fig. 3

Swing the bottom of the jar towards the audience to display the coin, retaining the right hand grip on the jar.

Now apparently dump the coin from the jar into the left hand. In reality, the coin simply slides directly into right-hand Finger Palm as the left hand apparently catches the coin as it falls from the jar. In other words, execute a Shuttle Pass from the jar into the left hand.

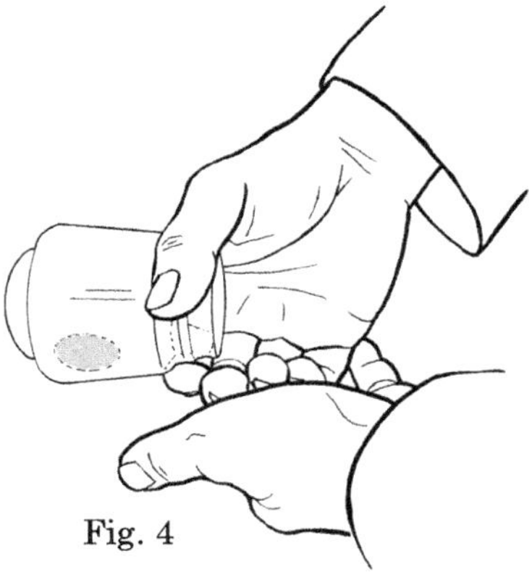

Fig. 4

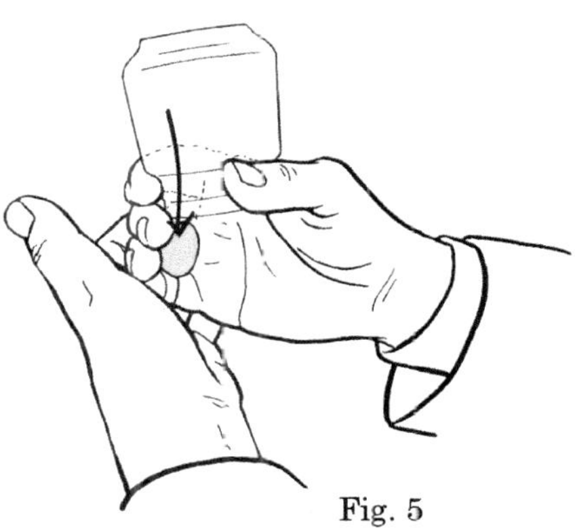

Fig. 5

You are set to repeat the penetration.

Slap the empty left hand against the bottom of the jar, dislodging the Finger-Palmed coin into the jar—the coin has penetrated the bottom of the jar for a second time.

Dump the coin onto the table, transfer the jar to the left hand, and pick up the lid with the right hand. Screw the lid onto the jar, again being careful not to dislodge the concealed coin. Place the jar on the table and pick up the coin with the right hand. Execute the **Basic Pivot Vanish**, apparently taking the coin in the left hand.

With the coin concealed in Finger Palm, pick up the jar by its sides—the lid is pointing up, the bottom of the jar down. Smack the left hand against the bottom of the jar.

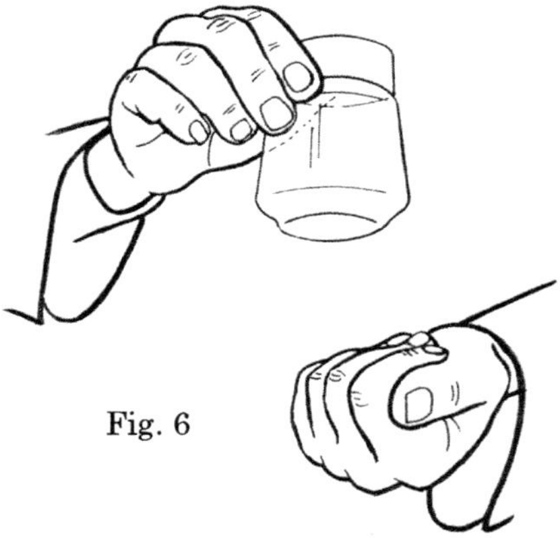

Fig. 6

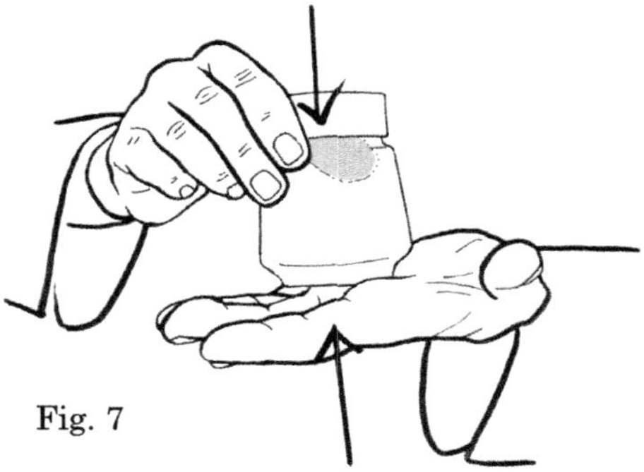

Fig. 7

This automatically dislodges the duplicate coin concealed in the lid and creates the perfect illusion of the coin penetrating the bottom of the jar.

Hand out the jarred coin for examination and secretly drop the extra coin into your pocket.

BABY JARRED COIN

Since Sol's developed "**The Jarred Coin**," magnetic (as opposed to simply metallic) coins have become readily available. This allows for a slightly different approach to the same basic plot that is suitable for walk-around performances. You simply need a magnetic quarter, a regular quarter, and a miniature jar that fancy restaurants sometimes use to serve marmalade or jam. The jar is about an inch and a half high and should have a metal lid.

There is no need to gaff the jar—simply stick the magnetic coin to the inside of the lid, drop the regular coin into the jar, and replace the lid. In this presentation, the coin will only penetrate the sealed jar a single time.

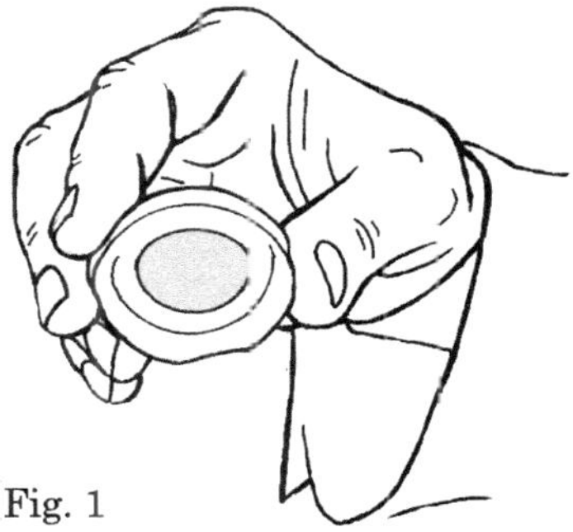

Fig. 1

When ready to perform, hold the jar in your left hand, unscrew the lid with your right hand, and pour the regular quarter from the jar onto your right hand.

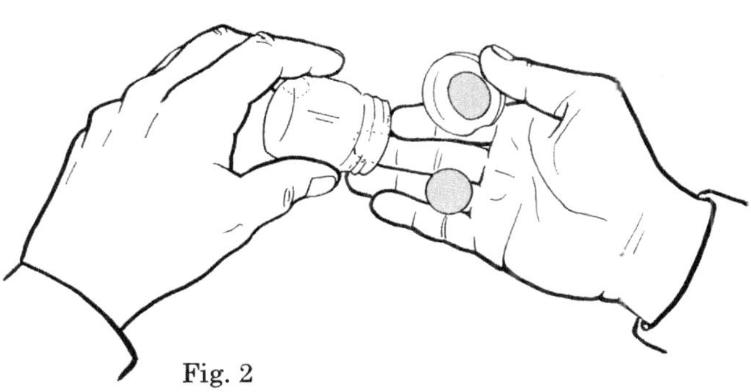

Fig. 2

Replace the lid on the jar, being careful not to expose or dislodge the magnetic quarter concealed inside the lid. Hold the jar by its sides between your right thumb and first and second fingers. Display the quarter in your left hand—Sol tosses it up and down a few times. When you are ready to perform the penetration, swing your right hand downward, Thumb Palming the quarter as you do so.

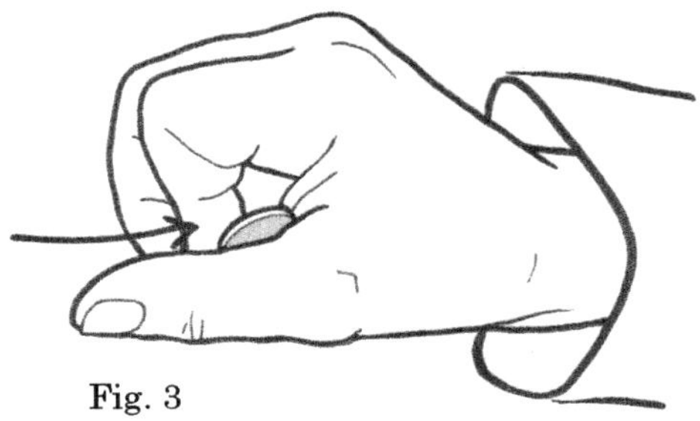

Fig. 3

Swing the hand upward, opening the hand and smacking the fingers against the bottom of the jar. Note that the top edge of the right thumb is toward the audience at this point, concealing the Thumb-Palmed coin from view.

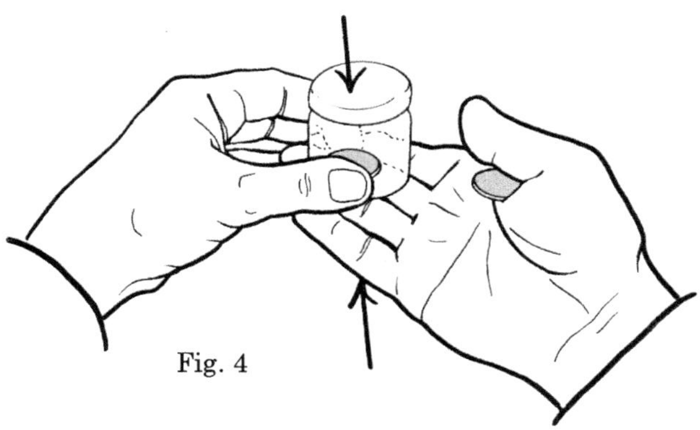

Fig. 4

The impact dislodges the magnetic coin inside the jar—the illusion of the quarter penetrating the glass is perfect.

As you display (and rattle) the coin in the jar with your left hand, drop your right hand to your side and let the quarter fall from Thumb Palm to Finger Palm. Transfer the jar to the right hand (where it helps to conceal the Finger-Palmed coin), and unscrew the lid with the left hand. Dump the coin from the jar onto the left hand.

Set the jar (but not the lid) aside and execute a Shuttle Switch, apparently tossing the coin from the left hand into the right hand. To do this you pretend to dump the coin from the left hand into the right, in reality retaining the coin in the left hand Finger Palm and bringing the right-hand's coin into view.

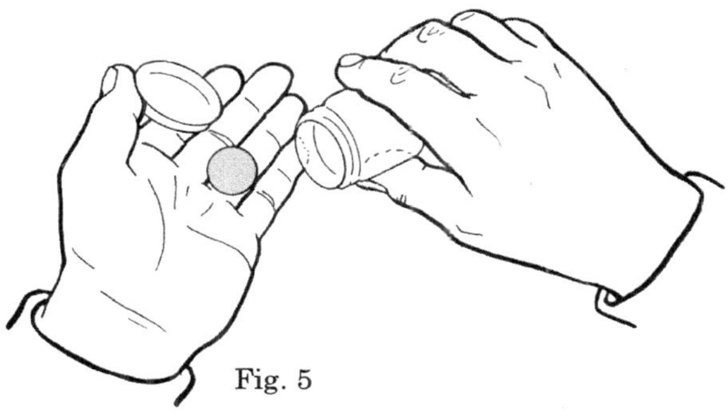
Fig. 5

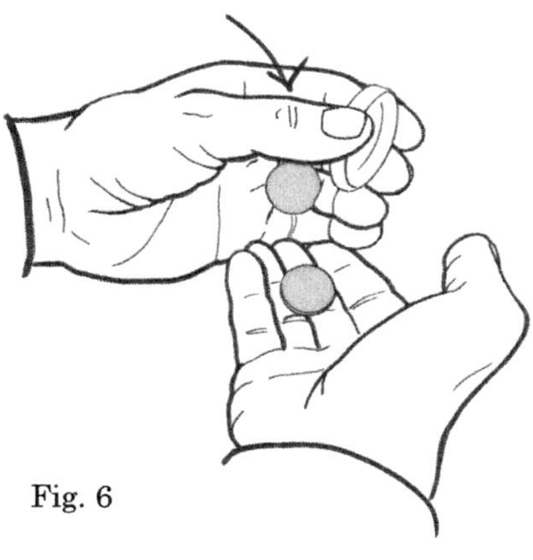
Fig. 6

Because the lid is still held in the left hand, the action of the Shuttle Switch is perfectly motivated.

Conclude by screwing the lid onto the jar and placing everything into your pocket, dropping off the magnetic coin at the same time.

Alternatively, if you are working from table to table, you can allow the magnetic coin to slide into the lid which is then dropped into your pocket. As you walk to the next table, simply screw the lid onto the jar and you are ready to repeat the effect.

Sweet and Low

This is a mini-classic of impromptu magic—a coin vanishes and reappears inside a sugar packet. It is the kind of trick that you can perform at a restaurant on the spur of the moment to stunning effect. The only requirement is that there are some sugar packets within easy reach and that you have a pencil readily available.

Borrow a quarter and have a spectator write his initials on the coin with the pencil. Take the coin from the spectator and hold it in right-hand Pinch Grip. Ask the spectator to pick up one of the sugar packets and place it on the table in front of him. He is then to place his palm-down hand over the packet. Do not have the spectator examine the sugar packet—you don't want to tip the climax of the effect. Say something like, "*What I am going to try and do is push the coin through the back of your hand so that, without spilling a single drop of your blood, it ends up on top of the sugar packet.*"

Apparently take the coin into the left hand, actually executing the **Pivot Vanish**. Now pretend to press the coin against the back of the spectator's hand. Rub the fingers in small circles and then lift your hand to reveal that the coin has vanished. Touching the spectator's hand is important—it opens the possibility, however far-fetched, that you somehow sneaked the coin under his hand and onto the packet. Have the spectator lift his hand to "reveal" the coin on top of the sugar packet. Act surprised when it isn't there. Say, "*Oh, I know. I pushed too hard, the coin must be underneath the packet.*"

Pick up the packet with your left hand and act confused when you discover that the coin is not underneath the packet. Focus your attention on the packet. Slowly turn your left hand over a few times—displaying both sides of the packet—as you "realize" what might have happened.

You now rip one end of the packet off with your right hand. The palm of the hand is toward the audience as you do this, the coin concealed in **Ramsay Subtlety**.

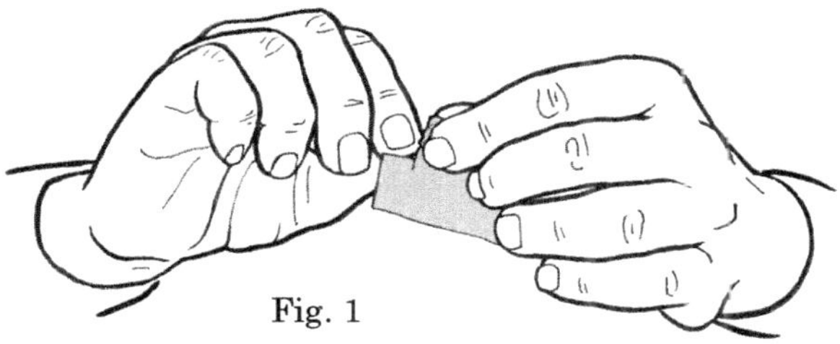

Fig. 1

Having torn off the end of the packet, drop it to the table. Close your right hand into a loose fist with the thumb hole uppermost. Pour the contents of the packet into your right fist and toss the empty packet aside.

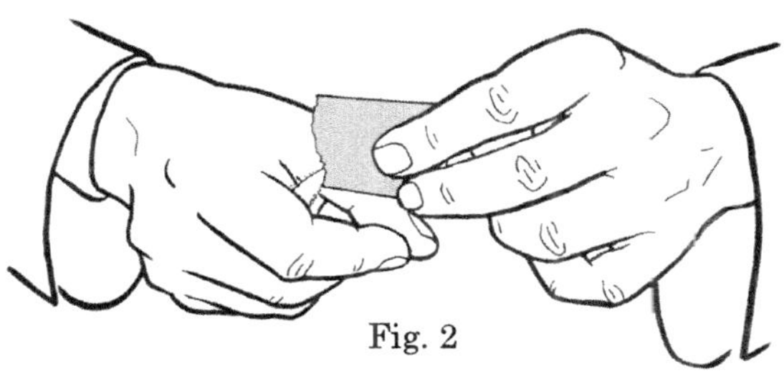

Fig. 2

Open the right hand and pour the sugar from the right hand onto your palm-up left hand. The coin remains behind in right hand Finger Palm and is not yet seen by the audience.

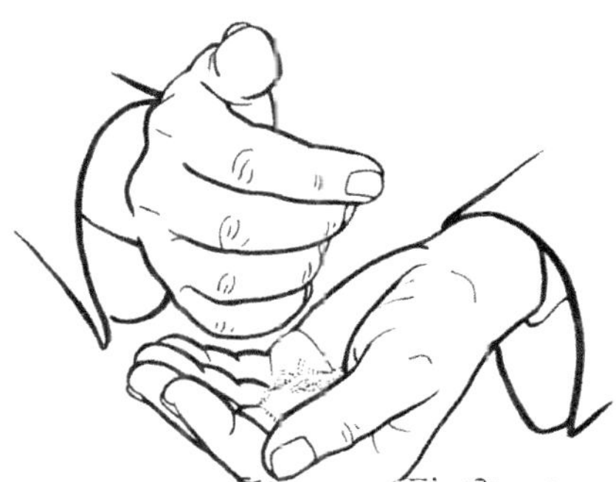

Fig. 3

Immediately, pour the contents back into the palm-up right hand, directly onto the coin (which is still concealed in **Ramsay Subtlety**). Poke around in the sugar with the tip of your left first finger, brushing some of the sugar off the coin so that it is clearly visible.

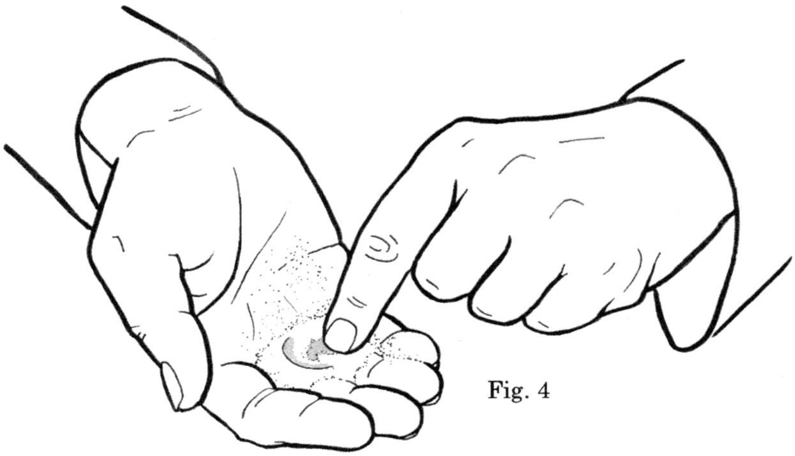

Fig. 4

Have the spectator remove the coin and verify that it bears his initials. Dump the sugar from your hand into an ashtray, plate or napkin and you are finished.

Cointemplate

There are just not enough adjectives to describe how good this routine is. It is simply the best coin-through-solid-object effect that I have ever seen. You apparently pass a coin through a clear glass plate which is held by a spectator. The routine can play small and very intimate, but is also suitable for larger groups. Moreover, you end completely clean—the spectator can immediately examine everything.

The price you pay is the use of a gaffed coin. You need a **Gibson Magnetic Copper-Silver Coin**. This gaffed coin set consists of a magnetic copper-silver coin (the "insert") that nests and locks in a shimmed silver shell. When the insert is in the shell the gaff appears to be an ordinary silver coin. Sol keeps the shell and insert inside a small wallet, each in a different compartment within the wallet.

Stuck inside the wallet is a piece of rubberized magnet. Sol uses this magnet to free the insert from the shell, in preference to banging the shell on the table or rattling it inside a glass—the Magnetic Copper-Silver is a fairly expensive item, worth it for this routine alone, but also worth taking care of.

You will also need a duplicate copper coin and a clear glass plate. The glass plate should have a gentle, sloping lip running around its circumference.

Before beginning, secretly Classic Palm the duplicate copper coin in the left hand. The copper-silver shell and insert are, of course, unnested at this point.

Invite a spectator to assist you and have her stand facing the audience. Give her the plate to hold, instructing her to grasp it firmly by opposite sides at about stomach level.

Fig. 1

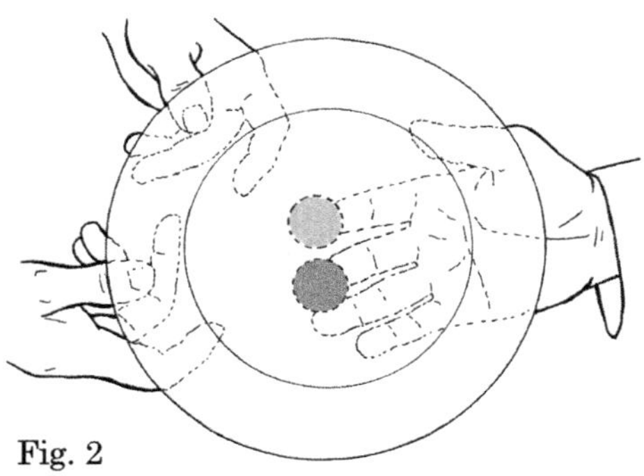

Fig. 2

Bring out the shell (silver) coin and the copper-silver insert (copper side up) coin and display them. Extend your right first and second fingers and balance the shell on the first finger and the copper-silver insert on the second finger. Place the right hand beneath the plate and allow the spectators to get a good look at both coins below the plate. Do not, however, touch the coins against the plate.

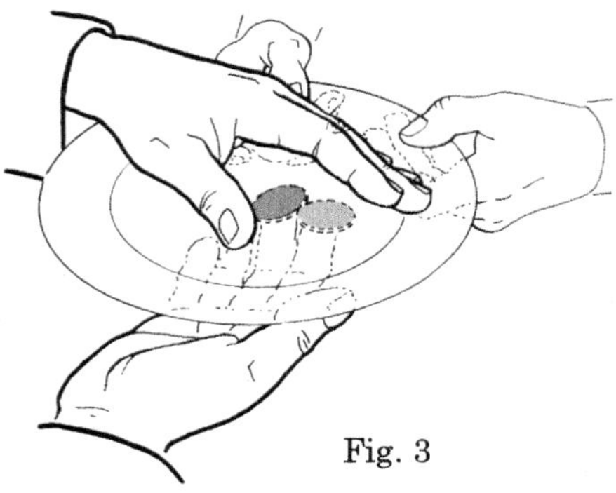

Fig. 3

Bring the left hand palm (with the secretly palmed copper coin) over the plate. Move the left hand so that it is directly above the right hand.

As soon as the right hand is screened from view—and it doesn't take much to do so—the right thumb presses down onto the shell coin resting on the right first finger. The thumb slides the coin directly to the left and onto the copper-silver coin, where it locks into place and becomes, for all intents and purposes, a silver coin.

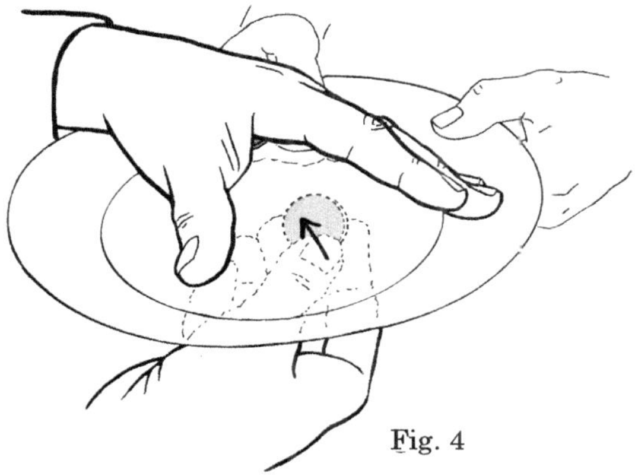

Fig. 4

At the same time, the left hand presses down against the plate from above, snapping the Classic-Palmed coin against the glass. This noise not only signifies that the penetration has taken place, but covers any noise caused by the shell locking onto the copper-silver insert. If you like, you can then snap the locked copper-silver coin against the bottom of the plate.

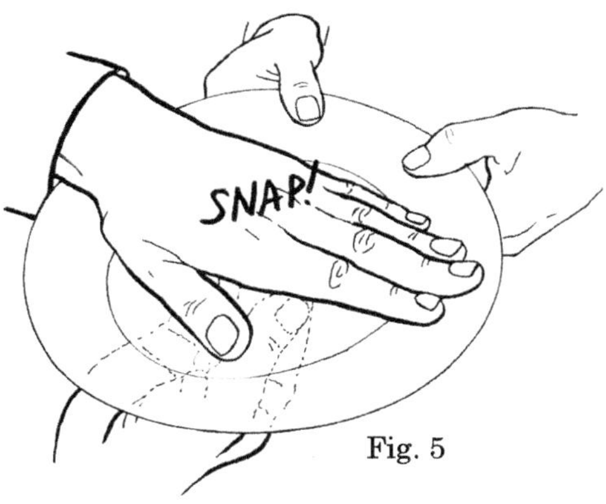

Fig. 5

Immediately raise the left hand, leaving the copper coin resting on top of the plate. The right hand presses the silver coin against the bottom of the plate. Pause for a moment.

Because it is difficult for the spectators to perceive relative depth in this situation, it is not immediately clear what has occurred.

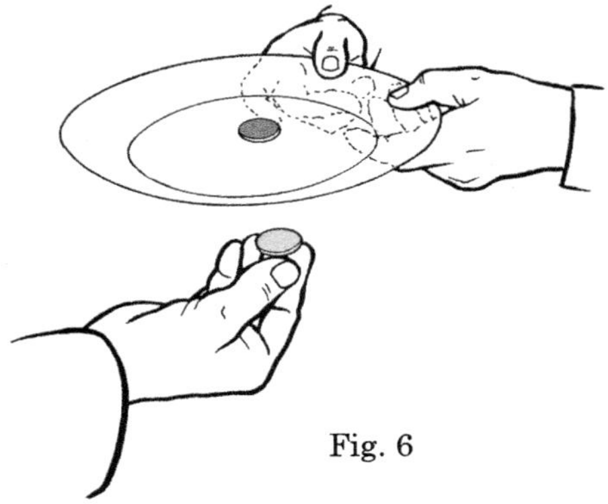

Fig. 6

Slowly lower the right hand, revealing that the copper coin is in fact resting on top of the glass.

Remove the right hand from beneath the plate and casually display both sides of the coin. Now, if the glass you are using has a gentle lip, you can rest the coin on the lip and allow it to slide onto the plate. Do not simply drop the coin in the plate because it will not ring true. Your hands are empty and the spectators can examine everything. The Magnetic Copper-Silver will withstand scrutiny, but obviously do not let this go on for too long. You will find, however, that the spectators are much more interested in the plate and the copper coin which apparently passed through it.

A few observations concerning "Cointemplate"...

First, the use of the plate allows you to do the effect under almost any circumstances and makes the routine play "big." Of course, it does require that you carry a glass plate with you. Occasionally, when caught without a glass plate, Sol has used an ordinary China plate—but the visual element is absent and the routine is not nearly as strong. If there is a glass table present, it can also be used to great—and apparently impromptu—advantage. Second, you can naturally offer the spectator a "magician's choice" as to which coin will travel through the glass. Sol has found, however, that this really isn't necessary. He prefers that the entire penetration come as a complete surprise. Finally, consistent with his belief that an effect should not be repeated, Sol does this once and then stops. Really, repetition in this context is bound to be anti-climatic.

STRANGE TRANSPOSITIONS

Two-Timing Transpo

This is a two-phase transposition in which a silver coin, placed in your pocket, changes places with a copper coin. Not only does it flow smoothly from moment to moment and phase to phase, but the effect is done entirely in the hands—no table or other surface is required. At the heart of the routine is **Sol's Spellbound Sequence**, with which I will assume you are familiar. The "**No Table" Pivot Vanish** is also employed. The rest is just solid routining.

To begin, have two silver coins in your right jacket pocket and a copper coin in your left jacket pocket. Sol always uses fifty-cent size coins for this routine. Both hands reach into their respective pockets. The right hand Finger Palms one of the silver coins and comes out with the other silver coin in Pinch Grip. The left hand comes out with the copper coin in Pinch Grip. Display both coins, concealing the extra silver coin in **Ramsay Subtlety**.

First Transposition: Say, *"I am going to make these two coins change places. How would you like me to do it—visibly or invisibly?"* It doesn't matter how the spectator responds because you will do the same thing in either case—simply exchange the two coins so that the silver coin is at the left fingertips and the copper coin is at the right fingertips. Sol has two similar lines to cover both responses. If the spectator said visibly, Sol exchanges the coins and says, *"That's efficient, but not very magical."* If the spectator said invisibly, he exchanges the coins and says, *"I'm glad you said 'invisibly.' If you had said 'visibly' I would have done it this way, which is efficient, but not very magical."*

Continue, saying, *"It's much more magical when done invisibly. To make this easier to follow, I will place the silver coin in my pocket."* Allow the silver coin to fall from the left fingertips onto the left palm. Display it for a moment and then give it a slight upwards toss as you close your left fingers around the coin. This is important as it sets up a very subtle throw-off in a moment.

Place your hand in your left pocket, depositing the coin. Remove your left hand and casually let it be seen empty. (Sometimes, Sol does not let the audience immediately see that the hand is empty. Instead, he keeps it palm down with the thumb pressed against the side of the hand. The audience—magicians particularly—are suspicious. He pauses a beat and then casually turns his hand over and spreads his fingers, dispelling all suspicion and throwing the audience momentarily off-track.)

Transfer the copper coin to left-hand Spellbound position, then immediately go into Phase One of **Sol's Spellbound Sequence**, exactly as described in the **Basic Coin Sleights** section. Don't forget to include the preliminary rotation of the coin (to dispel thoughts of a copper-silver coin) and to end by snapping the newly visible silver coin into Pinch Grip. As the right hand moves away from the left, Sol mimes throwing the invisible coin towards his pocket and then casually gestures with the palm-up right hand to show that it is empty.

Transfer the silver coin to right-hand Pinch Grip. The apparently empty left hand (it really has a coin in Finger Palm) enters the left pocket, pretends to search around, and removes the copper coin which is displayed in left-hand Pinch Grip. The first transposition is complete!

Take advantage of the fact that you now only have two coins to let the audience see that you are not holding out any extra coins. The best way to do this is to casually lower your hands to waist level, while still holding both coins in Pinch Grip, so that the spectators can see the entire inside of both hands. Do not, of course, make a big deal out of this display.

Second Transposition: Say, *"Perhaps that confused you, let me do it again."* You will now repeat the transposition, using only two coins. The silver coin is in right-hand Pinch Grip, the copper coin in left-hand Pinch Grip.

Pretend to take the silver coin into the left hand, in reality executing the "**No Table" Basic Pivot Vanish**. Without pausing, the right hand takes the copper coin at the left fingertips in Pinch Grip. You now apparently have the silver coin in your curled left fingers and a copper coin in right-hand Pinch Grip. In reality, the silver coin is concealed in right-hand Finger Palm. Say, *"Again, the silver coin goes into my pocket."*

Pretend to toss the (imaginary) silver coin in the left hand slightly upwards, catch it, and place it in your left pocket. Of course, there is no coin in your left hand—this is pure acting. Done properly, however, it really sells the fact that you have a coin in your hand.

Sol generally just removes the left hand from the pocket and lets it be seen empty. There are, however, two other options. You can quickly retrieve the silver coin already in the pocket, momentarily remove it, flash it to the audience, and drop it back in your pocket. This works best if you are working out of a jacket pocket. If you are working out of your pants pocket, you can grab the silver coin already there and press it outwards against the cloth of the pocket. The audience sees the circle of the coin through the cloth. Tap the coin through the cloth with the right-hand copper coin and then remove your empty left hand.

At this point Sol casually turns both palms toward the audience, concealing the silver coin in palm-down **Ramsay Subtlety**. *"And the copper coin is in my hand."*

Turn both hands palm up and place the copper coin in left-hand Spellbound position. Immediately go into the Spellbound sequence, exactly as before. Remember to include the pantomime toss of the "invisible" coin in the right hand towards the left pocket. Transfer the silver coin to right-hand Pinch Grip. Reach into your left pocket, pretend to fish around, and remove the copper coin to conclude.

Again, I can only reiterate that this is a superbly structured routine. During the first phase of the effect you are "one ahead" of the audience with the extra silver coin. However, any thoughts of an extra coin are completely dispelled during the second phase of the routine which, although it appears to exactly mimic the first in structure, clearly uses only two coins. Sometimes, when a table is available, Sol replaces the second phase of the routine with the "**Direct Transposition, First Version**." See below for details.

THE DIRECT TRANSPOSITION

THREE HANDLINGS

First Version: A silver coin is in right-hand Pinch Grip, and a copper coin in left-hand Pinch Grip. Pretend to take the silver coin into the left fist, actually executing the "**No Table" Pivot Vanish**. Then take the copper coin in right-hand Pinch Grip. Gesture with the closed left fist and say, "*Ignore the half, keep your eye on the penny.*"

You now apparently toss the copper coin to the table. In reality, as the right hand turns palm down execute an in-the-air **One Hand Thumb Palm Turnover Switch**—that is, the copper coin is slid directly into Thumb Palm and the silver coin tossed to the table as you say, "*I said ignore the half, keep your eye on the penny.*" The copper coin has apparently been transformed into the silver coin.

In the mind of the audience, the effect is basically over, all that remains to be done is to show that the silver coin in the left hand is now the copper coin. To do this, execute the **Hot Potato Shuttle Pass**—only here there is no extra coin concealed in the left hand. Just pretend to toss a coin from the left hand onto the right fingertips—actually releasing the copper coin in right-hand Thumb Palm and letting it fly onto the right fingers. Toss the coin from hand to hand once or twice and then drop it on the table to conclude.

Sun and Moon Patter

Recently, Sol has begun using the following patter as he performs the above two-coin transposition. You need a "gold" (we will assume copper) coin and a "silver" coin.

"The ancient civilizations of Peru believed that gold is the Sun's sweat and silver is the Moon's tears. When a warrior-priest is buried, they bury his gold possessions on his right side and his silver possessions on his left side. [Place the gold coin on the table to your right; the silver coin on the table to your left.]

"If a member of the burial party makes a mistake and buries a gold object on the left and a silver object on the right. . . [Pick up the gold coin and hold it at the right fingertips; pick up the silver coin and hold it at the left fingertips. The gold coin is apparently taken by the left hand using the **"No Table" Vanish**. The silver coin is then taken at the left fingertips.]

" . . . the warrior-priest's spirit can't rest until a magician comes and magically moves the gold object to the right . . . [Perform the in-the-air **Thumb Palm Turnover Switch**, tossing the gold coin from the left hand to the table and secretly transferring the silver coin to left-hand Thumb Palm.]

Second Version: Begin with a silver coin in left-hand Pinch Grip and a copper coin in right-hand Pinch Grip. An extra silver coin is Classic Palmed in the left hand. Pretend to take the copper coin in the left fist, performing the **"No Table" Pivot Transformation**. Be sure to keep the back of the left hand toward the audience so as not to expose the extra coin in Classic Palm, just as you do when executing the standard **Pivot Transformation**. Take the visible silver coin in right-hand Pinch Grip.

Pretend to toss the silver coin to the table, executing the in-the-air **One Hand Thumb Palm Turnover Switch**. The copper coin falls to the table. Turn your left hand palm up and open it—the audience sees the silver coin lying on your palm—a most direct transposition.

To clean up, execute a standard **Hot Potato Shuttle Pass**, apparently tossing the silver coin onto the right fingers—in reality retaining the coin in left-hand Classic Palm and allowing the coin in right-hand Thumb Palm to fly onto the right fingertips. Toss the coin from hand-to hand (concealing the Classic Palmed coin in **Malini Subtlety**) and then drop it on the table. Because the audience immediately sees the silver coin in the left hand, there is very little heat on the Shuttle Pass.

Third Version: A silver coin is in left-hand Pinch Grip, a copper coin in right-hand Pinch Grip, and a copper-silver coin in left-hand Classic Palm, silver side against the palm. Execute the **"No Table" Pivot Transformation**, apparently placing the copper coin into the left hand. Take the silver coin in right-hand Pinch Grip. You can now turn your left hand palm up and open it. Everything appears as it should—there is a copper coin (really the copper-silver coin) on the left palm and a silver coin at the right fingertips. Close your left hand and turn it palm down. As you do so, the copper-silver coin is flipped over inside the fist.

There is really nothing to this -- just allow the coin to slide across the heel of your thumb and then fall onto your left fingers so that the silver side of the double-faced coin is against the tips of the fingers.

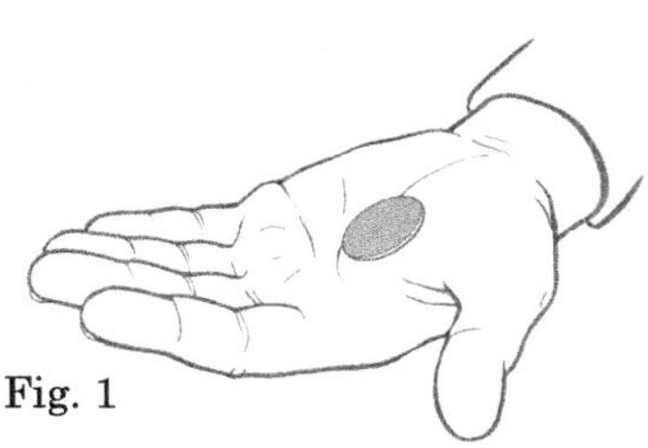

Fig. 1

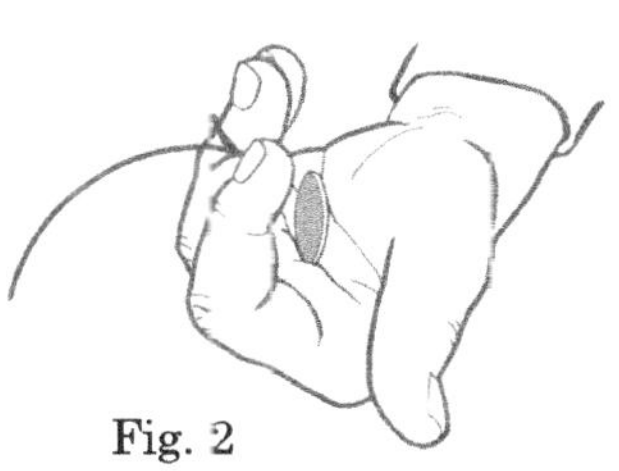

Fig. 2

With the right hand, toss the silver coin to the table, executing the in-the-air **One Hand Thumb Palm Switch**. The silver coin has been transformed into a copper coin. Immediately turn your left hand palm up and open it to display a silver coin (the other side of the copper-silver). As you open the hand, position the coin so that it is in Position to be Classic Palmed. Finally, execute the **Hot Potato Shuttle Pass**, retaining the silver-copper coin in left-hand Classic Palm and releasing the silver coin in left-hand Thumb Palm onto the right fingers. Casually turn the right hand palm down and place the silver coin on the table.

I'D RATHER BE RICH

This is a simple Spellbound routine with a twist. At the end of the effect you roll the coin down the backs of fingers, displaying it on both sides, and then cleanly show the backs and fronts of both hands—there is only one coin. There is no sleeving or lapping—you could do this in your birthday suit. The price is the use of a magnetic copper-silver coin, the same sort of coin employed in the routine "**Cointemplate**" (see that routine for a description of this gimmick).

Begin with the copper-silver insert in left-hand Pinch Grip, copper side toward the audience. The silver shell is hidden in right-hand Finger Palm, with the face of the shell against the fingers.

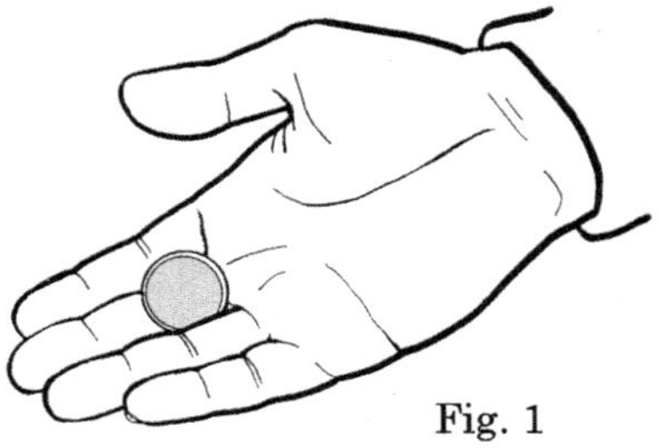

Fig. 1

Display the copper coin and then execute the first phase of the **Brush Change**—the right hand moves in front of the left hand and the copper coin is taken directly into right-hand Thumb Palm; as the right hand moves away from the left the silver shell is taken in left-hand Pinch Grip. As this transformation takes place, say, "*When I change copper into silver I feel rich.*"

As you display the silver shell at the left fingertips (keeping the face of the shell toward the audience, of course), secretly allow the copper-silver insert to slide from Thumb Palm to Finger Palm (copper-side against the fingers). Repeat the Brush Change, say, "*When I change silver into copper I feel poor.*"

While displaying the copper coin at the left fingertips, let the shell concealed in the right hand slide from Thumb Palm to Finger Palm so that the face of the shell ends up against the fingers.

Secretly press your right thumb against the shell and slide it toward the tips of the first and second fingers. From the front, the shell should be completely concealed behind the fingertips.

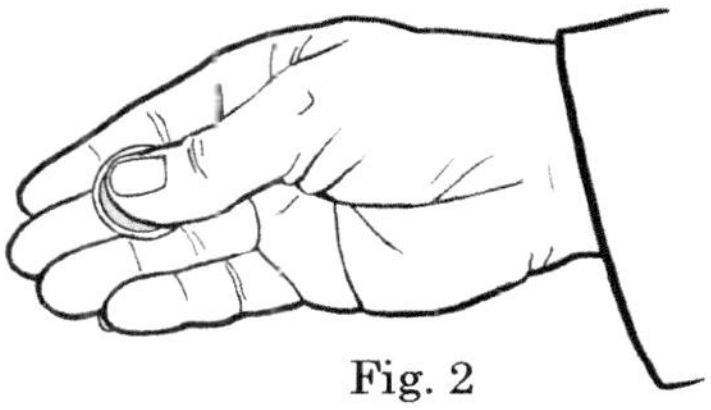

Fig. 2

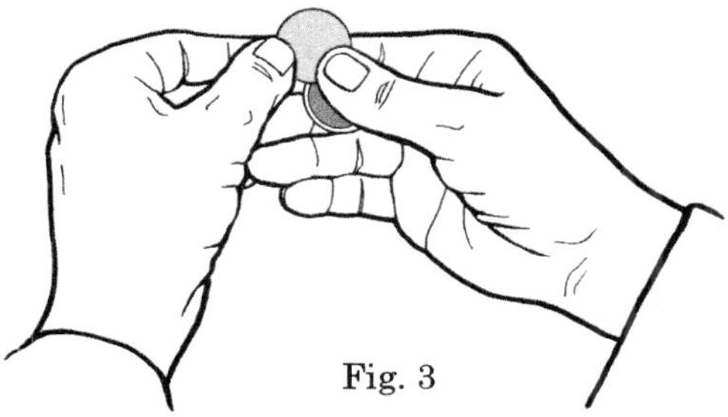

Fig. 3

Keeping the copper side of the insert toward the audience, transfer it to right-hand Pinch Grip so that the lower edge of the insert is resting over the upper lip of the shell, where it is held in place with the right thumb.

Slowly pull the insert behind the right fingers with the right thumb, sliding it directly into the shell. When the insert is fully in the shell it will be locked in place by the magnet and becomes, for all intents and purposes, a silver coin.

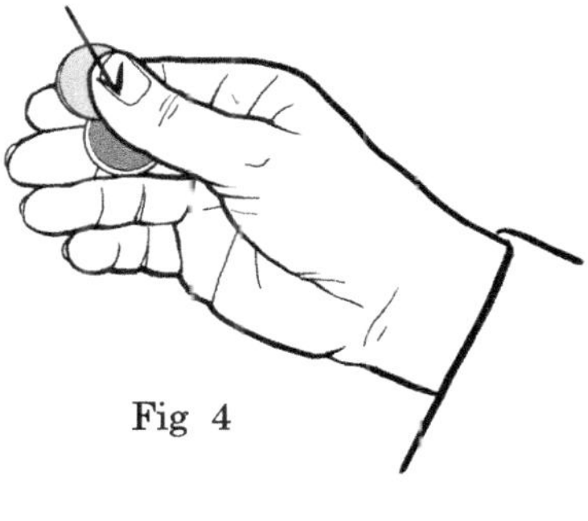

Fig 4

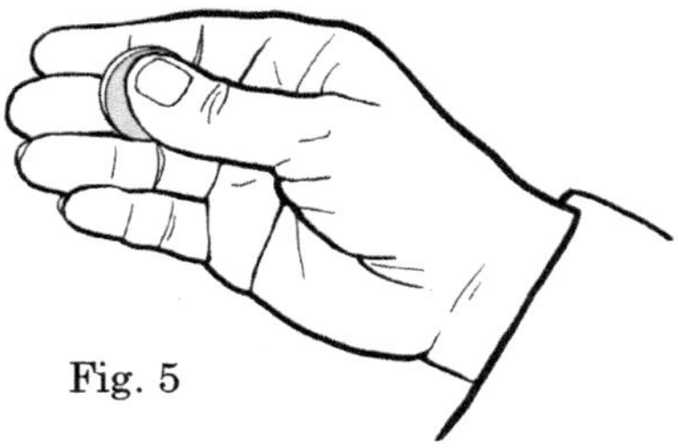

Fig. 5

Use the right thumb to push the silver coin into view at the fingertips. It appears as if you have caused the coin to change by simply pulling the coin behind your fingers and pushing it back into view. As this change takes place, say, "*Rich feels better!*"

Without pausing, immediately go into a Coin Roll, sending the coin cascading down the backs of the right fingers. Repeat the Coin Roll once or twice and then drop the coin into your left hand and turn both hands palm up with the fingers slightly spread. You clearly have only one coin and any attempt by the spectators to "walk back the cat" is frustrated before it even begins.

Fifty-One Cents And Counting

During World War II, before he was sent overseas, Sol was briefly stationed in Nashville, Tennessee. While there, he met T. J. Crawford. This was the same T. J. Crawford who contributed effects to T. Nelson Downs' The Art of Magic and had a section devoted to his coin work in Hilliard's Greater Magic. Sol was very much surprised to find that he was still alive.

Crawford showed Sol several interesting coin moves and, after he was shot down and "bumming his way through the Balkans," Sol used these moves as the starting point for his "Fifty-One Cent Routine." The routine has evolved over the years as Sol replaced obsolete sleights with new, improved techniques.

I am going to describe Sol's original handling—which contains two of Crawford's coin sequences—as well as Sol's new, streamlined handling.

These routines are more "manipulative" than, say, Sol's copper-silver transposition effects—the audience is intended to sit back and simply enjoy the various transportations and transformations. Sol says very little while the routines are in progress, limiting his comments to the occasional reminder as to the supposed location of the coins. For ease of learning, I divided these routines into steps or phases. Remember, however, that each phase flows smoothly and seamlessly into the next.

Fifty-One Cent Routine

Original Handling

Begin with a silver (fifty cent) coin in left-hand Pinch Grip and a copper (English penny) displayed in right-hand Pinch grip. An extra silver coin is secretly Classic Palmed in the right hand.

Phase One: Say, "*Keep your eye on the half dollar because it's worth forty-nine cents more than the penny.*" Lower both hands to your sides and say, "*Up my sleeve* (1), *across my chest* (2), *and down into my hand* (3)."

Fig. 1

Fig. 2

In time to your words you perform the following actions: (1) Shrug your left shoulder and jerk your left arm stiffly upwards for an inch or two—this is meant to suggest that you might be "sleeving" the coin. Under cover of this action, Classic Palm the silver coin in your left hand. (2) Simply say, "*Across my chest.*" Then reach over with your left hand and tug your right sleeve just above the elbow. This subliminally suggests that your left hand is empty. (3) Allow the silver coin in right-hand Classic Palm to fall onto the copper coin, creating an audible "clink." Turn your right hand palm up to display both coins.

Phase Two: Transfer the copper coin to the left hand and display both coins in Pinch Grip, copper on the left and silver on the right. The extra silver coin is concealed in left-hand Classic Palm. You are now in position to repeat Phase One only in reverse—the silver coin travels from the right hand to the left. The words and timing are essentially identical to that described in Phase One. Just Classic Palm the silver coin in the right hand, tug the left sleeve with the right hand, and allow the extra silver coin in left-hand Classic Palm to fall onto the copper coin. Phases One and Two are Crawford's first contribution to the routine.

Phase Three: You are now going to get rid of the extra silver coin in a very expeditious fashion. Transfer the copper coin to the right fingertips. Say, "*If I drop the half dollar in my pocket, it melts right through the cloth.*" Openly drop the silver coin at the left fingertips into your left trousers pocket. Bring your right hand against the left trouser pocket, allowing the Classic Palmed coin to fall onto the copper coin. Slowly turn your right hand palm up to show the copper and silver coins, spreading them between your thumb and first two fingers. Pause a beat, and then turn your left hand palm up and take the copper coin between your left thumb and first finger.

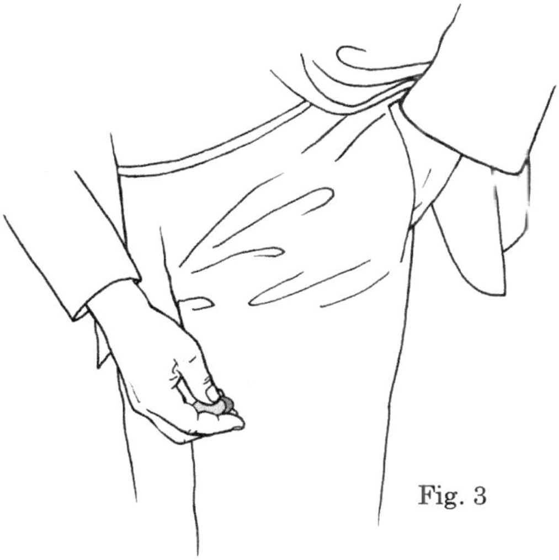

Fig. 3

Phase Four: Display the copper coin in the left hand and the silver coin in the right hand, both in Pinch Grip. Pretend to place the silver coin into the left hand and close the left fingers around the imaginary coin, leaving the copper coin pinched between the extended thumb and first finger. Consistent with sleights he was using when he developed this routine, Sol does a **Classic Palm Vanish** here—the coin is simply snapped into Classic Palm as you pretend to place it in the left hand. (You could, of course, use the **Pivot Vanish**.)

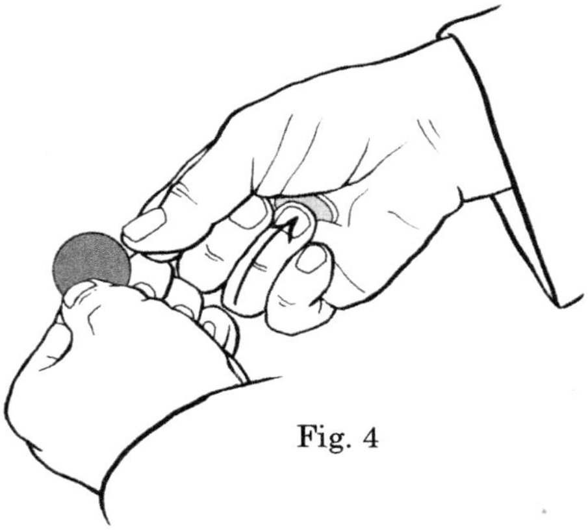

Fig. 4

Now transfer the copper coin from the left to the right fingertips. Display it and then execute a **Classic Click Pass**, allowing the silver coin in Classic Palm to fall onto the copper coin (creating a "click") and then into the left hand. All this occurs behind the semi-curled left fingers. The audience believes that the noise they hear is the copper coin falling onto the silver coin in the left hand.

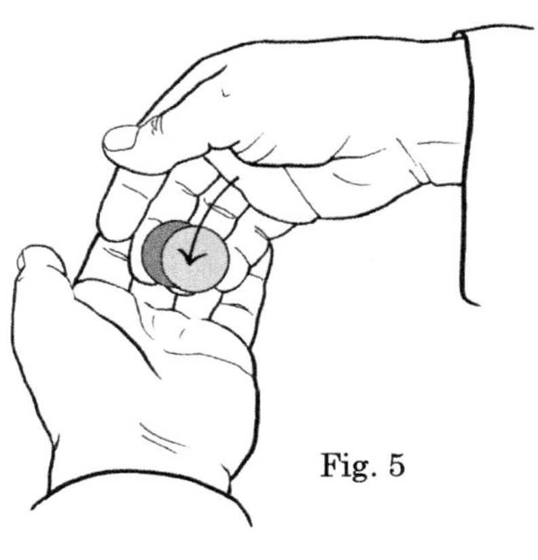

Fig. 5

In reality, only the silver coin is in the left hand; the copper coin is resting on the right fingertips. (My descriptions of these standard techniques has been rather terse, for more detailed explanations see Bobo's ***CoinMagic*** or any other standard coin text.)

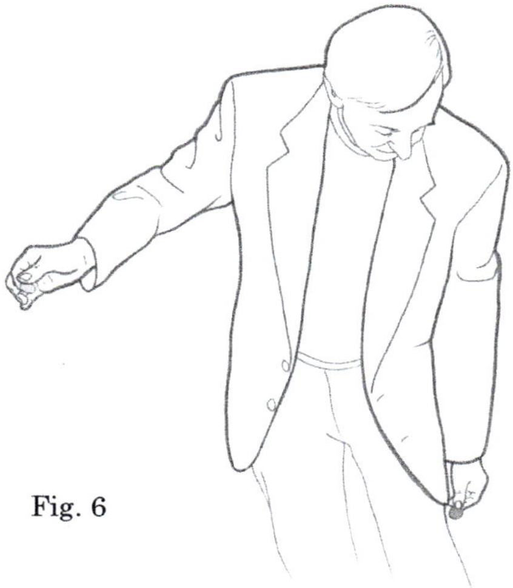

Fig. 6

Make a tossing motion with the left fist, following the imaginary path of the coin with your eyes. Reach out with your right hand and make a grabbing motion in the air, keeping the back of the hand toward the audience as you do. Slowly open the right hand to reveal the copper coin. Open your left hand to reveal that only the silver coin remains.

Phase Five: Place the copper coin between your lips (don't worry, its there for only a moment). Pretend to toss the silver coin from the left hand into the right hand, actually retaining it in left-hand Finger Palm. Close your right hand into a fist around the imaginary coin. Reach up with your left hand and take the copper coin from between your lips, displaying it in Pinch Grip. Make a tossing motion with the right hand and a beat later allow the copper coin in Pinch Grip to fall onto the silver coin in Finger Palm. The audience hears a nice loud "clink." Open your right hand to show that the coin has vanished and then open your left hand to reveal the copper and silver coins. Phases Four and Five are also T. J. Crawford's.

Phase Six: At this point Sol does the **Back Clip Double Vanish**, exactly as described in the section **On the Miser's Dream**. He reproduces the coin in right-hand Back Clip by reaching up and producing it at the fingertips via **Back Clip Retrieval Number Two**. The left hand then reproduces the second coin from behind the left knee. It doesn't matter in which order the copper and silver coins are vanished or reproduced. If you are not comfortable with this sequence, you can proceed directly to Phase Seven.

Phase Seven: For the final phase, Sol now relies upon a technique he has developed since the War, believing it to be considerably superior to his original handling. Display one coin in each hand in Pinch Grip. Execute the **Pivot Click Pass**. That is, the left hand apparently takes the coin from the right hand, actually executing the **"No Table" Pivot Vanish**. The right hand takes the left hand coin and apparently drops it onto the coin in the left fist. In reality, the coin is allowed to fall onto the coin in right-hand Finger Palm, creating a "clink"—both coins end up in right-hand Finger Palm. For complete details, see the description of this sequence in the **Coin Sleights** section.

The left hand (which supposedly contains both coins) reaches up and apparently rubs the coins into the left eye.

Fig. 7

Fig. 8

As the audience is reacting, reach up with your right hand and pinch your nose between the thumb and first finger.

At the same time, let the two coins fall out the bottom of the right fist, catching them in the left hand. Display the two coins to conclude.

ANOTHER FIFTY-ONE CENT ROUTINE

This is another handling of the "**Fifty-One Cent Routine**" that incorporates techniques that were not available to Sol in the 1940's. Begin with a silver coin in right-hand Finger Palm and a copper coin in left-hand Finger Palm.

Phase One: Cross your arms and produce each coin from opposite elbows, pushing the coins to the fingertips. They are not visible until you uncross your arms. Display both coins in Pinch Grip, silver on the right and copper on the left.

Fig. 1

Fig. 2

Phase Two: Do the "**No Table" Pivot Vanish**, apparently placing the silver coin into the left hand. Immediately transfer the copper coin to right-hand Pinch Grip. Make an upward tossing motion with the left fist, but do not open the hand.

Make a catching motion with the right hand, at the same time allowing the copper coin in Pinch Grip to fall onto the silver coin in Finger Palm—causing an audible "clink"—and then closing the hand into a fist. Slowly open the left hand to reveal that the silver coin has vanished. Open the right hand to show that it has joined the copper coin.

Phase Three: Take the copper coin in the left hand and display both coins in Pinch Grip. Now perform Sol's **Pivot Click Pass**, apparently placing the silver coin into the left fist, transferring the copper coin to the right fingertips, and apparently dropping the copper coin into the left hand. Both coins end up in right-hand Finger Palm. Make a tossing motion with the left hand without opening the fist. Make a catching motion with the right hand, allowing the two coins to clink against each other. Slowly open the left hand to show that the coins have vanished, then open the right hand to show that both coins have jumped across.

Phase Four: Transfer the copper coin to the left hand and display both coins in Pinch Grip. Say, "Up on the ceiling!" as you make an upward tossing motion with the right hand. Under cover of this action, the right-hand coin is snapped into Thumb Palm.

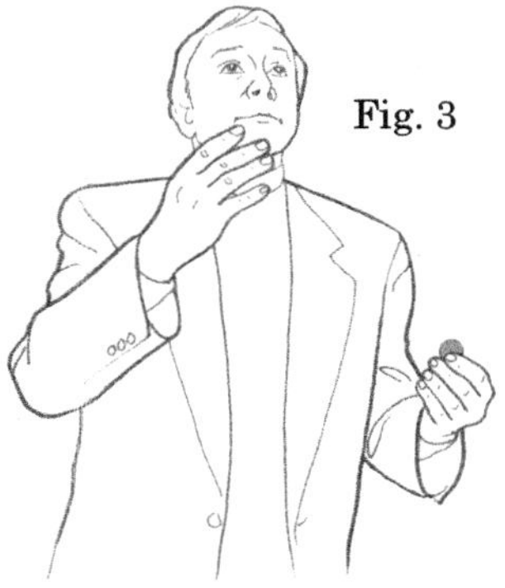

Fig. 3

Naturally, you must keep the back of your hand toward the audience as you do this or the coin in Thumb Palm will be exposed. Follow the upwards path of the (invisible) coin with your eyes and "watch" it disappear.

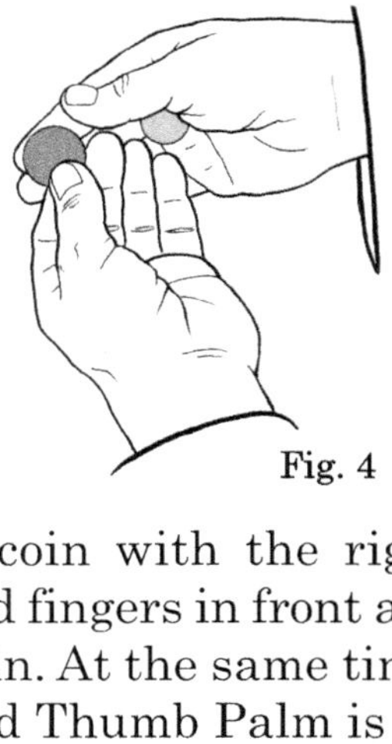

Fig. 4

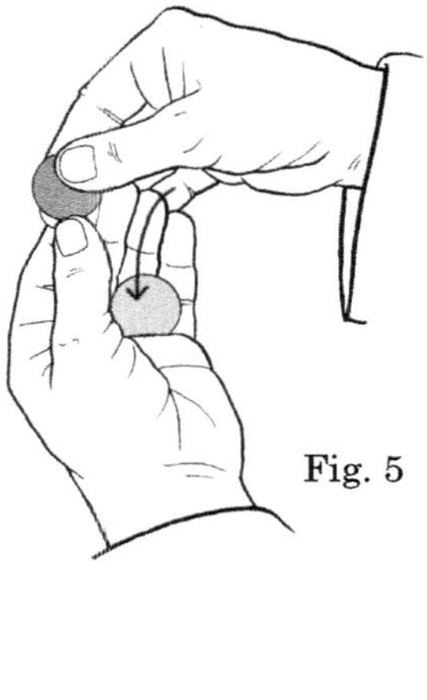

Fig. 5

Bring your hands together so that the backs of the left fingers rest against the front of the right finger. Take the left-hand coin with the right hand, first and second fingers in front and thumb behind the coin. At the same time, the coin in right-hand Thumb Palm is allowed to fall into left-hand Finger Palm.

Separate the hands, turning the right hand palm up to display the copper coin resting on the fingertips. Done properly this unloading of the Thumb-Palmed coin is natural in appearance and undetectable in execution.

Fig. 6

Say, "*Down on the floor!*" as you make a downward tossing gesture with the right hand. Under cover of this larger action, the right-hand coin is Thumb Palmed. Pretend to grind out the (invisible) coin as it hits the floor with your foot. Both coins have apparently disappeared.

Phase Five: Cross your arms and reproduce the coins from the elbows (as was done at the beginning of the routine). Display the coins and then place the right-hand coin at the left fingertips so that both coins are in left-hand Pinch Grip. The two coins should overlap each other for about half their width as you display them. The left thumb then slides the inner coin of the pair into alignment with the outer coin. Execute Sol's **Simplified Spider Vanish** with both coins and then immediately go into the **Townsend Acquitment Sequence**. (See the **Basic Coin Sleights** section for notes on handling two coins during the **Spider Vanish** and the **Townsend Acquitment Sequence**.)

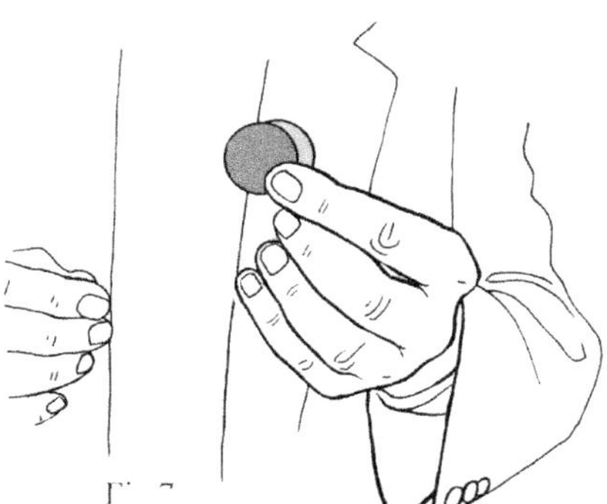

Fig. 7

Conclude by displaying both hands palm up (the two coins are concealed in left-hand Finger Palm) as you gently rub the tips of your fingers and thumb together. Sol ends the routine on this note—having produced two coins at the start, both coins are caused to vanish at the conclusion of the effect.

Psychological Splits

Coin-Fusion

This is a very strong, easy-to-do routine in which two quarters are transformed into a fifty-cent piece. The fifty-cent piece is then split back into two quarters. Harvey Rosenthal and Dr. Sawa introduced Sol to this basic premise. The effect is both visual and audible—the audience "sees" and "hears" the coin split apart. It is a great example of the sophisticated effects that can be achieved with Sol's basic coin techniques. The routine is structured around the **Brush Change**, with which I will assume you are familiar.

A fifty-cent piece is secretly concealed in right-hand Finger Palm. Have or borrow two quarters. One quarter is held pinched between the thumb and first fingers of each hand, in **Fingertip Pinch Grip**, the fifty-cent piece concealed by the **Ramsay Subtlety**. You want as much of the quarters visible as possible.

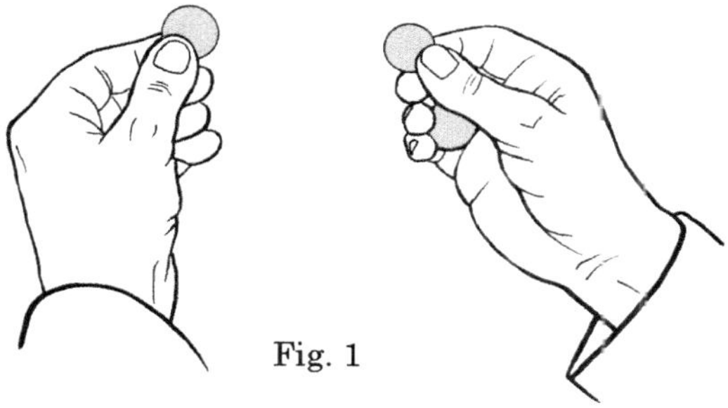

Fig. 1

Say, "*Let me show you the difference between fusion and fission.*" Display the two coins and then place the right-hand quarter in front of the left-hand quarter so that the two are roughly (but not completely) aligned. The coins are held between the left thumb and first finger in Pinch Grip.

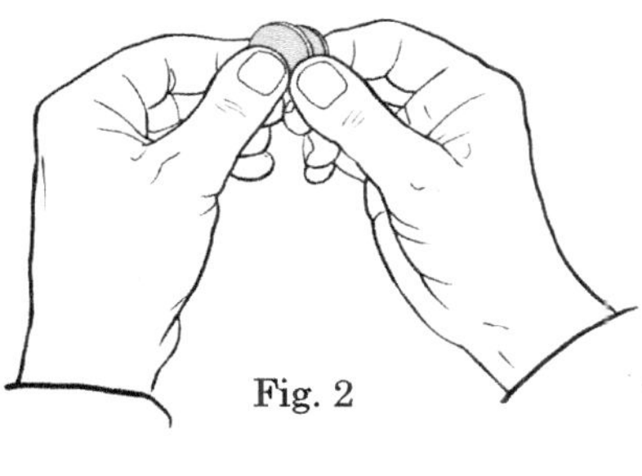

Fig. 2

Now you simply perform the first phase of the **Brush Change**. The right fingers cover the two quarters which are immediately taken into right Thumb Palm. The two quarters must be held firmly as they are placed into Thumb Palm, or they will "talk."

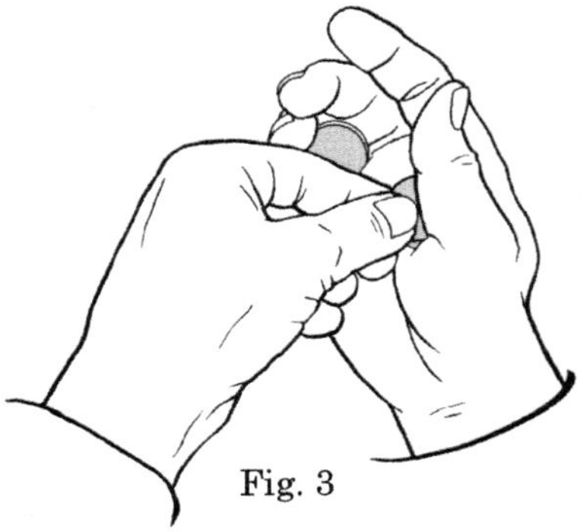

Fig. 3

The left hand picks up the Finger-Palmed fifty-cent piece in Left Hand Pinch Grip, and then brings the coin into view past the right fingertips. *"That's fusion!"* Display both sides of the fifty-cent piece by lowering your left hand at the wrist.

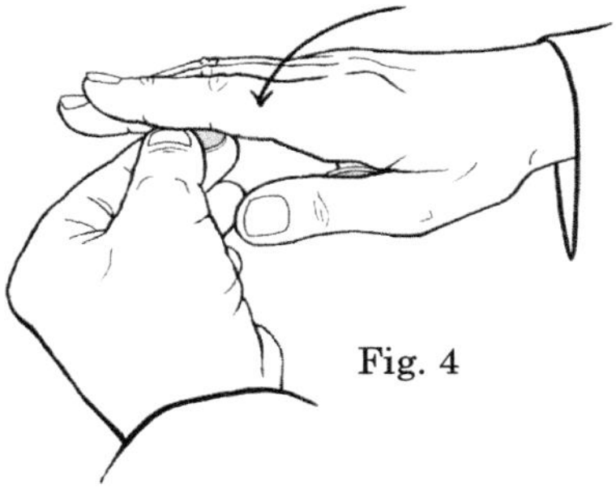

Fig. 4

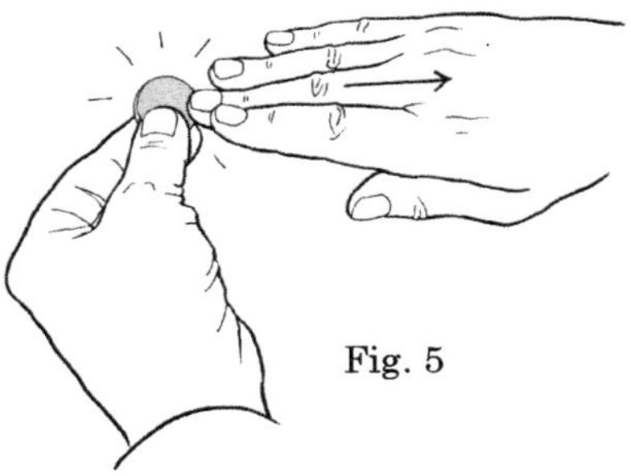

Fig. 5

Now execute phase two of the **Brush Change** as you say, *"And this is fission!"* In other words, the right hand comes over the fifty-cent piece and secures it in Finger Palm. The left first finger and thumb then retrieve the two quarters from Thumb Palm.

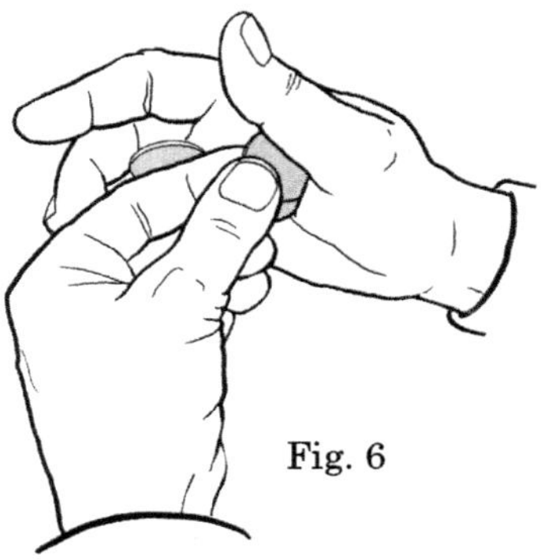

Fig. 6

The coins are not immediately carried into view, however. Instead, they are brought to the tips of the right fingers and both hands grip the coins between the first and second fingers and thumb.

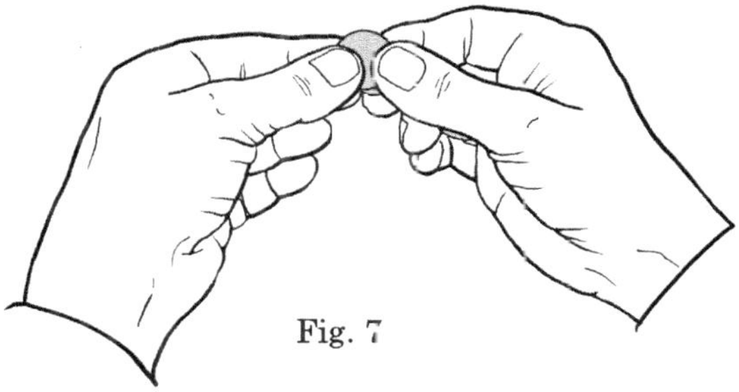

Fig. 7

The hands then rotate sharply inward, snapping one coin off the other and providing audible proof of the "fission." Relax the hands, displaying the two quarters while keeping the fifty cent piece concealed in **Ramsay Subtlety.**

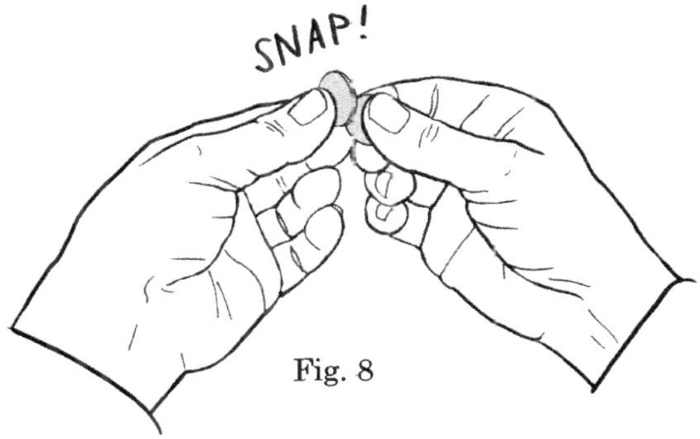

Fig. 8

If he is seated, Sol will lap the fifty-cent piece and use the two quarters in another effect.

Pulling Silver

This is an expanded version of "**Coin-Fusion**." This time, a silver dollar is split into two fifty-cent pieces, which in turn are split into four quarters. While not easy, it is the ultimate blend of Sol's basic coin techniques. In Richard Kaufman's words, it's a "standup, no sleeving, no lapping, in-the-hands miracle."

You will need a silver dollar, two fifty-cent pieces, and four quarters.

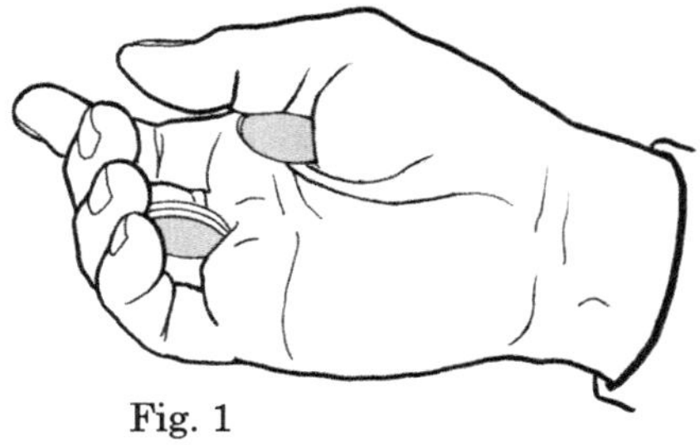

Fig. 1

Place the four quarters in your right thumb crotch in Downs Palm. The two half dollars are also concealed in the right hand in Curl Palm. Some variation is acceptable here: I find it easier to simply retain the fifty-cent pieces in Finger Palm or you may prefer to use the **Angled Finger Palm** described in the description of the **Brush Change**. Finally, take the silver dollar in **Fingertip Pinch Grip**. With all of the coins concealed in your right hand, you cannot rely on the **Ramsay Subtlety**. So keep the back of your right hand toward the audience, with the fingertips and coin pointing toward the left.

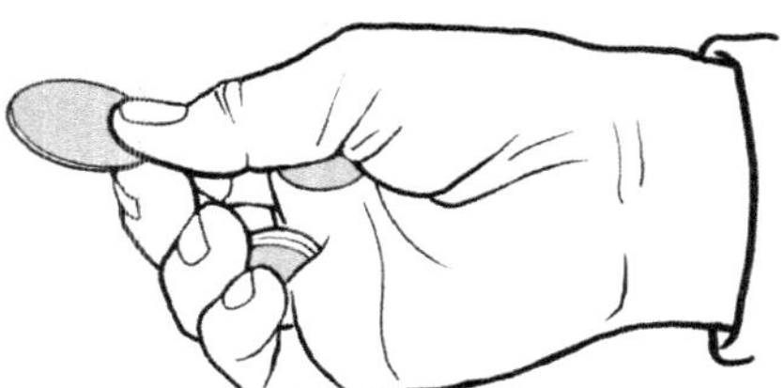

Fig. 2

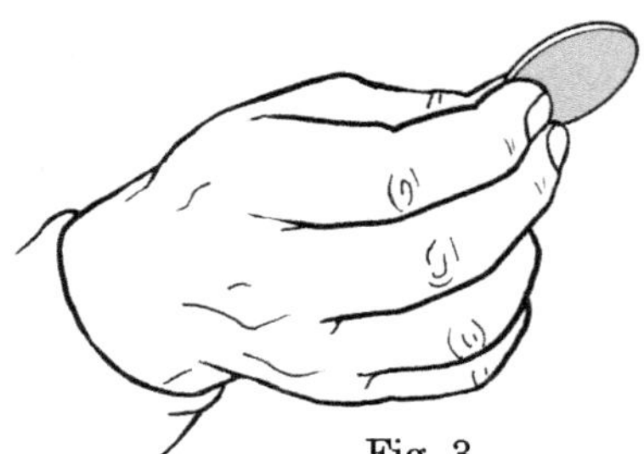

Fig. 3

Casually show your left hand empty. Grasp the silver dollar between your left fingertips and thumb, turn it over, and retake it at the right fingertips. This lets the audience see both sides of the coin. Turn your left hand palm up and place the silver dollar in Spellbound position—in this case, Sol places the coin so that it is perpendicular to the length of the fingers.

Fig. 4

The First Break: Tap the coin with your right first finger. Move your right hand in front of the silver dollar and immediately allow the silver dollar to fall backward into left-hand Finger Palm. Without pausing, the left hand grasps the fifty-cent pieces, thumb above and fingers below. Begin to move your right hand to the right. At the same time, rotate your left hand so that the fingertips are pointing to the right.

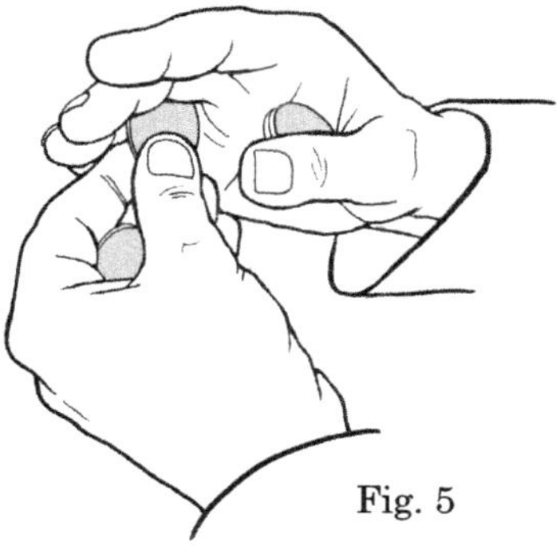

Fig. 5

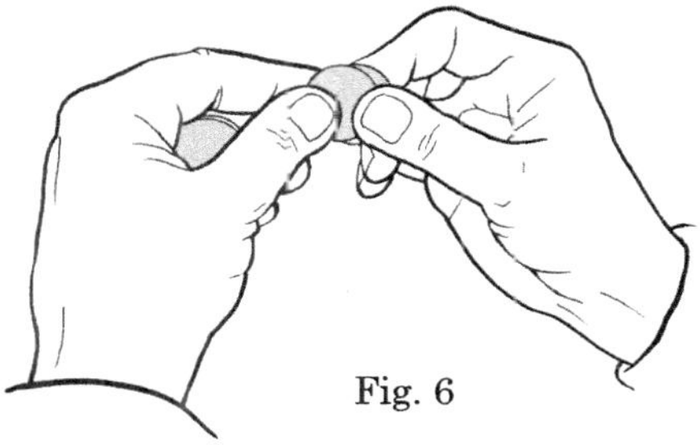

Fig. 6

The fifty cent pieces should not be in view just yet. Pull the innermost coin a little to the left with your left thumb, allowing the right thumb and fingers to grasp the right edge of the outermost coin.

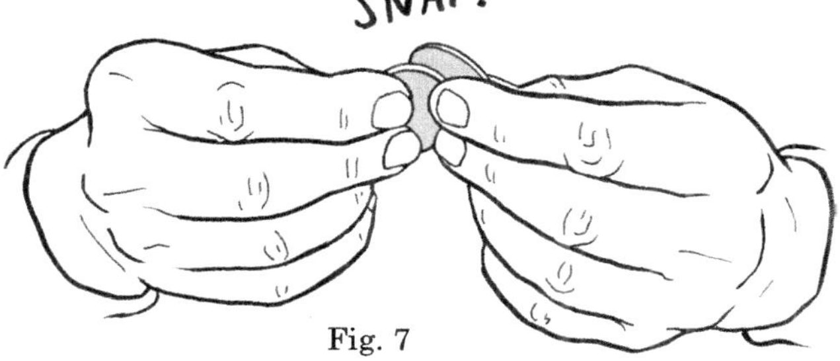

Fig. 7

Bend both hands sharply inwards at the wrist, allowing the two coins to audibly snap off each other. Separate your hands and display both coins.

The Second Break: Place one fifty-cent piece behind the other and then place both coins in left-hand Spellbound position. The right hand moves in front of the two coins, fingers straightening in the process. Move the right hand to the left until you can easily grasp the two coins in right-hand Finger Palm.

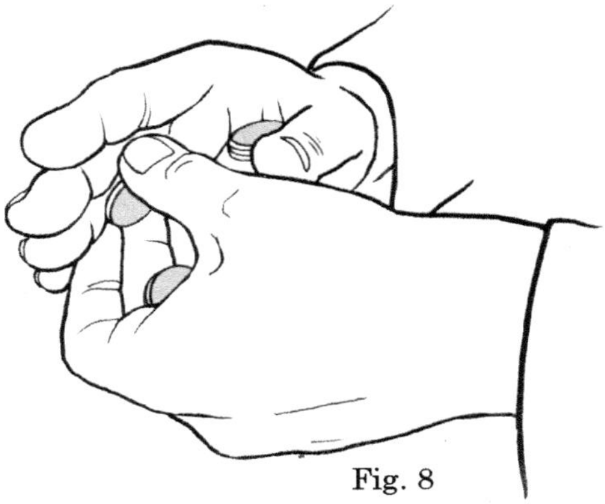

Fig. 8

Take the coins in Finger Palm and continue to move the right hand to the left until the left fingers and thumb can grasp the stack of quarters. Grip the stack between the left thumb, above, and fingers, below.

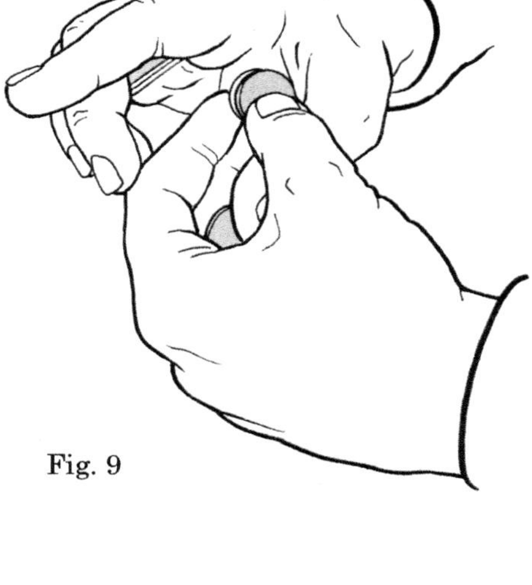

Fig. 9

The hands now reverse directions, the left hand moving to the left and the right hand moving to the right. During this movement, the left fingers spread the stack of quarters in a small fan.

The quarters are not quite in view at this point. As the right hand thumb and fingers pass the quarters, they grasp two of them .

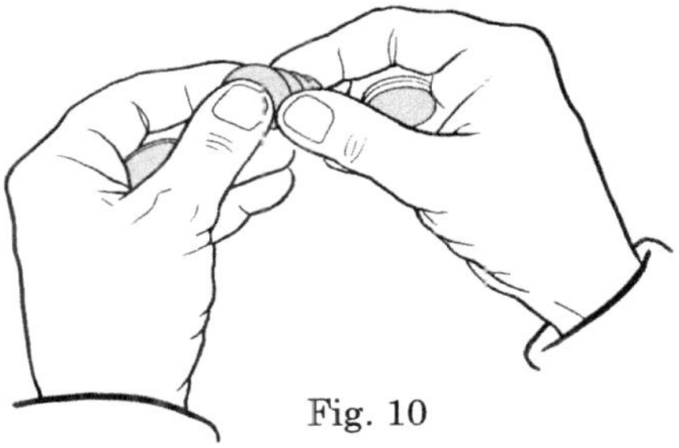
Fig. 10

This brings into view the four quarters, which are audibly snapped off the two in the left hand as explained in The First Break, two in each hand. To conclude, drop the quarters to the table.

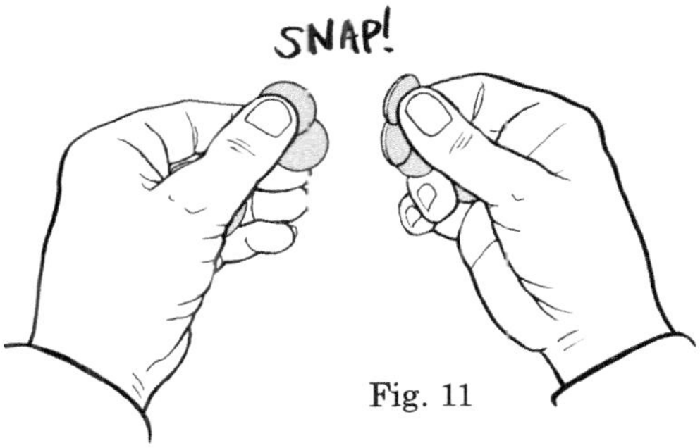

Fig. 11

Cleaning Up: Sol has two approaches to cleaning up: Usually, he picks up two of the quarters, one in each hand, and drops them in his jacket pocket, getting rid of the half dollars and silver dollar at the same time. This leaves two quarters on the table which Sol uses in his next effect (often his handling of the **Tenkai Pennies** routine).

Sometimes, however, Sol leaves the quarters on the table. He then reaches behind his right elbow with his left hand and produces the silver dollar, which is held in Spellbound position. The First Break is performed leaving a half-dollar in Fingertip Pinch Grip in each hand and the silver dollar hidden in Finger Palm in his left hand. Both half-dollars are placed on the table. Finally, the silver dollar is produced, displayed, and placed on the table with the other coins.

Soft Sleeving

Sol uses sleeving sparingly but effectively in his coin work. He has developed a handling he calls "Soft Sleeving." The action is perfectly natural—there is no jerking, snapping, or excessive raising of the wrist commonly associated with most sleeving techniques. Even if you dislike or are afraid to sleeve, give Sol's sleeving technique a try -- you may be pleasantly surprised at the results.

"If you can Sleeve a handful of BB's while standing on a corrugated iron roof without hearing any noise -- you're doing it right."

Emil Jarrow

Basic Soft Sleeve Technique

First, let's focus on the basic **Soft Sleeving** mechanics—it's really very simple. You must, of course, be wearing a jacket with sleeves that are not uncomfortably tight. It will help if you roll up your right shirt sleeve. Hold a coin between the tips of your right thumb and first finger. The position of the hand is important, and leads us to the **First Rule of Soft Sleeving**: ***The palm-down hand is always raised upward at a slight angle***. This means that the path the coin will travel to the sleeve is partially downward. The coin does not move along a horizontal line, nor does it drop directly downward into the sleeve.

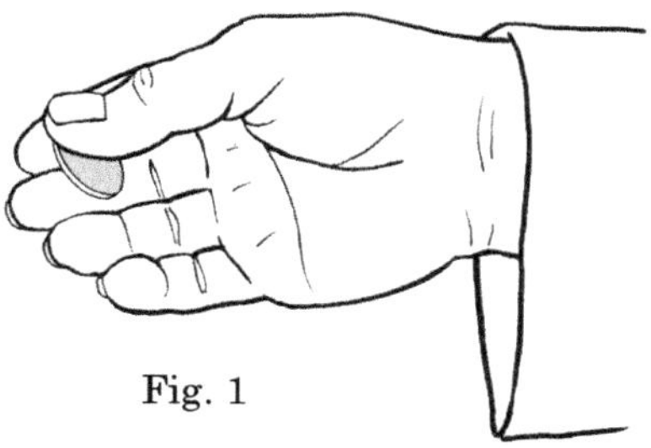

Fig. 1

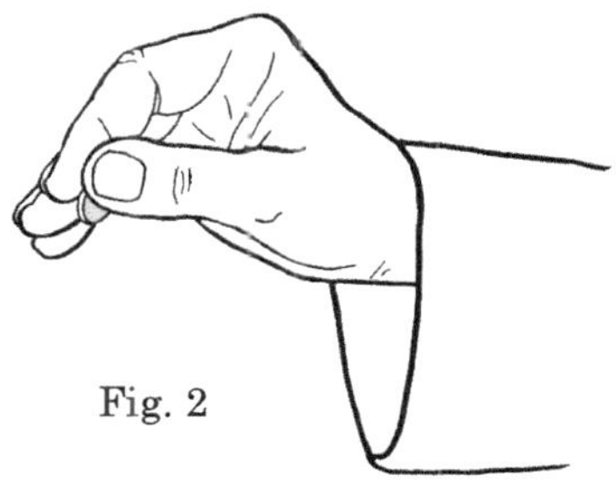

Fig. 2

The Second Rule of Soft Sleeving now comes into play: ***The coin is always rubbed, never snapped, into the sleeve.***

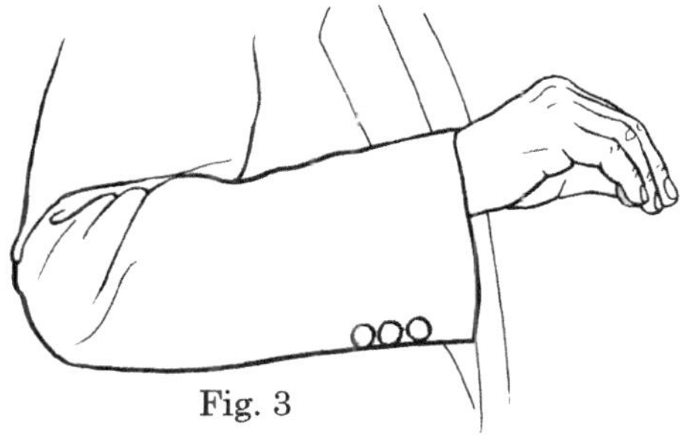

Fig. 3

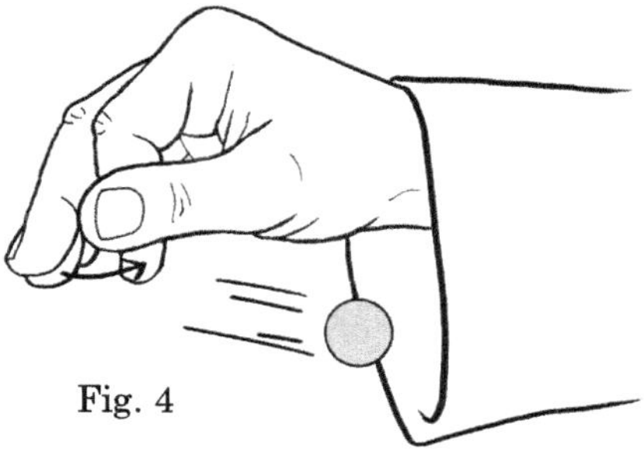

Fig. 4

The first finger gently rubs the coin along the length of the thumb—with very little force the coin will be propelled into the sleeve.

There is a "feel" to this move that will only come with practice, but it is not difficult to do. Again, the action is soft and effortless, the coin practically moves into the sleeve by itself. As you will see in the "**Soft Sleeve Short Routine**," Sol often sleeves coins in this way with very little cover—a simple motion or gesture with the hand will suffice.

Soft Sleeve Cover

If you are worried about the lack of cover and still want to practice the **Soft Sleeving** technique, this simple idea will be of interest. A coin—and it can be a fairly large one—is displayed in right-hand Pinch Grip. The left hand throws a handkerchief over the coin. The outline of the coin is clearly visible through the cloth and you can have a spectator touch the coin through the handkerchief as well.

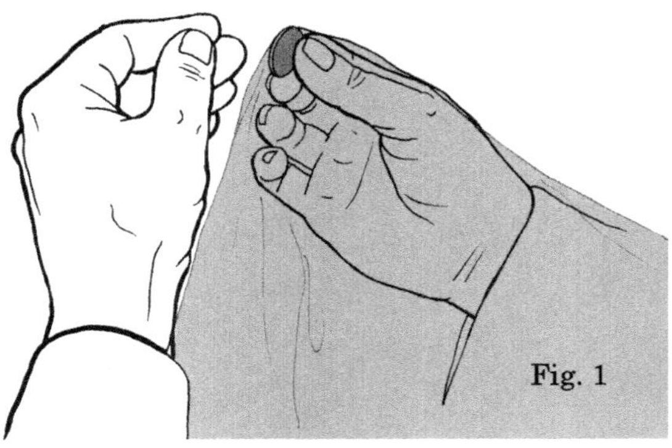

Fig. 1

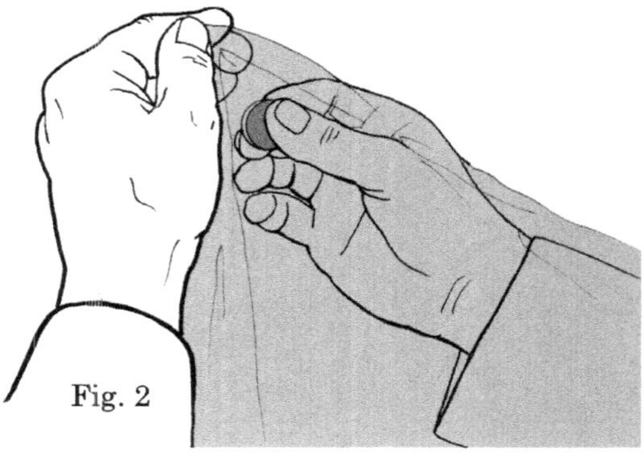

Fig. 2

The left hand now apparently lifts the coin and handkerchief away from the right hand. In reality, the left hand only takes the handkerchief—the coin is left behind at the right fingertips.

As the left hand raises the handkerchief, the right hand moves down toward one of the handkerchief's inner corners. It is at that moment that the coin is **Soft Sleeved**.

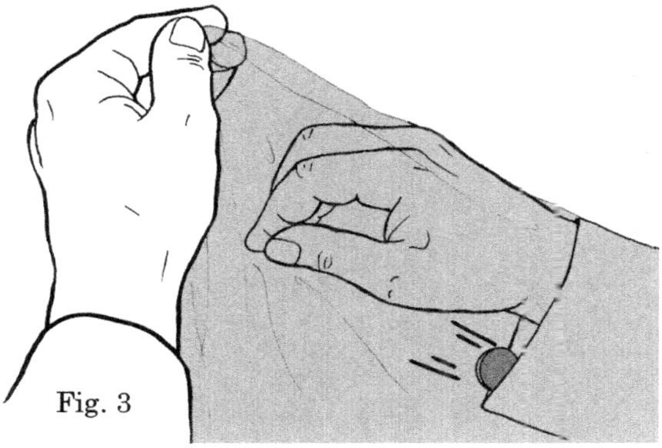

Fig. 3

The sleeving action occurs while the hand is still underneath the handkerchief, naturally pointing diagonally upward. In this context, the act of sleeving is obviously invisible.

Without pausing the right hand grasps the corner of the handkerchief. The left hand releases the center of the handkerchief which then flutters down—the coin has apparently melted away. Drop the handkerchief to the table or hand it to a spectator to examine as you casually make it clear that your hands are empty.

Soft Sleeve Turnover Vanish/Change

In a sense this is another way to disguise the **Soft Sleeve** action. The coin disappears as it is turned over from hand-to-hand. This sequence is done to five distinct beats...

One: Display a coin resting on the tips of the first and second fingers. The right thumb moves onto the edge of the coin, the right hand turns over, and the coin is deposited on the tips of the left first and second fingers.

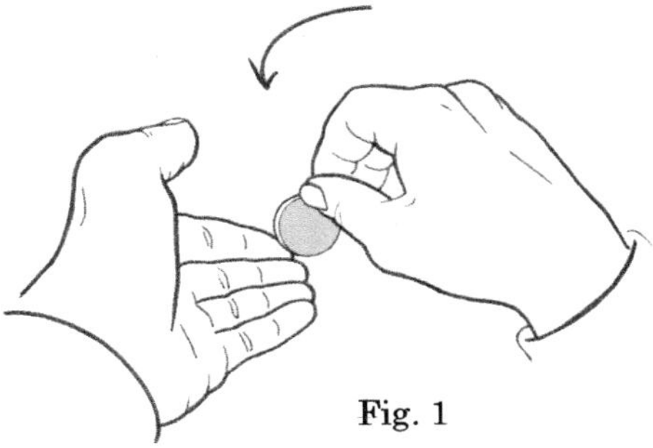

Fig. 1

The right hand moves away and the coin is displayed.

Two: The left thumb is placed on the coin, the hand turns over, and the coin replaced on the right fingertips. This is the exact reverse of step two. The first three steps establish the rhythm of the sequence.

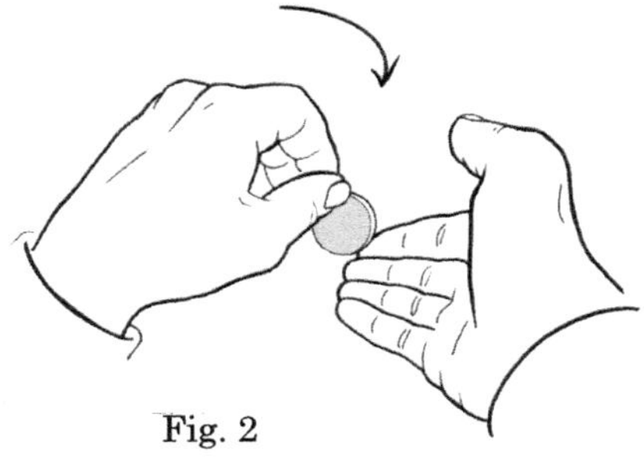

Fig. 2

Three: Place the right thumb on the edge of the coin, holding it in place. Turn the right hand palm down. Do not, however, turn the left hand palm up to receive the coin.

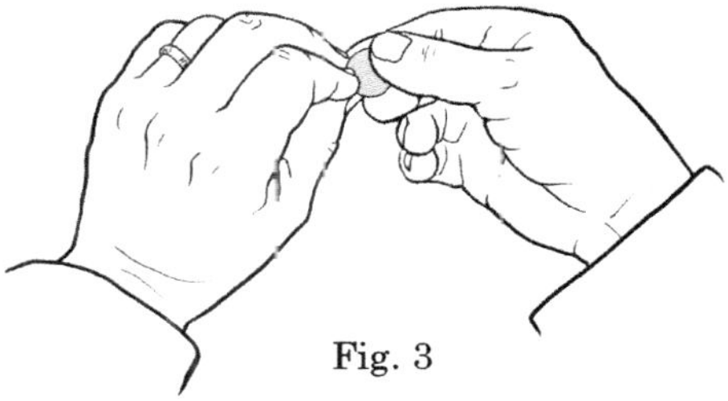

Fig. 3

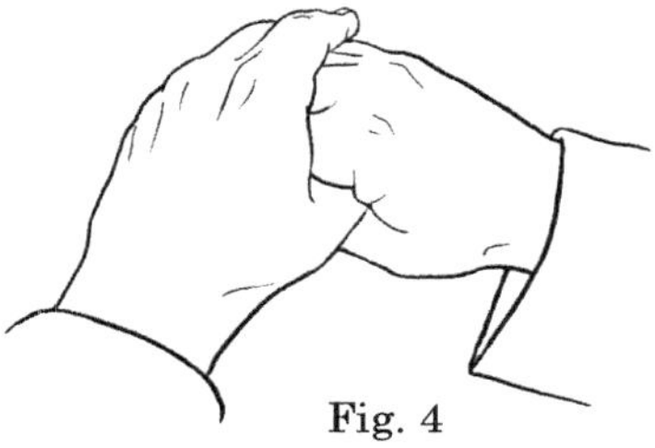

Fig. 4

Instead, the left fingers move over the backs of the right fingers, screening them from view. To do this, the left thumb naturally moves into the circle created by the right thumb and first finger.

Four: With the tips of the fingers covered by the left hand, the right hand is free to **Soft Sleeve** the coin. The presence of the left thumb is no impediment to this action.

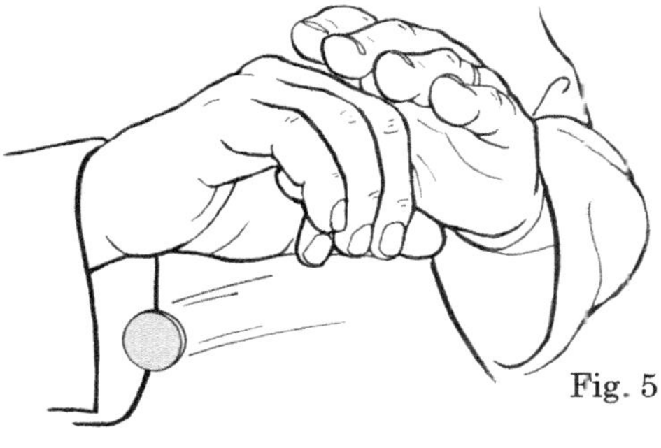

Fig. 5

Five: Slide the left fingers across the back of the right hand until they clear the right fingertips. Smoothly rotate the left hand palm up, closing it. Slowly separate the hands and crumple the left fingers, then open them to reveal that the coin has vanished. The right hand is also shown empty.

Sol sometimes uses this sequence as a change. To do this, a coin must be concealed (using the **Malini Subtlety**) in left-hand Classic Palm throughout the turnover sequence. This is quite difficult to do, but you may want to experiment with it after mastering the basic vanish.

One-Hand Spectator Sleeve Change

This is a sophisticated handling of the cover used in "**Soft Sleeve Turnover**." The difference is that instead of using your hand to cover the sleeving action, you will use the *spectator's hand.* Begin with a silver coin displayed in right-hand Pinch Grip and a copper coin Finger Palmed in the same hand concealed by the **Ramsay Subtlety**.

Have a spectator to stand to your left. As she approaches, turn your right hand palm down, adjusting the silver coin so that it is held only between the thumb and first finger. The spectator can still see the silver coin at the fingertips, but the copper coin is completely hidden from view. Ask the spectator to extend her *left hand* and turn it palm down. Grasp her wrist with your left hand and guide her thumb into the circle created by your right thumb and first finger.

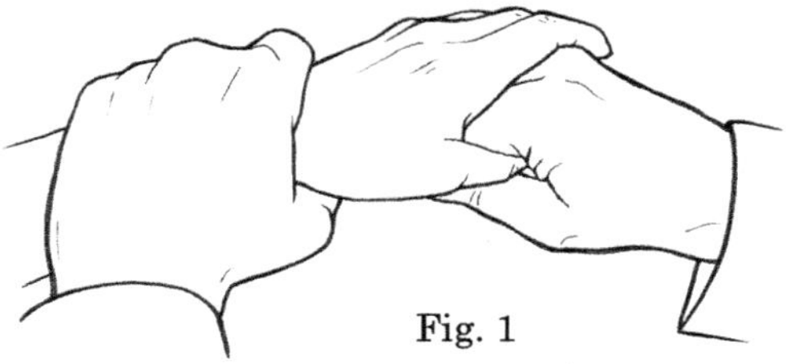

Fig. 1

When the back of your right hand is covered by her fingers raise her wrist very slightly, moving your right hand upwards as you do so, and **Soft Sleeve** the coin. This may sound crazy, but the action is completely hidden. When Sol did this to me, I had no idea that he was sleeving the coin.

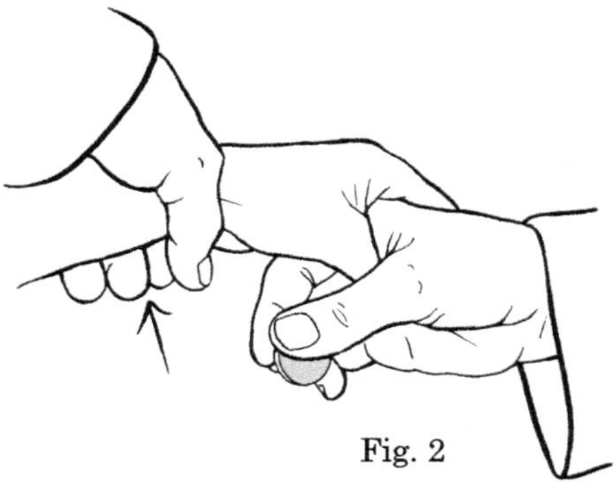

Fig. 2

As soon as the coin has been sleeved, the right thumb moves onto the copper coin in Finger Palm and slides it to the fingertips.

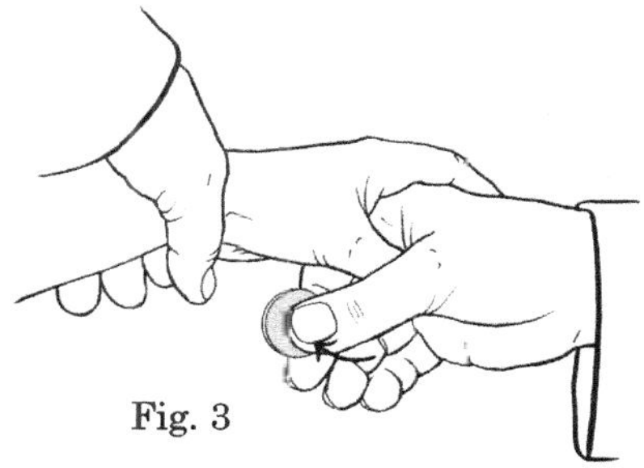

Fig. 3

Now use your left hand to guide the spectator's hand over the coin. Use both hands to press her fingers firmly around the coin.

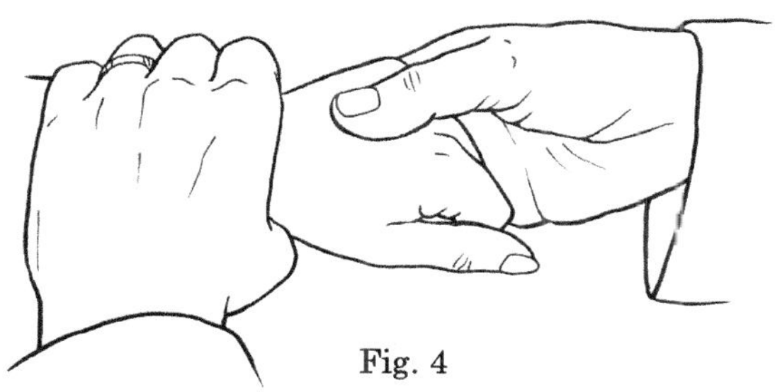

Fig. 4

She holds onto the supposed silver coin until you are ready to reveal the transformation.

Soft Sleeve Short Routine

A nickel begins in the left hand in modified Finger Palm; simply gripped at the base of the curled third finger. Borrow a penny and openly display it in Pinch Grip at your right fingertips. Ask a spectator to hold out his hand and place the penny on his palm. Turn the penny over a few times with your right hand and then pick it up between the tips of the first finger and thumb.

Raise your left hand to about chest level, backs of the fingers toward the audience, and pretend to place the right-hand penny into the left hand. The left fingers apparently curl around the penny. In fact, the right hand never releases the penny, but moves out and away from your left hand. As the right hand is moving away from the left hand, **Soft Sleeve** the penny. This may seem very bold, but the larger (although still soft) movement of the right arm, combined with the new focus of attention on the left hand (see next paragraph), perfectly conceals the very small action it takes to sleeve the coin. Also remember that you are sleeving a very small object—a penny—and that object is concealed by the back of the right hand at the critical moment of the sleight.

As the coin is being sleeved by the right hand, the left hand opens to reveal the nickel. Allow the nickel to slide onto your right palm and from there onto the spectator's outstretched palm. This subtlety shows both hands to be empty. As the coin rests on the spectator's palm, drop your right hand to your side and let the penny fall from your sleeve into your cupped right hand where it is Finger Palmed.

Reach out with your right hand and take the nickel between your thumb and first finger, in position to **Soft Sleeve**. In a continuing action, move your hand upward (about six inches) and slightly outward (away from your body). At the same time, **Soft Sleeve** the coin.

The upward movement of the arm brings the hand to the correct diagonal position for sleeving the coin. The presence of the nickel in Finger Palm does not interfere with the sleeving action at all.

The instant the coin is sleeved the hand rotates palm up and the fingers close into a fist. It should look like you simply turned your hand palm up and closed the fingers around the nickel. Massage your fingers together and then slowly open your hand to reveal that the nickel has changed back to a penny, which is placed back on the spectator's hand.

BACK FINGER CLIP STEP BY STEP

One of Sol's specialties is the **Back Finger Clip**. Indeed, Sol is responsible for pioneering work in this area of coin magic—he began his experimentation in 1936 when he was fourteen years old. Unfortunately, the **Back Finger Clip** (or **Back Clip**) has a reputation for difficulty that is only partially deserved. It is true that Sol has developed some particularly demanding routines that rely on the **Back Clip** for successive, visible transformations. He has also, however, developed routines in which the **Back Clip** is employed in a hidden and very subtle manner.

The Sol Stone Back Finger Clip

We begin with the starting display position. The back of the hand is perpendicular to the floor and a coin is held between the first and second fingers and thumb. The outer edge of the coin should not extend much past the tip of the first finger. The thumb is near the inner edge of the coin so that the bulk of the coin's face is exposed.

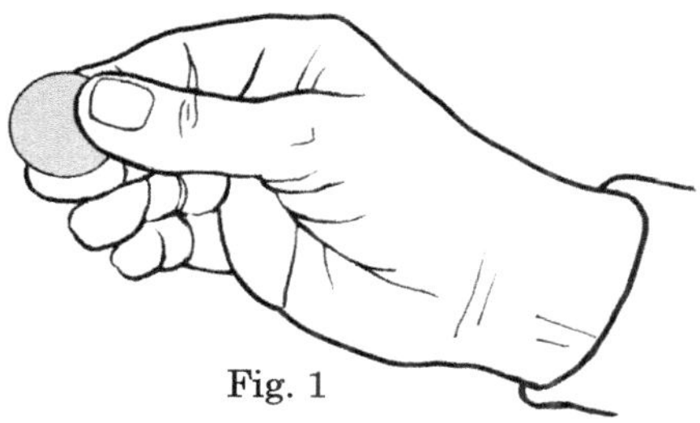

Fig. 1

Sometimes, in order to display the coin more fully, Sol moves his third finger slightly inward, creating a ledge upon which the coin can rest. The thumb can now be removed completely and the coin freely displayed.

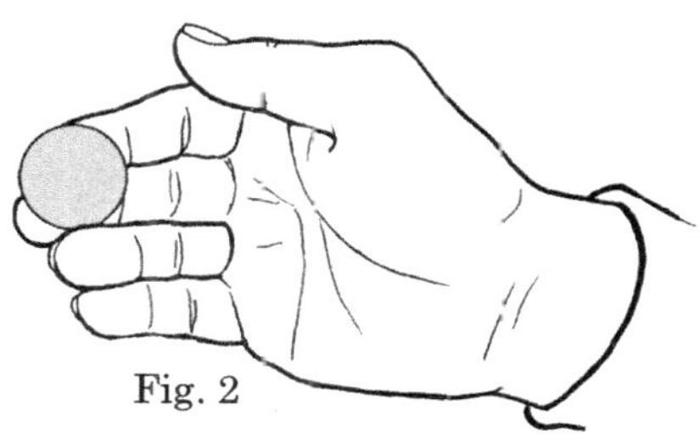

Fig. 2

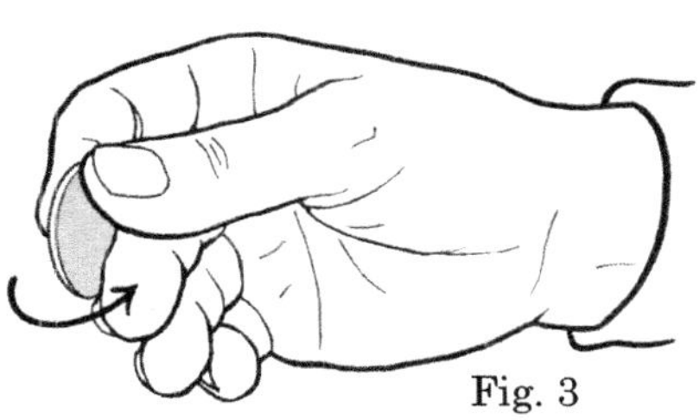

Fig. 3

When you are ready to proceed, the thumb is placed back onto the coin, and when you wish to transfer the coin to **Back Clip**, move the second finger from behind the coin onto the coin's visible face—the second finger moves in a small arc beneath the lower edge of the coin to do this. The back of the first joint of the second finger ends up resting against the face of the coin. During this action the first finger and thumb remain stationary.

As soon as the second finger is in position, the first and second finger press firmly together while the thumb relaxes its grip on the coin. This allows the coin to rotate from a vertical to a horizontal position, leaving it clipped between the two fingers.

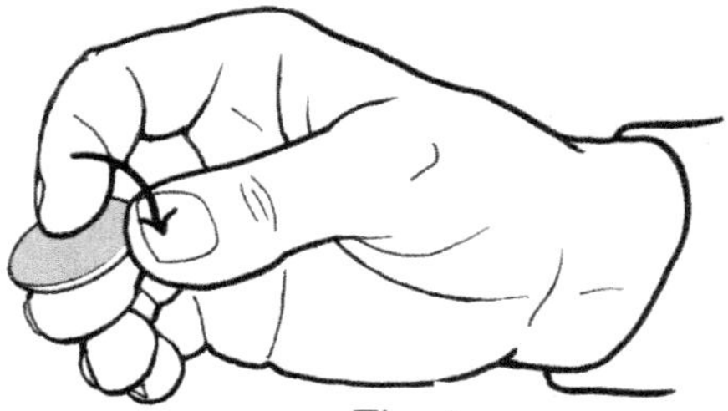
Fig. 4

The thumb remains stationary while the first and second fingers curl inward, automatically bringing the coin to the back side of the fingers. Do not use the thumb to push the coin through the fingers!

Fig. 5

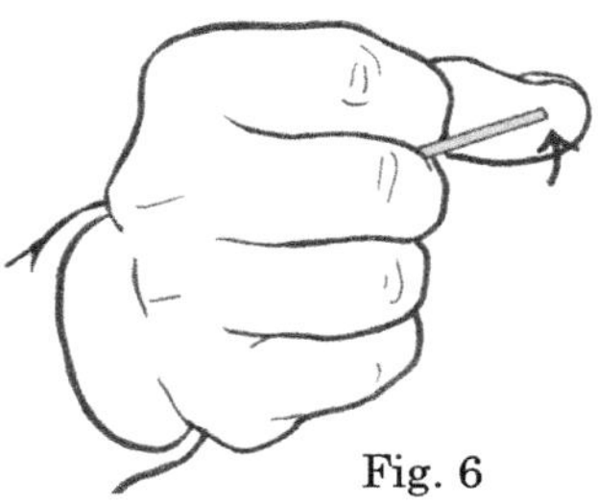
Fig. 6

If you were to release the thumb and straighten the fingers at this point, the coin would basically be in **Back Clip**. It is likely, however, that the edge of the coin would protrude from between the fingers and be visible from the front. In order to avoid this, after the fingers have curled inward, the thumb lifts up slightly on the edge of the coin.

While the coin is still in this slightly raised position, the thumb presses the edge of the coin against the upper side of the second finger. The lifting action moves the coin slightly so that its edge will not be visible from the front. Pressing the coin against the second finger provides tactile confirmation that it is in the right position.

Both actions take but a moment to accomplish and occur even as the first and second fingers are curling inward.

Squeeze the first and second fingers together, release the thumb, and straighten the fingers until they are naturally, not stiffly, open. The coin is now in **Back Clip**, pinched between the first and second finger at the outer joint.

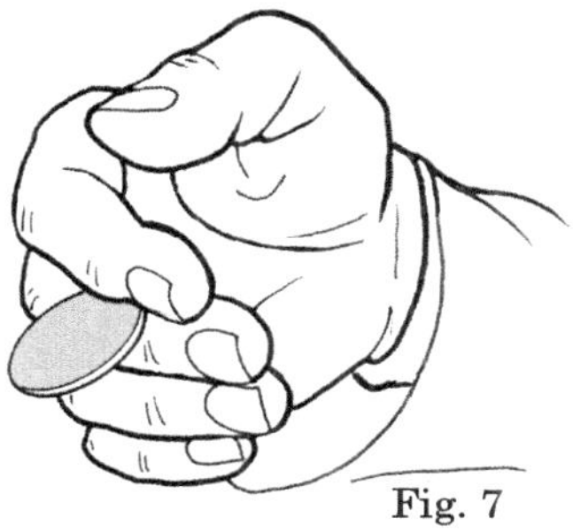

Fig. 7

An audience view is shown in Figure 8.

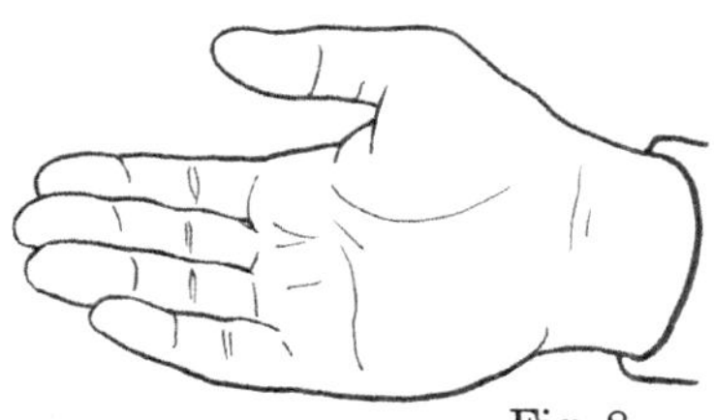

Fig. 8

It will take some practice to learn to correctly position the coin so that it cannot be seen from the front of the hand. In this regard, the action of the right thumb described above is crucial. Everyone's hand and fingers are different and some experimentation is required to find the exact position at which the coin can be securely gripped without peeking through the fingers. Once this spot is discovered, positioning the coin will soon become second nature.

Position of the Hand: Vertical v. Horizontal : In the above description it was assumed that the palm of the hand was perpendicular (vertical) to the floor. Starting with the coin in this position is necessary for many of the routines that employ the **Back Clip Changes** (described below).

The hand can also be parallel (horizontal) to the floor—the hand is palm up and the coin simply resting near the tips of the first and second fingers.

From this position the coin can be transferred to **Back Clip** exactly as described above. To ensure that the **Back Clipped** coin is not seen, keep your hands at waist level and make sure that the audience is looking directly down at your palms. This starting position is somewhat more natural and is employed by Sol in those routines in which the coin is transferred to **Back Clip** under the cover of some larger action.

Coin Size: Quarter v. Half-Dollar : When studying the **Back Clip** you should become comfortable with **Back Clipping** both half dollars and quarters. If he is working a few feet from the audience in a "manipulative" mode, Sol will use half dollars or similar size coins. If, however, the audience is right on top of him, Sol prefers to use quarters. The thinner thickness of the quarter compared to the half dollar means that there is much less chance of the coin "peeking" through the first and second fingers and being visible to the audience.

Second and Third Finger Back Clip

Once proficiency with the basic **Back Clip** is acquired, it is a simple matter to learn to **Back Clip** a coin between the second and third fingers. The action is identical to that described above, but the coin begins at the tips of the second and third fingers.

The third finger moves onto the face of the coin, the second and third fingers curl inward, and the coin **Back Clipped** as outlined above.

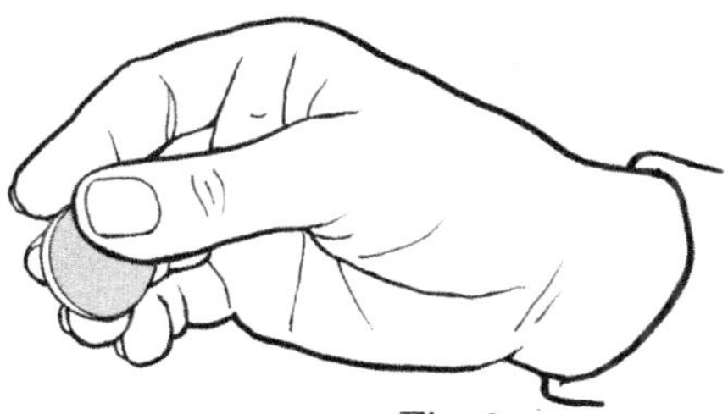

Fig. 9

Fig. 10

With the coin in this position, the "angles" at which a spectator can view the action are significantly improved. Moreover, the **Second and Third Finger Back Clip** frees the first finger, which can be an important factor in some routines (see, in particular, the "**Tenkai Pennies & Variations**").

Back Clip Recoveries

Once you have gotten a coin into **Back Clip** it's important—and useful!—to know how to get it out. Sol has three basic approaches to retrieving **Back-Clipped** coins.

Back Clip Retrieval No. 1 (Hand by Side): The most basic method is retrieve the coin on the off-beat, when your hand is at your side. As your hand drops to the side, you must curl your fingers inward, or else the coin will be clearly visible from the front.

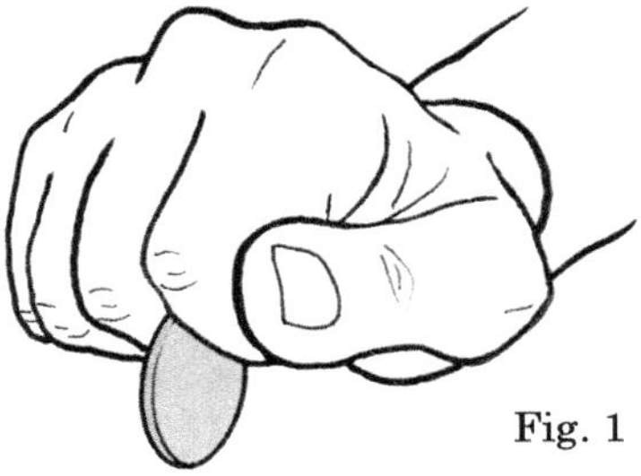

Fig. 1

When you need to recover the coin, simply extend your thumb until it contacts the coin, press the coin against the back of your fingers, and pull it into the fist.

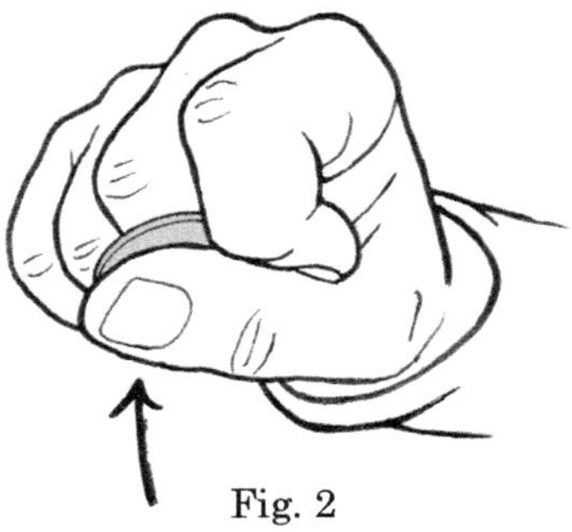

Fig. 2

Fig. 3

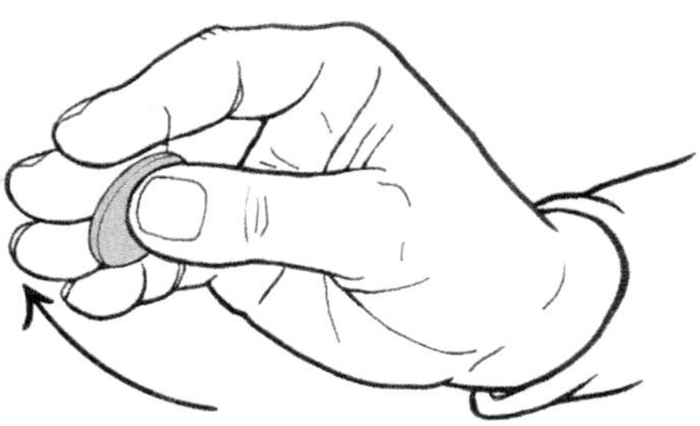

Fig. 4

There is really no "technique" here—just do it as quickly as possible with a minimum of finger movement. From this position you can maneuver it into any palm that you like. Sol often slides it into Thumb Palm and then follows up with a palms-down, fingers-open gesture which casually displays the backs of the hands.

Back Clip Retrieval No. 2 (Open Acquitment): This is similar in some ways to **Back Clip Retrieval Number One,** except that it is done in the open with the hand in full view. In a sense it is an open acquitment in which the front and back of the hand are shown. It relies primarily on good timing and smooth execution. Begin with palm up hands at waist level. This works best if both hands turn palm down at the same time—the action of the "off" hand takes some of the heat off of the "dirty" hand.

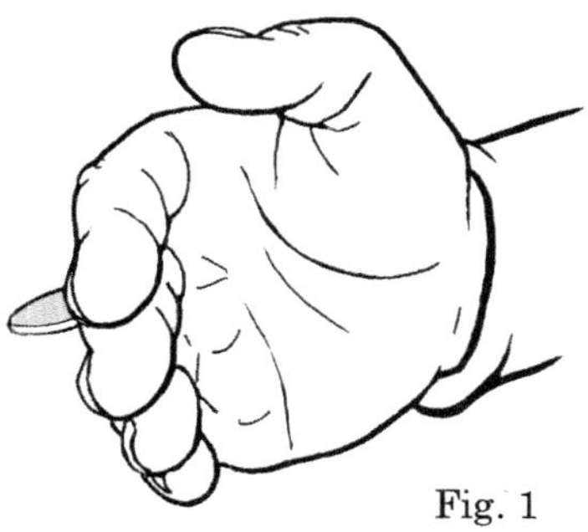

Fig. 1

Begin with a coin in **Back Clip**, your palm toward the audience. The hand rotates inward at the wrist. At the same time the fingers curl into a loose fist. Timing and coordination are crucial here, or you will expose the **Back-Clipped** coin.

Curl the fingers into a slightly tighter fist and extend the thumb until it contacts the edge of the coin.

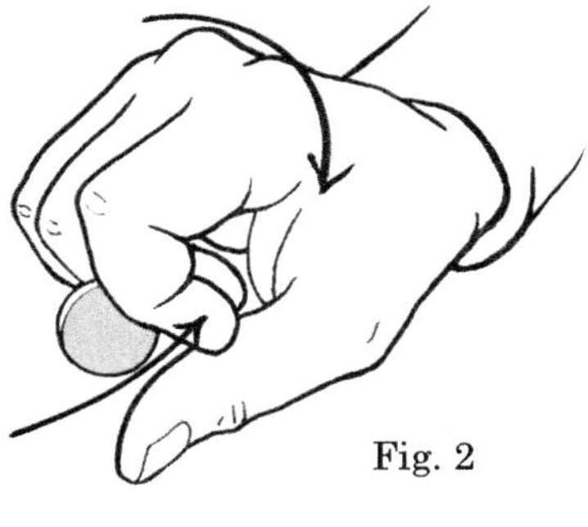

Fig. 2

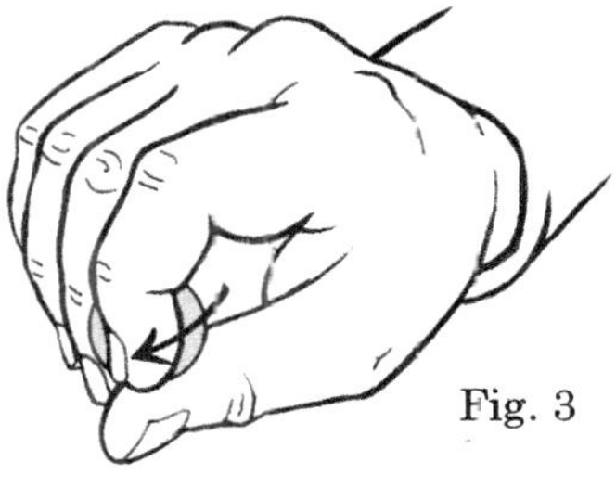

Fig. 3

The thumb then holds the edge of the coin as the fingers straighten.

The back of the hand is turned toward the audience as this happens.

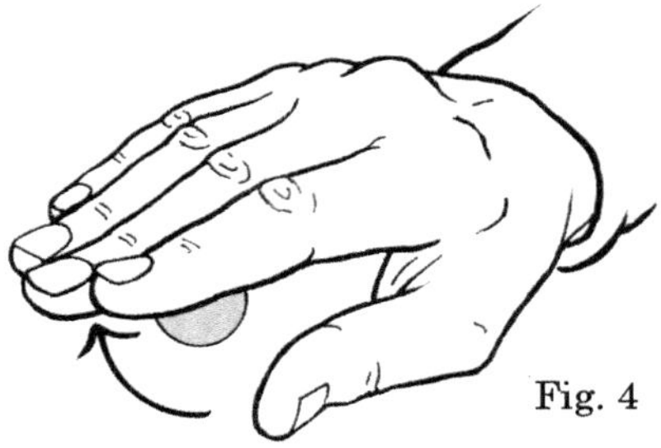

Fig. 4

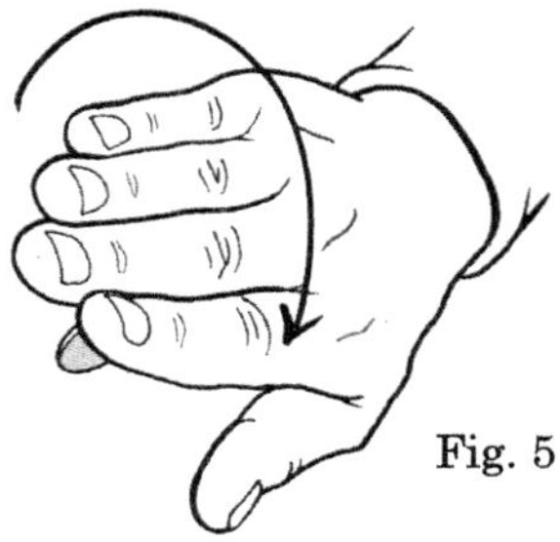

Fig. 5

From the audience point of view, the covering action is shown in Figures 6, 7, 8 and 9, like a Channing Pollack Back Palm.

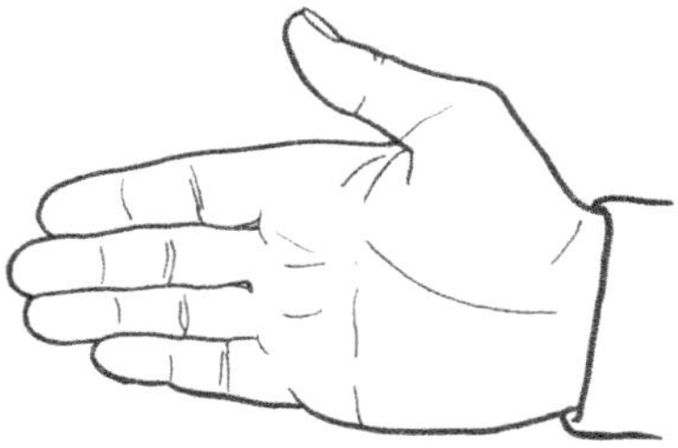

Fig. 6

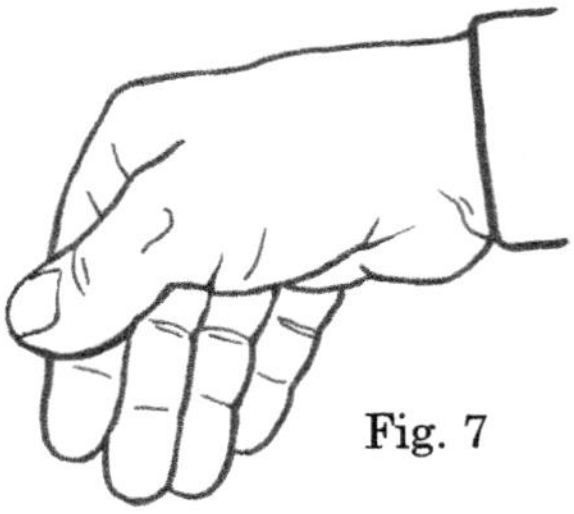

Fig. 7

Fig. 8

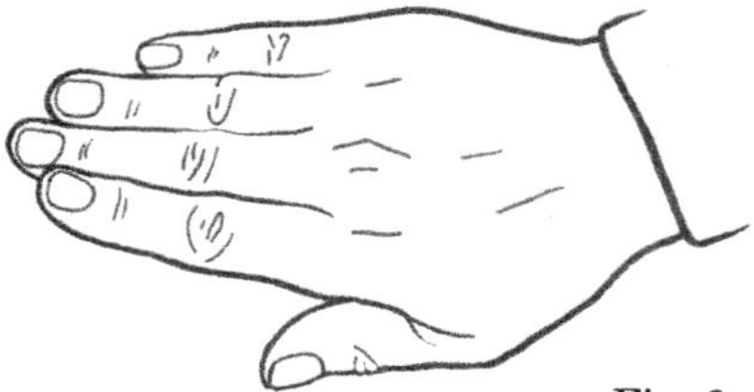

Fig. 9

It's also possible to move the coin from **Back Clip** directly into Thumb Palm by curling the fingers.

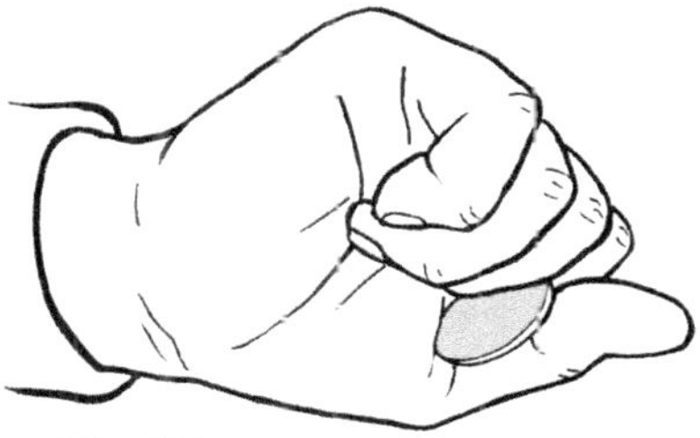

Fig. 10

The fingers of the palm down hand open completely.

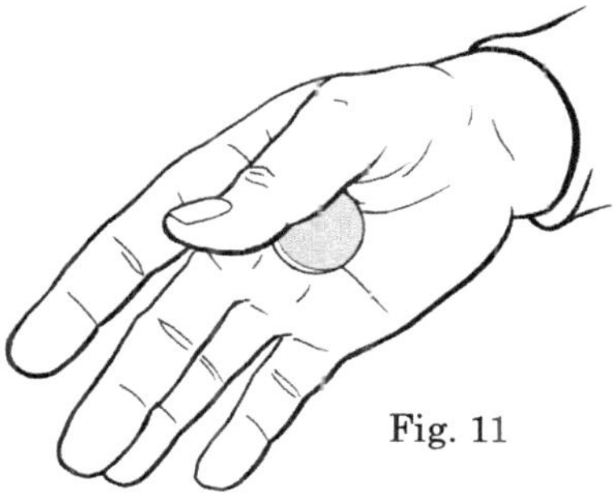

Fig. 11

Back Clip Retrieval No. 3 (Production): Sometimes, Sol prefers to reach out and produce the **Back-Clipped** coin at the fingertips. The action is basically simple. As the hand reaches out to the right (assuming the coin is in right-hand **Back Clip**) the first and second fingers curl inward and the thumb extends onto the upper edge of the coin.

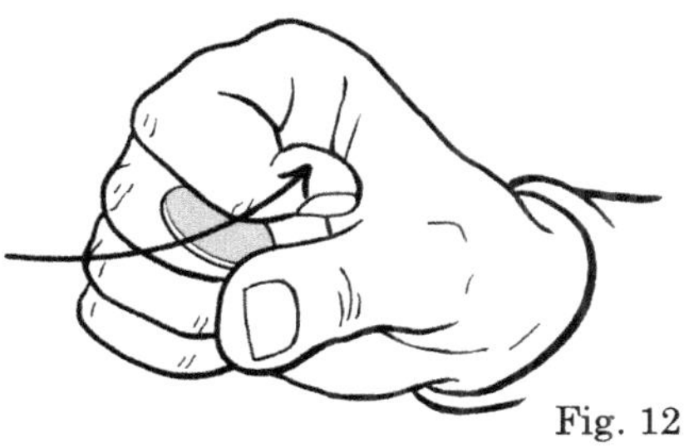

Fig. 12

The thumb presses the coin against the second finger, holding it in place, and then the fingers open.

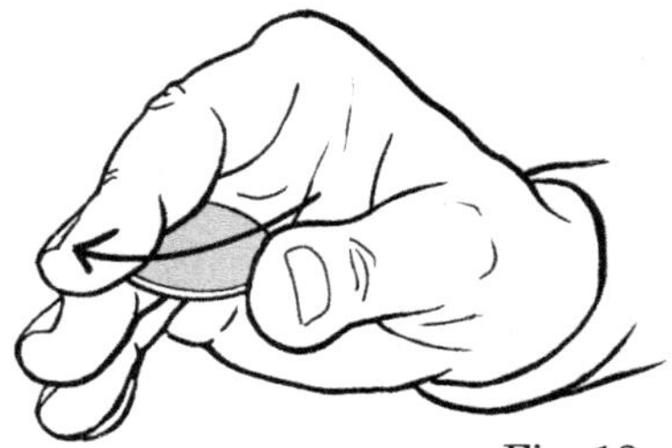

Fig. 13

To complete the production, the thumb pushes the coin to the fingertips.

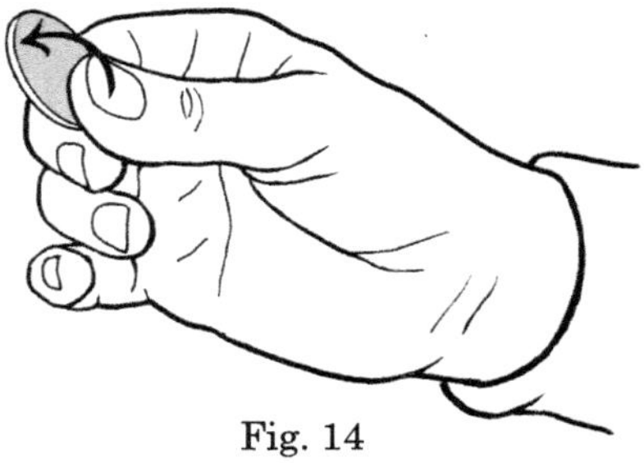

Fig. 14

Time these actions so that the coin is reproduced as your hand and arm reach their full extension. Naturally, a little acting as you produce the coin—seeing the invisible coin in the air, etc.—makes the production that much more believable.

Back Clip Change Number One

Strangely, the difficulty with this Change lies not so much in the actual technique—which is relatively simple—but in learning the proper timing to cover the action. At this point I am just going to describe the mechanics of the move—that is, just the action of the fingers. The larger, covering action of the hand is described below in the "One-Two-Three Cover."

Sol almost always uses fifty-cent size coins for this sequence. Begin with a copper coin concealed in **Back Clip** and a silver coin at the first and second fingertips in **Back Clip Display** position. You are going to **Back Clip** the silver coin and bring the copper coin into view. The action occurs in three beats.

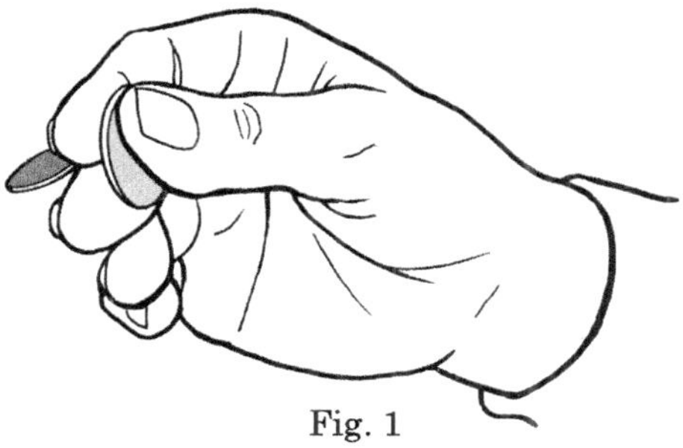

Fig. 1

Beat One: The third finger moves behind and on top of the **Back-Clipped** copper coin. The first finger releases its grip on the copper coin which automatically becomes pinched between the second and third fingers.

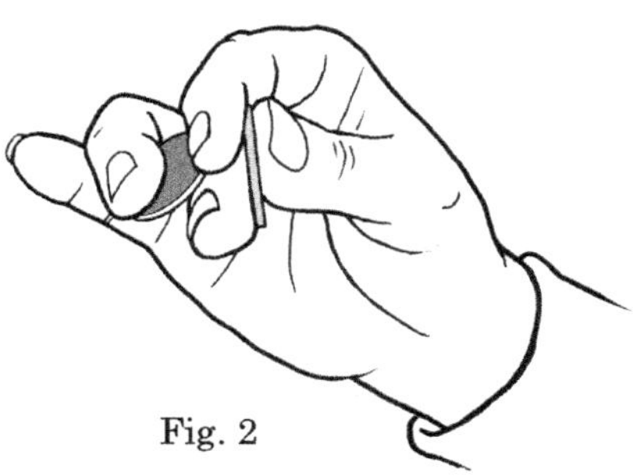

Fig. 2

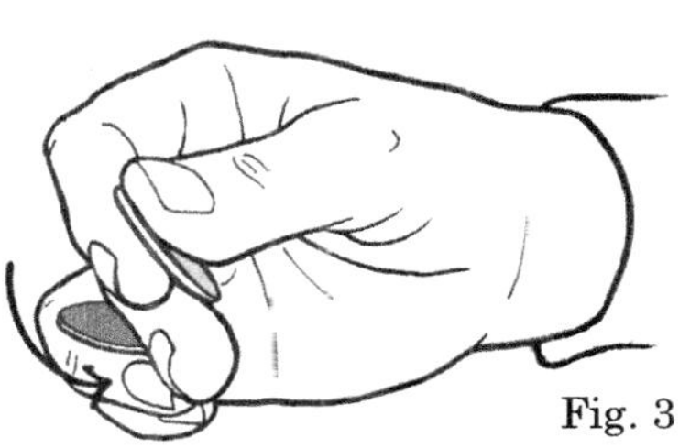

Fig. 3

The second and third fingers curl inward, toward the palm, taking the copper coin with them. The thumb and first finger remain partially extended, clipping the silver coin between them.

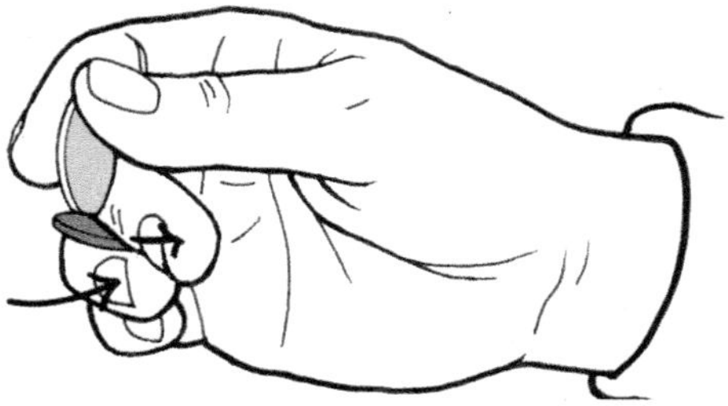

Fig. 4

At the end of this action, the back of the right second finger should be pressing against the lower edge of the silver coin.

Beat Two: The first and second finger squeeze together while the thumb relaxes its grip on the silver coin. The coin rotates to a horizontal position between the fingers. The thumb rests on the edge of the coin opposite the fingers.

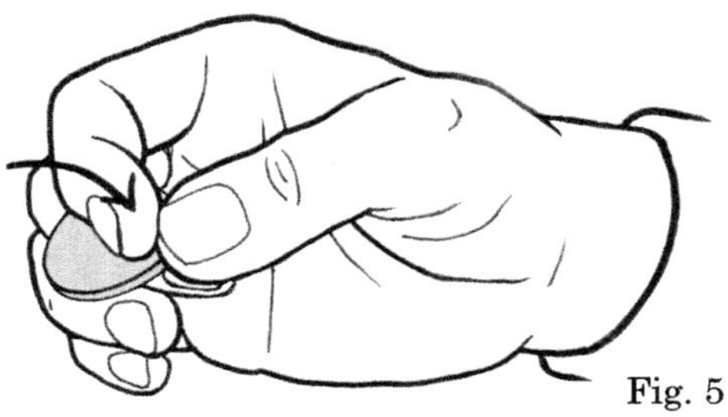

Fig. 5

The first and second fingers curl inward, while the thumb holds the coin in its same relative position.

Fig. 6

The coin is now in **Back Clip**. The thumb moves down and contacts the edge of the copper coin that protrudes from the curled second and third fingers. This is a very small movement.

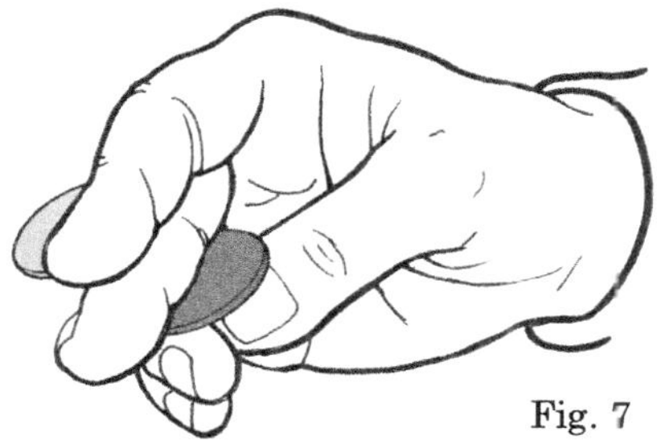

Fig. 7

Beat Three: Straighten the first, second and third fingers, the thumb holding the copper coin's edge so it ends inside the hand. Move the thumb under the copper coin. The thumb snaps the coin flat against the first and second fingers to complete the sequence.

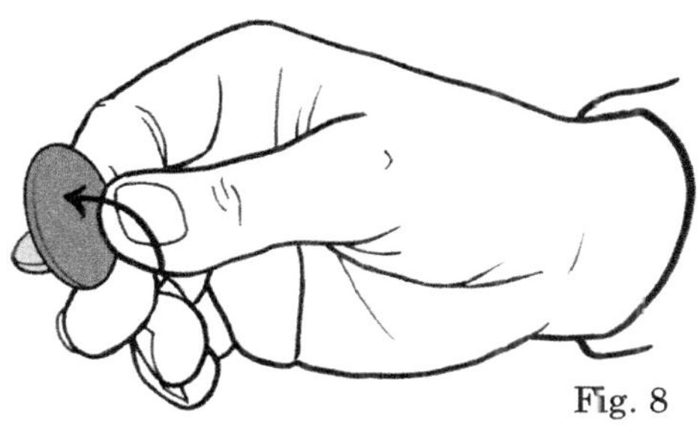

Fig. 8

You are now in position to repeat the Change as described, turning the copper coin into the silver coin. Indeed, the entire sequence can be repeated indefinitely.

This brings up an important point, which should allow you to check and see if you are doing the move correctly. ***Every time the coin comes into view, it should be showing a different face than was previously displayed.***.

So, if you begin with a silver coin at your fingertips, (head side showing) and a copper coin in **Back Clip** (head side up), the sequence will be as follows: The first change will bring the head side of the copper coin into view; the second change will bring the tail side of the silver coin into view; the third change will bring the tail side of the copper coin into view; and the fourth change will bring the head side of the silver coin into view, returning you to your starting position. This fact plays an important role in Sol's "**One-hand Triple Spellbound**" and "**Patriotic Poker Chip**" routines.

There is also some good news! Each successive change brings the new coin into **Display Position**—where it rests over the first and second fingers at the point where the other coin is **Back Clipped**. This means that you can be a little less precise in positioning the **Back Clipped** coin. Obviously it cannot protrude past the front of the fingers, but if it is slightly visible this fact will be hidden by the coin at the fingertips. This is an important point when you are trying to do the move smoothly and quickly.

This seems like a lot to master—and it is—but if you will take your time, you will be surprised at how soon you have the mechanics down. As soon as the move begins to flow, read "**The One-Two-Three Cover**" to learn how Sol executes this change while the spectators are staring at his hands.

Back Clip Change Number Two

Although it looks easier, this is probably more difficult than **Back Clip Change Number One**. Let's assume that you are going to change a silver coin into a copper coin. You will find this considerably easier if you use fifty-cent size coins.

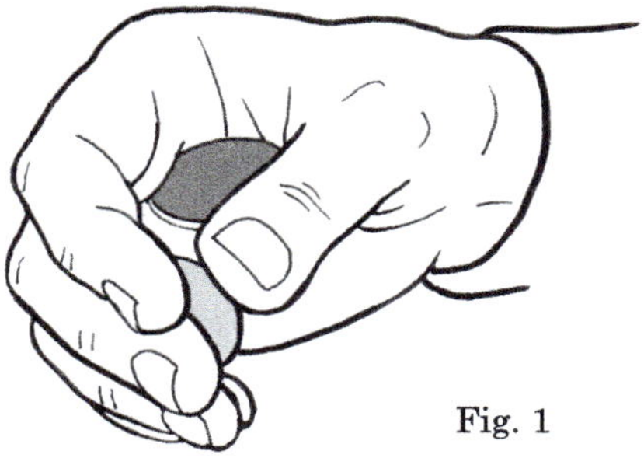

Fig. 1

The copper coin begins secretly concealed in Downs Palm. The switch is much easier if you are already comfortable with holding a coin in this position, otherwise it will seem impossibly awkward.

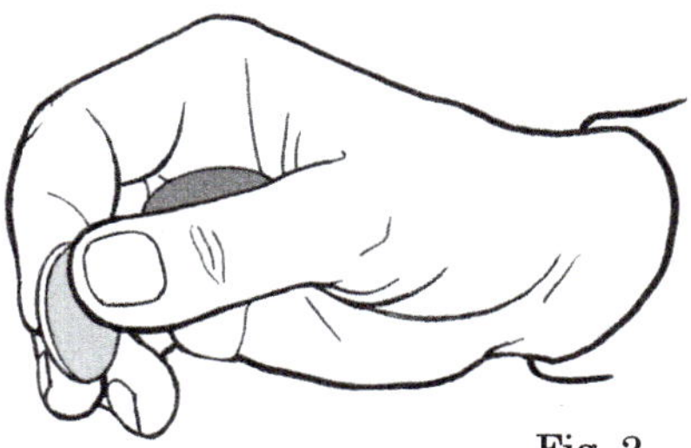

Fig. 2

The silver coin begins flat against the tips of the first and second fingers, held in position by the tip of the thumb—in other words, in **Display Position** ready to be **Back Clipped**.

Note the freedom you have here. With the extra coin in Downs Palm, and with tip of the thumb curled against the first and second fingertips, you can show all sides of your hand freely—flashing the back of your hand and then letting the audience have a direct view into the palm of the hand. You do, of course, have to be careful if spectators are staring straight up or down at your hand—you should be working on roughly the same "level" as the audience. Now for the action of the switch itself, which will be broken down into three "beats."

Beat One: Begin to **Back Clip** the silver coin. This is done exactly as described above—except that you have to maintain a light inward pressure with the thumb in order to keep the Downs Palmed coin in place. The second finger moves onto the face of the coin, the first and second fingers begin to curl inward as the thumb holds the coin in the same relative position.

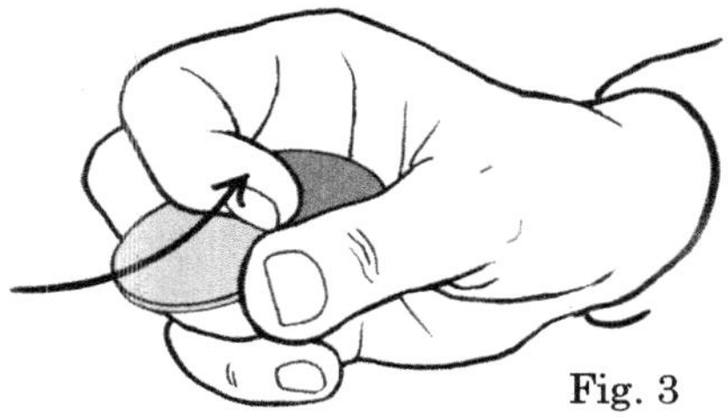

Fig. 3

Beat Two: The first and second fingers curl fully inward. As this happens, the tips of the fingers will naturally move above and below the copper coin. Or, to put it another way, the copper coin slides between the fingertips. (Note that the thumb at this moment is helping to position the **Back-Clipped** silver coin.)

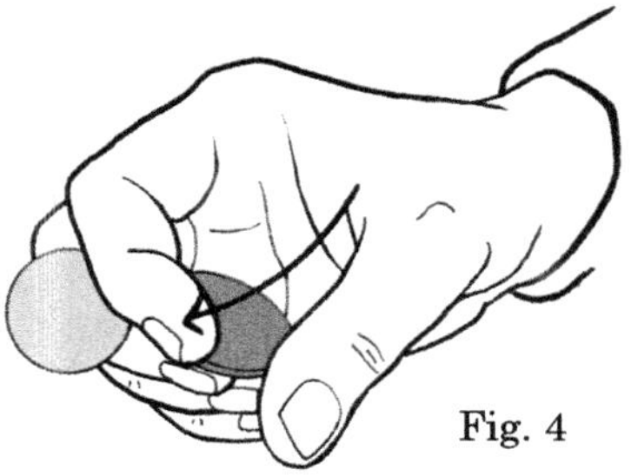

Fig. 4

The copper coin is gripped between the fingertips, which begin to straighten out.

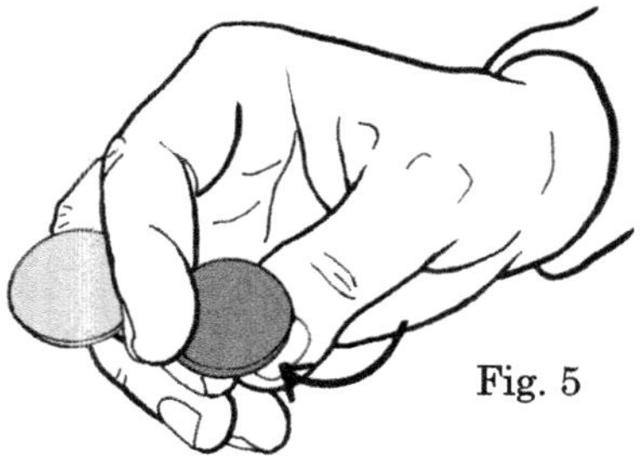

Fig. 5

Beat Three: The fingers continue to straighten fully out and the thumb moves beneath the lower edge of the copper coin.

The thumb flips the coin flat against the first and second fingertips to conclude.

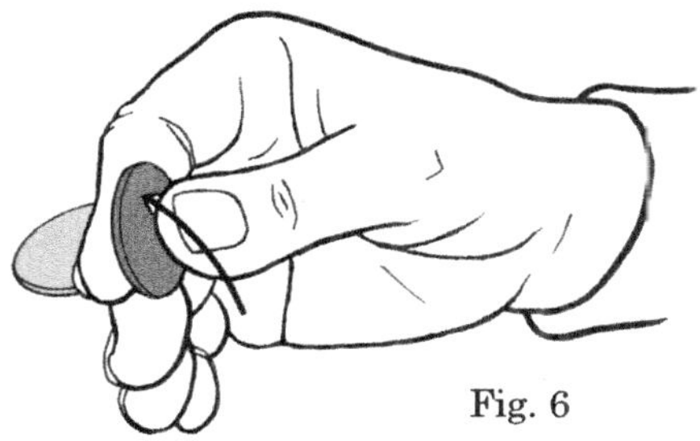

Fig. 6

Practice this switch until you can do it fast and effortlessly—do not worry about covering or disguising the action at this time. When you have it down, learn "**The Hung Coin**" (see Pg. 163). In that routine the action of the switch is masked—at the crucial moment—by the back of the left hand. When you want to learn to do the switch visibly, with no cover, practice the "**One-Two-Three Cover**."

The One-Two-Three Cover

So, how does Sol perform **Back Clip Changes** so that they are invisible? The secret is the **One-Two-Three Cover**. This is probably the hardest part of the **Back Clip Technique** to master—indeed, I have only seen one other person who can do it really well—and for this reason I have separated the covering action from the actual mechanics of the two Changes. I want you to have the mechanics down cold before you begin to focus on the larger action of the hand.

In the above descriptions, I broke the actions of changes **Number One and Two** into three beats. Each beat corresponds to one moment in the **One-Two-Three Cover**. The **One-Two-Three Cover** itself is very simple: On "one" you raise your hand (first beat), on "two" you lower your hand (second beat), and on "three" you raise your hand again (third beat). The trick is to complete each and every action described for that particular beat within the space and time assigned for it. This is more difficult than it sounds—there is a very strong tendency to perform the action in four beats (up - down - up - down) which for some reason is not nearly as deceptive. You must discipline yourself to perform the actions exactly as described.

Begin by practicing each sequence slowly. When you begin to get a feel for it, start to speed up. Finally, work up to a sort of shaking, or snapping action, which blends everything into a blur of transformation.

The drawings show the **One-Two-Three Cover** for both **Back Clip Changes**. Moreover, these are purely audience views, so you can more easily check your actions in the mirror. For a different approach to the by-no-means-easy task of illustrating this sequence, I urge you to check out Richard Kaufman's illustrations in ***CoinMagic***.

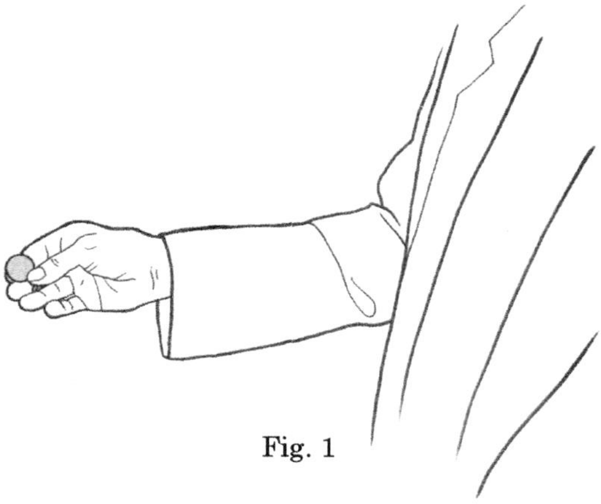

Fig. 1

Figure 1 is the starting position.

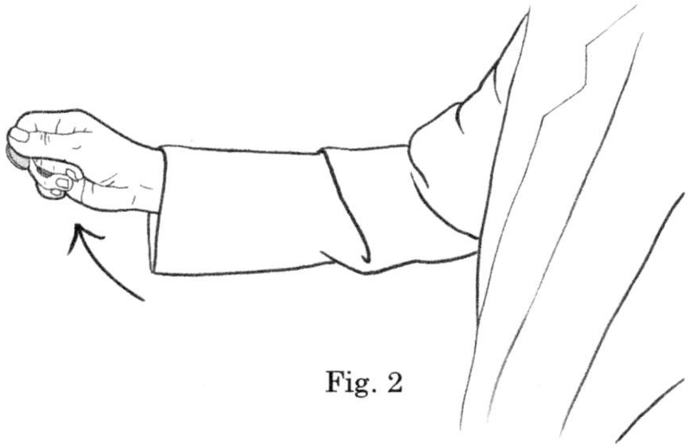

Fig. 2

Figure 2 shows the up swing as you begin to Back Clip the silver coin.

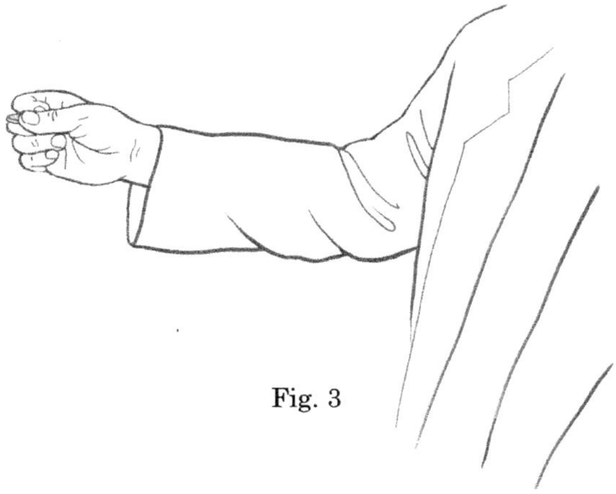

Fig. 3

Figure 3 shows the high point of the upward swing. The silver coin is now Back Clipped and the fingertips are grasping the copper coin.

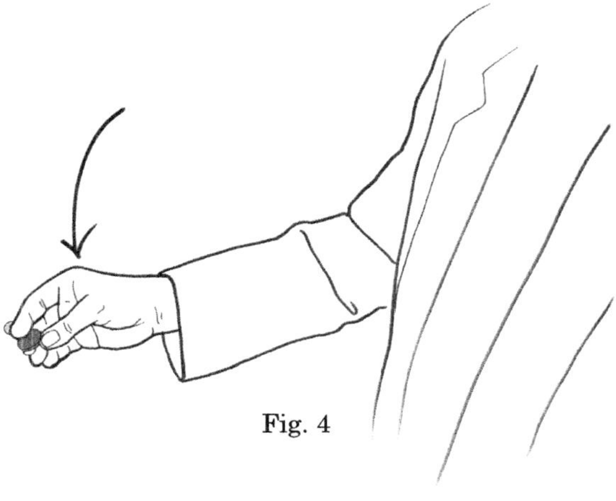

Fig. 4

Figure 4 shows the downward swing as the fingers straighten.

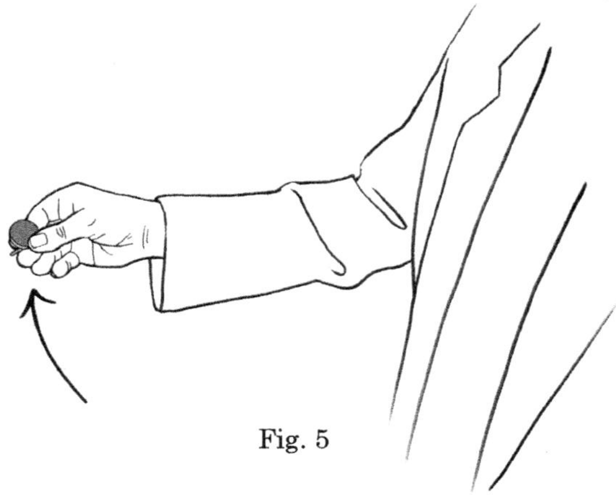

Fig. 5

Figure 5 shows the upward swing as the copper coin appears.

There are two final points worth mentioning: First, note that the hand ends up higher than it begins. This is a natural result of the three-beat action. If you are ending up in the same place you started, you are probably doing something wrong. Second, it helps if you keep your hand slightly tilted backward, away from the audience. This seems to obscure the actual moment at which the visible coin is Back Clipped.

Back Clip Routines

The Shrinking Coin

Sol brings out a miniature bottle containing "the last few drops of the formula that shrunk the kids." A few drops of this shrinking fluid are placed on "George" (a quarter), which slowly shrinks until it at last disappears completely.

The above description was, shall we say, "psychologically valid." The audience does not actually see the coin shrink—but, if you properly establish the premise, the audience will be convinced that this is what takes place. In this regard, the role of the miniature bottle is very important. It helps to create a fun and playful mood and smoothly introduces the "shrinking" premise.

It does not really matter what type of bottle or container is used—Sol uses a miniature baby bottle (that came, I believe, with a set of girls' dolls). The size of the bottle in relation to the quarter is shown in Figure 1. Finally, the bottle contains no liquid, you simply mime placing a few drops on the coin.

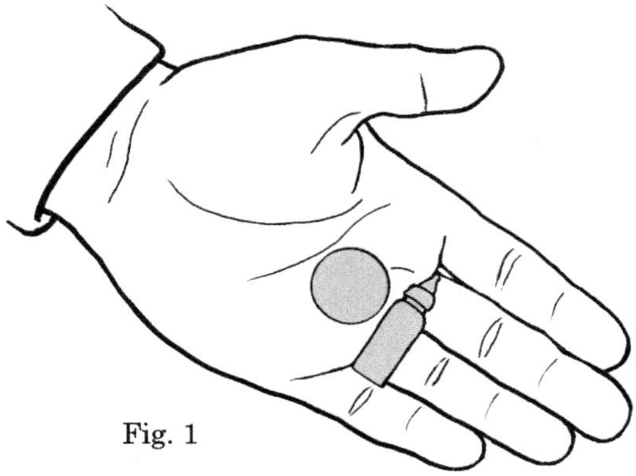

Fig. 1

So, borrow a quarter, talk about the shrinking formula, and pretend to place a few drops on the coin. Set the bottle aside.

You will now apparently turn the coin over from hand to hand three times, finally opening your hands and showing that the coin has vanished. The hands are palm up at waist level. The quarter should be resting on the tips of your right first and second fingers. The right thumb presses down against the coin holding it in position.

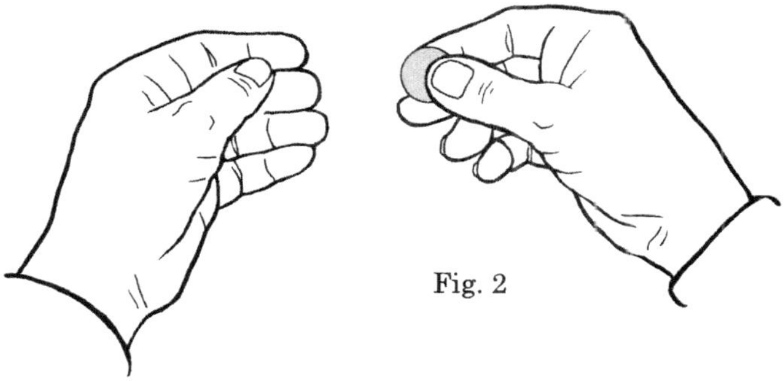

Fig. 2

Although the coin is turned over three times, there are five "beats" to the action.

One : The right hand turns palm down and places the coin on the tips of the left first and second fingers. The right hand moves away and the left thumb clips the coin in position against the left fingertips.

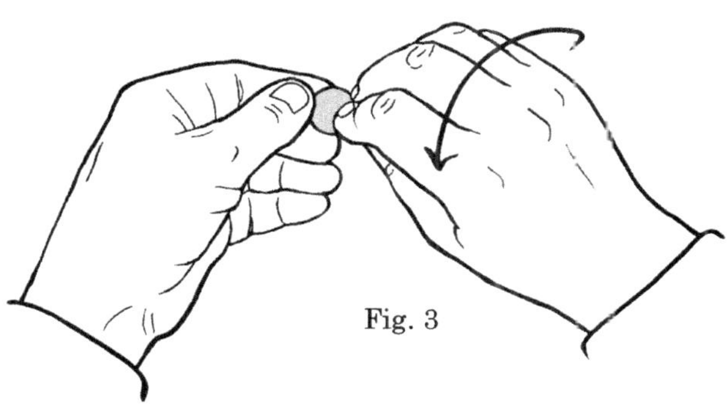

Fig. 3

Two : The left hand turns palm down and places the coin on the right first fingertip as the right hand turns palm up. The coin is clipped in place with the right thumb. This action is simply the reverse of the first action, except that the coin is placed on the first finger.

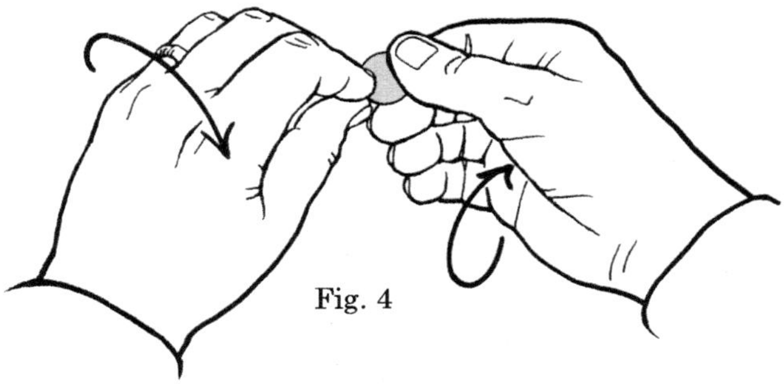

Fig. 4

Three : The right hand turns palm down and apparently places the quarter on the left fingers. In reality, as the right thumb holds the coin against the right first finger, the second finger moves onto the face of the coin. As the hand turns over, the thumb releases its grip, the first and second fingers squeeze together, and the coin ends up in Front Finger Clip—one edge of the coin ends up pinched between the right first and second fingers, while the opposite edge is pressed lightly against the thumb.

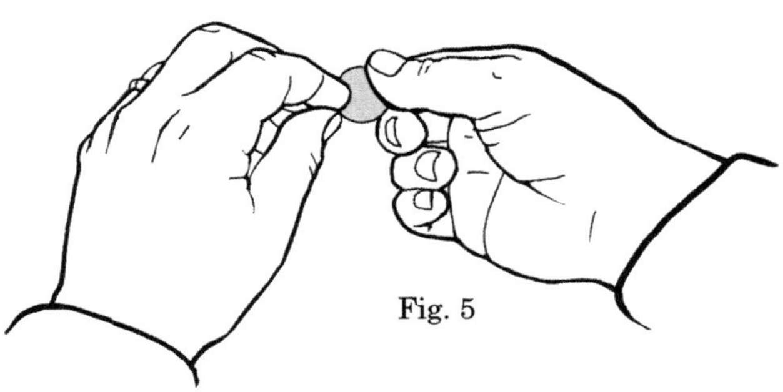

Fig. 5

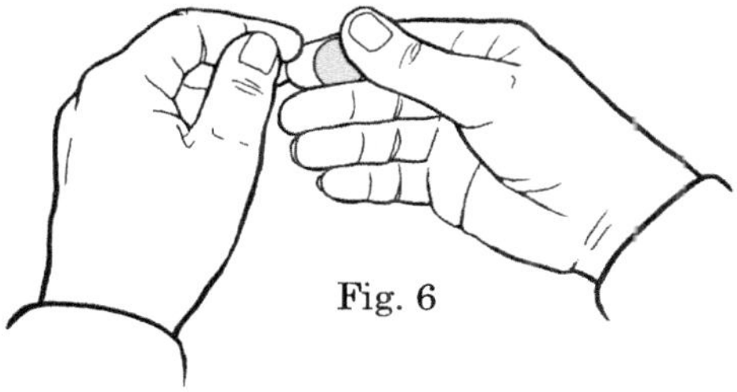

Fig. 6

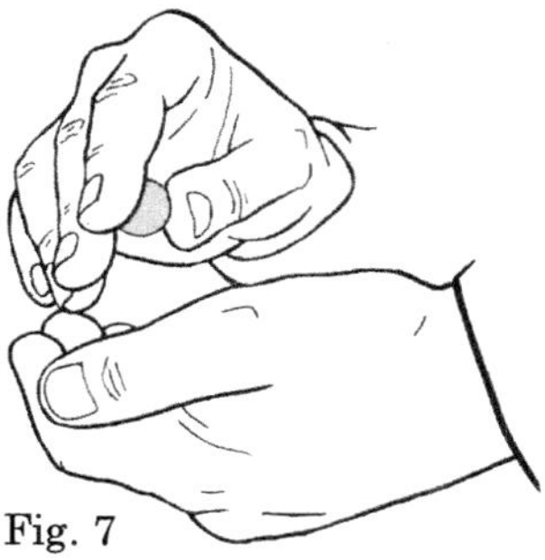

Fig. 7

This takes place as the hand turns over and simply pretends to place the coin on the left fingers. The left fingers lower slightly to allow the back of the right hand to move parallel to the floor. At this point, the coin is completely concealed from the audience by the back of the right fingers.

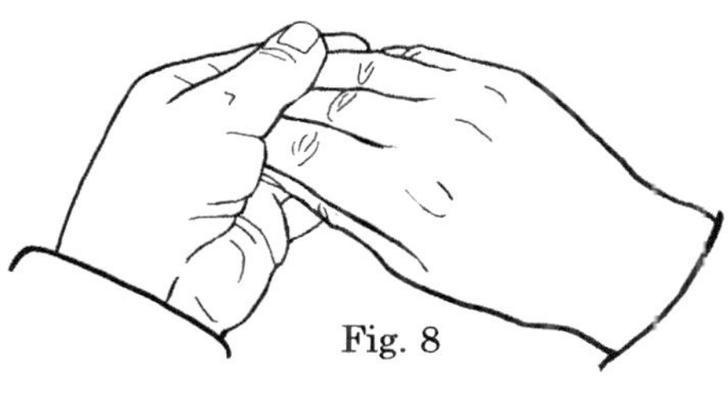

Fig. 8

Four : While the right hand remains stationary, the left hand turns palm down, moving over the back of the right fingers. As soon as it is covered by the left fingers, the right hand begins to turn palm up, Back Clipping the coin between the first and second fingers at the same time.

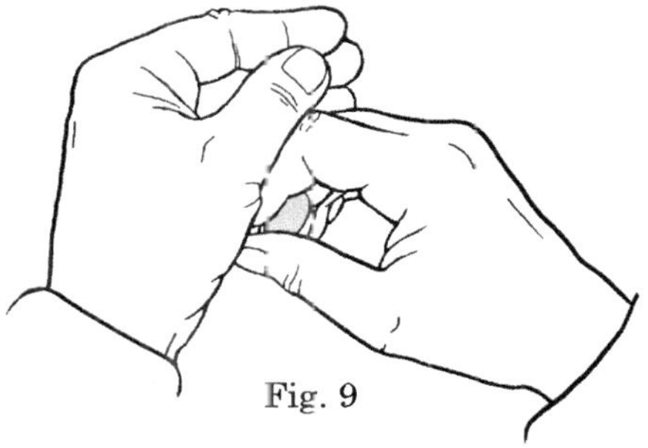

Fig. 9

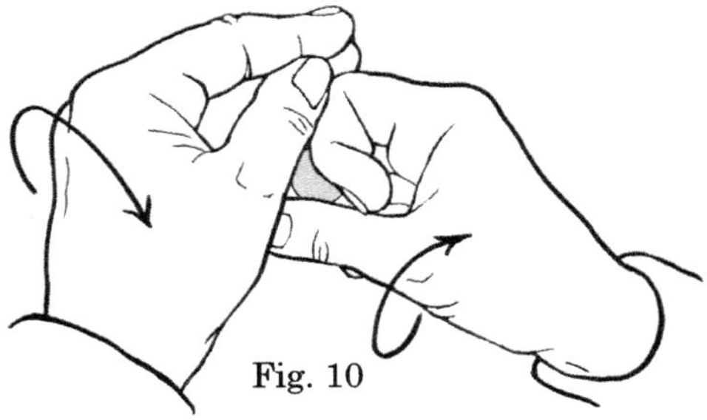

Fig. 10

Fig. 10 is an exposed view. The left hand actually covers the right fingers.

The left fingers now press flatly on the right fingers, as if trapping the coin between them.

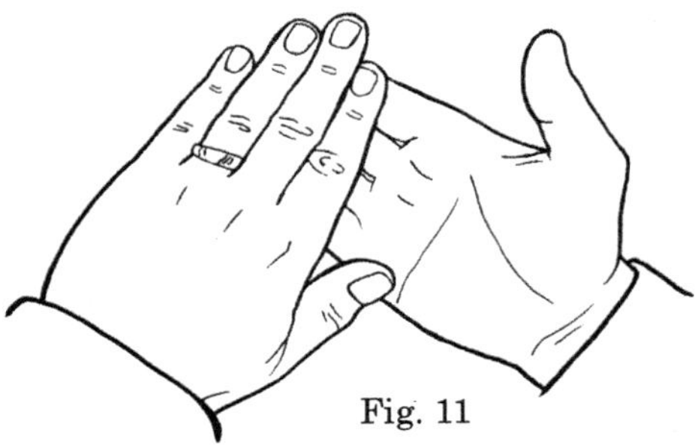

Fig. 11

Five : The left hand rotates at the wrist, turning palm up to display two empty hands. Both hands are relatively flat and their positions should mimic each other (in other words, don't hold the left fingers wide apart because you can't do the same with the right fingers).

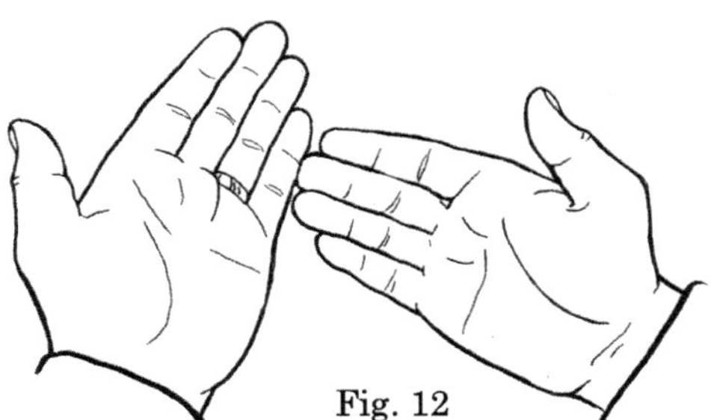

Fig. 12

What is really happening in this sequence is that the action of Back Clipping the coin is broken into two stages. The coin is levered into Front Clip as the hand turns over during step three.

This is essentially the first stage of the Back Clip, except that the fingers are not curled inward because doing so would expose the coin from the spectator's viewpoint. During step four the coin is actually moved to Back Clip under cover of the left hand.

Sol now shrugs and then drops his hands to his sides, recovering the coin. He generally does not reproduce the coin. After transferring the coin to thumb palm, he casually gestures with his palm down hands and then proceeds with another effect.

Sol's patter as he turns the coin over and over is straightforward and serves to draw the audience's attention to the coin and emphasizes its apparent shrinking. Sol simply says, "*Watch! Each time I turn the coin over it gets smaller and smaller, until it completely disappears.*"

"Right There" Revisited

This is Sol's handling of a Nate Leipzig effect published in ***Vernon's Tribute to Nate Leipzig***. Sol believes that in general a production is weaker than a vanish, and that the re-production of a vanished object is weakest of all. Thus, he feels that to reproduce the coin in this effect would be anti-climatic and prefers to let its whereabouts remain a mystery.

In this regard, Sol often prefers to reverse the normal vanish-production sequence. For instance, he will produce a coin from behind someone's ear and then vanish it. The mysterious disappearance of the coin will cause people to follow you around all evening, trying to discover where the coin went.

Begin by displaying a quarter pinched between the left first finger and thumb. The second, third, and fourth fingers are curled loosely against the fist. The hand is palm down with the tips of the fingers pointing to the right. Call this the "starting position."

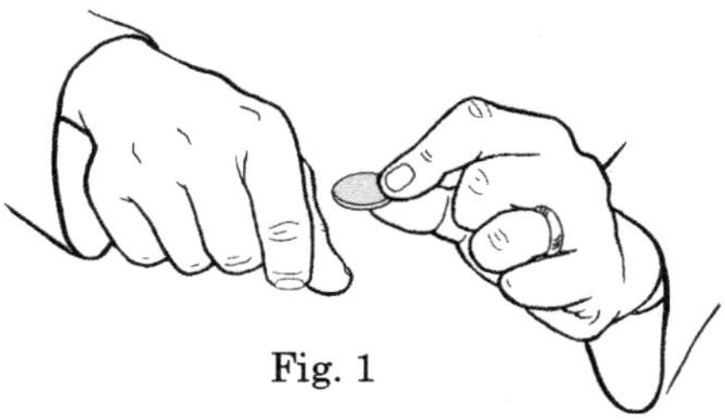

Fig. 1

The Feint : At this point, the head side of the quarter should be uppermost. Say, "*When I place the quarter in my hand Washington side up and push it in like this, nothing happens.*"

As you speak, the palm-down right hand closes into a loose fist. The left hand places the quarter through the thumb hole and into the fist, where it rests at the base of the second and third fingers. The left first finger pretends to push the coin a little further into the fist. In reality, the first finger simply slides over the right fingers (and coin) until the left first and right second finger touch.

The left first finger begins to withdraw from the fist. When the tip of the finger reaches the quarter, both hands turn palm upward, open, and separate to reveal the quarter resting at the base of the right second and third fingers. This sequence is simply a feint intended to condition the audience to your upcoming actions. Naturally, the sleight described in the next phase should mimic the foregoing movements as closely as possible.

The Vanish : Retrieve the quarter with the left hand and hold it in the starting position, described above. This time, the tail side of the coin is uppermost.

Your words and actions are now closely meshed:

1) Say, "*But if I place the quarter in my hand American Eagle side up and push it in like this. . .*" The palm down right hand closes into a loose fist. The left hand pushes the quarter through the thumb hole, over the right first finger and under the right second finger. The extreme right edge of the quarter comes to rest against the edge or side of the right third finger.

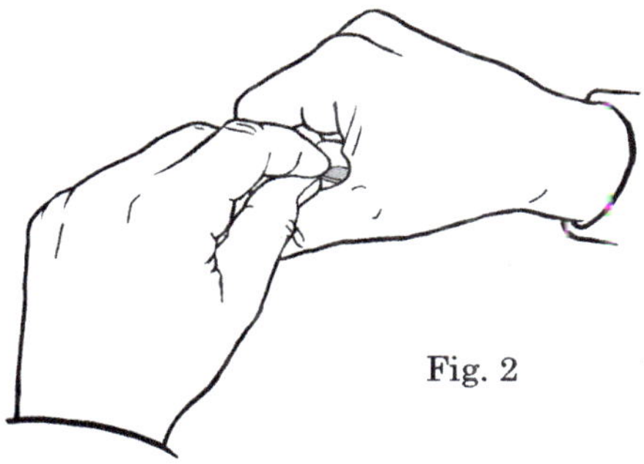

Fig. 2

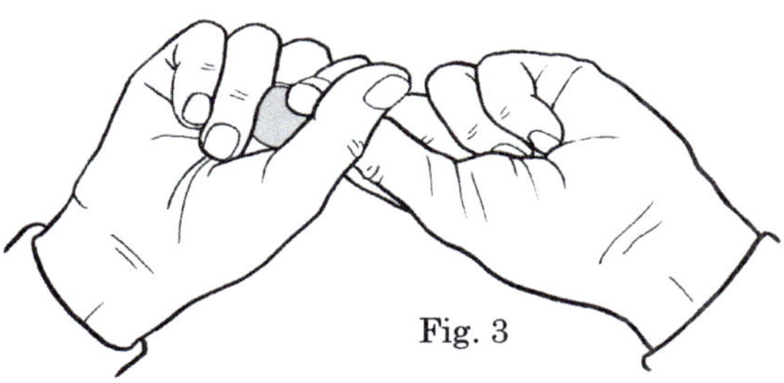

Fig. 3

The quarter is now regripped against the back of the second finger by the right first and third fingers, which hold it by opposite edges. (Fig. 3 is an exposed view.).

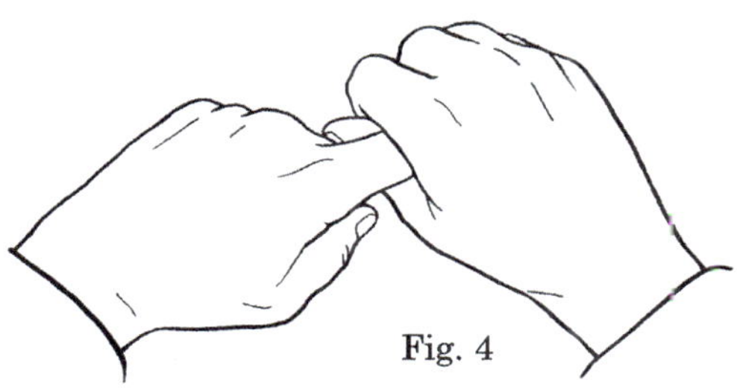

Fig. 4

The left first finger pretends to push the quarter further into the fist. In reality the left first finger simply glides over the right fingers until its tip touches the tip of the right fourth finger.

2) ". . . *it flies away and stays away. . .*" The left first finger begins to withdraw from the fist. Both hands rotate palm up and open, but do not separate. For a moment, the right fingers are hidden by the left fingers.

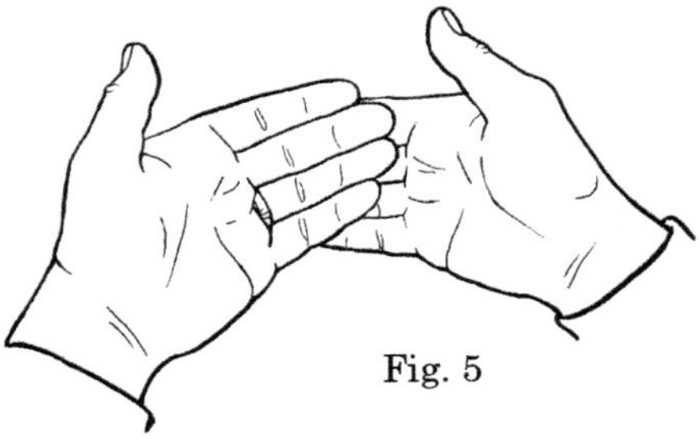

Fig. 5

The right third finger releases its hold on the quarter which immediately pops into Back Finger Clip between the first and second fingers.

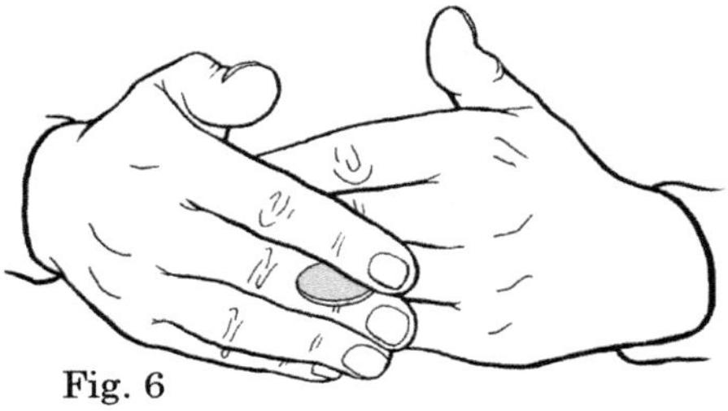

Fig. 6

The palm-up hands now separate, revealing two empty hands.

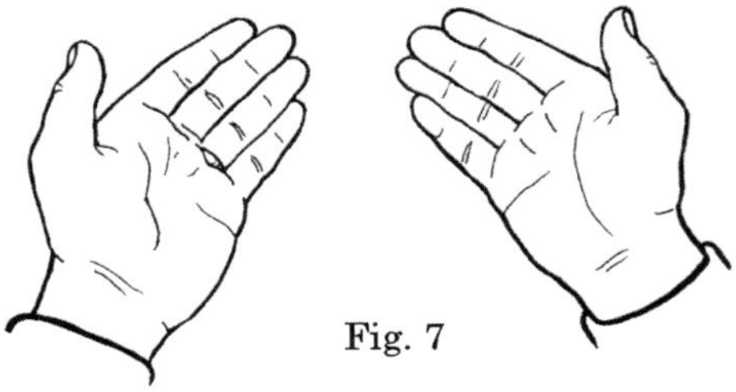

Fig. 7

3) ". . . *until it decides to return.*" You have just shown the palms of your hands to be empty. Now you are going to casually show that there is nothing on the backs of your hands. Turn your hands palm down and close them into loose fists, performing **Back Clip Retrieval No. 2**. To do this, you must keep the backs of your fingers pointing to the floor and turn your hands inward at the wrist in order to prevent the spectator from seeing the quarter. The quarter is transferred to right Thumb Palm—an action which is almost automatic—and the fingers of both hands immediately open. Gently spread the fingers of both hands to show that there is nothing concealed on the backs of the hands. Let this register and then casually drop your hands to your sides to conclude.

The Invisible Coin

"H.G. Wells wrote a book called **The Invisible Man** *and Claude Rains starred in the motion picture of the same name. I happen to have the last few drops of the secret formula that he took to make himself invisible. I am going to give 'George' (a quarter) just one little taste and, in a moment, he becomes transparent, and disappears completely. As the secret formula wears off, he becomes first transparent and finally he becomes completely visible."*

You will need a quarter, a plastic or glass disc the size of a quarter, and a small bottle that contains the (purely imaginary) invisibility compound. The glass disc begins in right-hand Finger Palm.

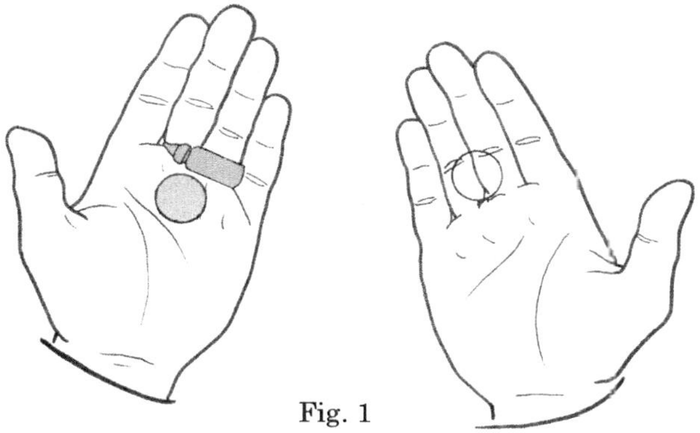

Fig. 1

After telling the introduction to the story, place the quarter in classic Spellbound position—gripping it by opposite edges between the left thumb and first finger. Execute **Sol's Spellbound Change**, transforming the coin into a glass disc—which represents the intermediate stage of invisibility, if you will.

Take the disc in the right hand and display it resting on the tips of the first and second fingers. Place the right thumb on the disc and begin to massage the disc between fingers and thumb.

Turn half-right and swing the right hand so that it is about a foot in front of the body at about waist height. At the same time, Back Clip the disc between the right first and second fingers. Continue to massage the "disc"—the fact that it has already disappeared is blurred by its transparency. After a few moments, remove the right thumb from the fingertips to show that the disc has actually vanished.

All attention is now on the right hand. Take advantage of this fact to Classic Palm the quarter in the left hand. Casually swing the right hand in front of your body and, under cover of this larger action, retrieve the disc using **Back Clip Retrieval Number Two**. Do not reveal it immediately, instead, knead or massage the fingers together and then slowly push the disc to the tips of the fingers where it is displayed in Pinch Grip. (Sometimes, Sol simply reaches out and produces the disc using Back Clip using **Retrieval Number Three**.)

Finally, pretend to take the disc in the left hand, in reality executing the **Pivot Transformation**. Rub the left fingers together and then open the hand to display the fully-visible quarter.

THE HUNG COIN

This is an excellent routine with which to practice the Back Clip. Causing a Chinese coin to penetrate onto a loop of string is both offbeat and visual, and the fact that the ends of the string are tied together makes this much more impressive than most ring on string effects. Although this has appeared in print several times, I have yet to see anyone use it (with the exception of Harvey Rosenthal, who has a much longer routine loosely based on the same premise). Give this a try—it is really good!

You will need a piece of soft string or cord that is about two feet long and two Chinese (brass) coins with holes in their centers. Thread one of the coins onto the string, leaving it near one end, and place it in your right jacket pocket. Place the other coin in your left jacket pocket.

When you are ready to perform, both hands reach into their respective pockets. The left hand openly removes the brass coin. The right hand maneuvers the brass coin on the string into Downs Palm and grasps the end of the string nearest the coin. Hand the visible brass coin to a spectator to hold for a moment. The right hand brings the string out of the pocket. The extra brass coin is concealed in Downs Palm, so the angles are very good except from directly above. Just to be safe, however, keep the back of your hand toward the audience at this point.

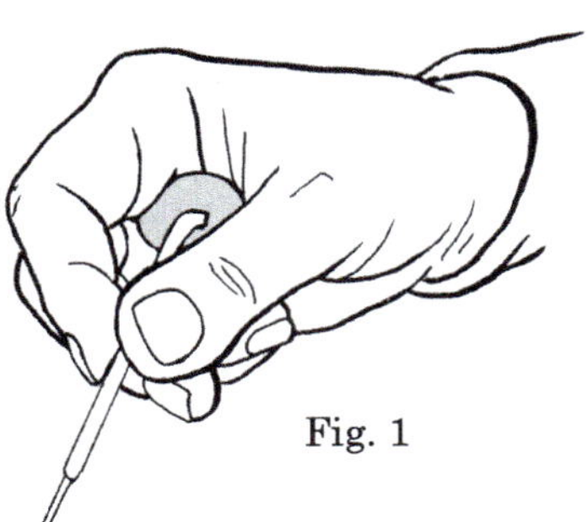

Fig. 1

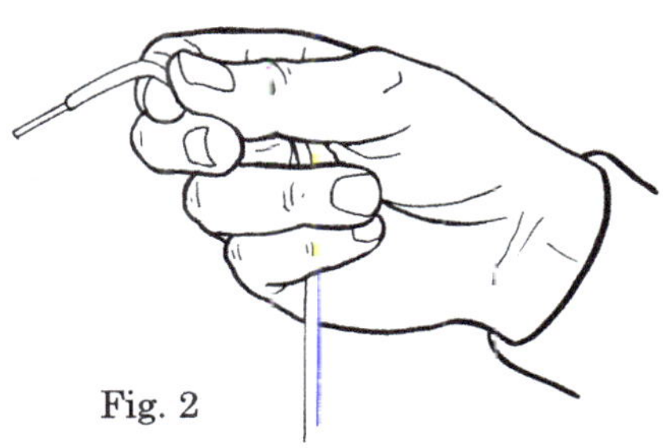

Fig. 2

Your left hand grasps the dangling end of the string and brings it up so that you can tie the two ends together. The right hand remains relatively stationary while the string is knotted, with the left hand doing most of the work.

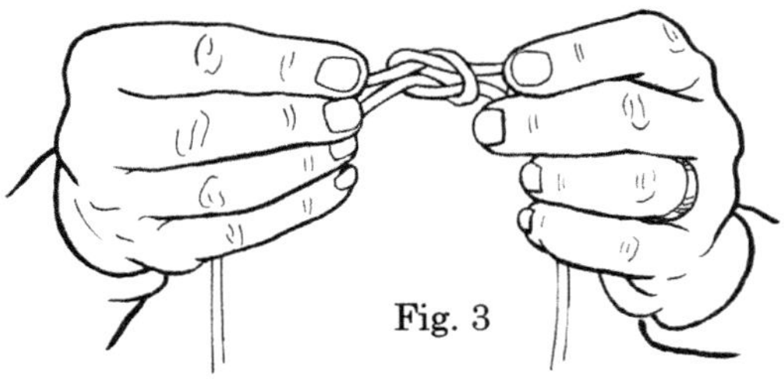
Fig. 3

With the ends tied together, allow the loop of string to drape over your right thumb. With the coin in Downs Palm, you can safely pivot to the right so that the palm of your right hand is toward the audience—everything looks as it should.

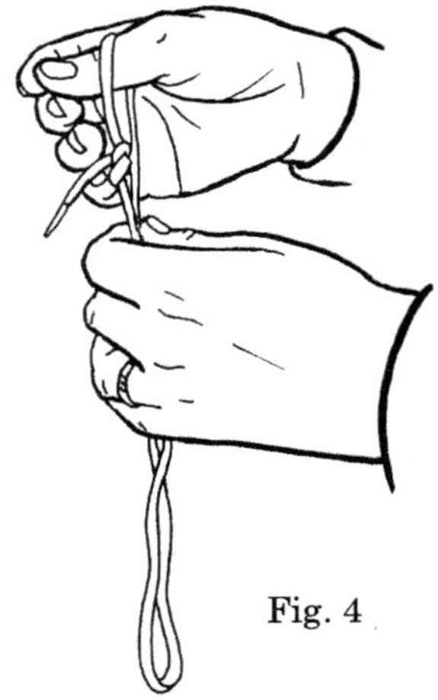
Fig. 4

Take back the brass coin and place it between the first and second fingers and thumb in Back Clip Display position.

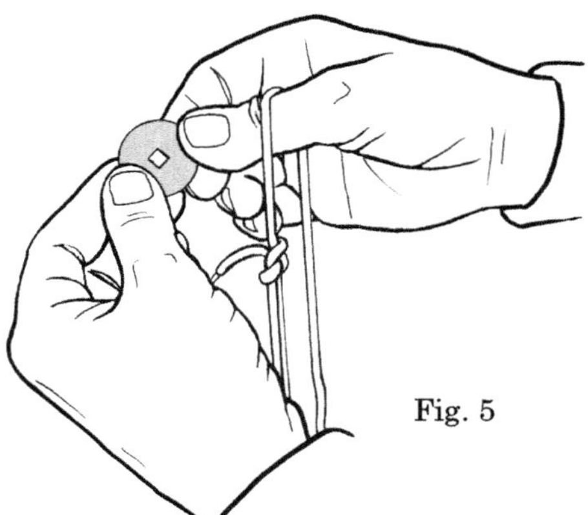
Fig. 5

You will now apparently transfer the loop of string from your right thumb to your right fingers. At the same time you will secretly exchange the two coins—moving the visible coin to Back Clip and bringing the coin in Downs Palm into view. In other words, execute **Back Clip Change Number Two**. For ease of learning, this sequence is best broken down into stages, though in performance it should be one smooth series of actions.

The left hand grasps the strand of the loop that is nearest you and just below the right thumb.

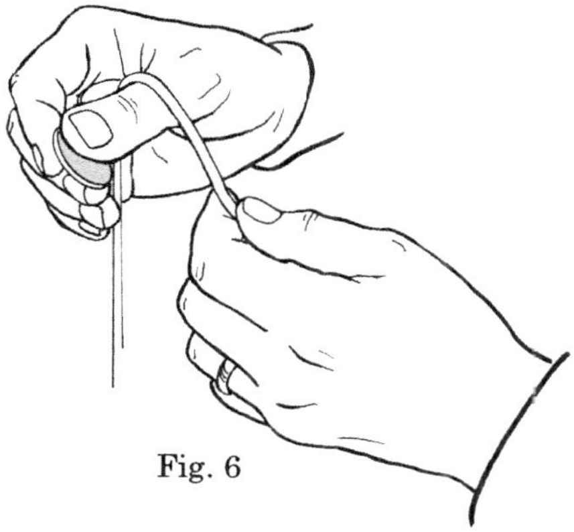

Fig. 6

Begin to Back Clip the coin. That is, move your second finger onto the face of the coin, release the grip of your thumb, pinch the coin between your first and second finger, press the thumb against the projecting edge of the coin, and begin to curl the first and second fingers inward.

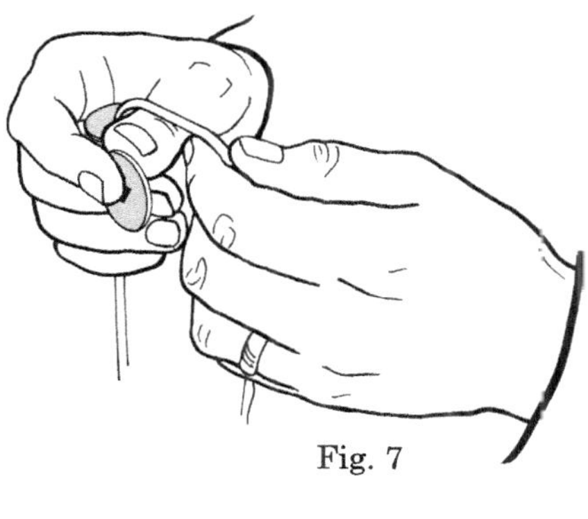

Fig. 7

Continue Back Clipping the coin, curling the fingers all the way in. You will find that this automatically brings the Downs-Palmed coin between the tips of the right first and second.

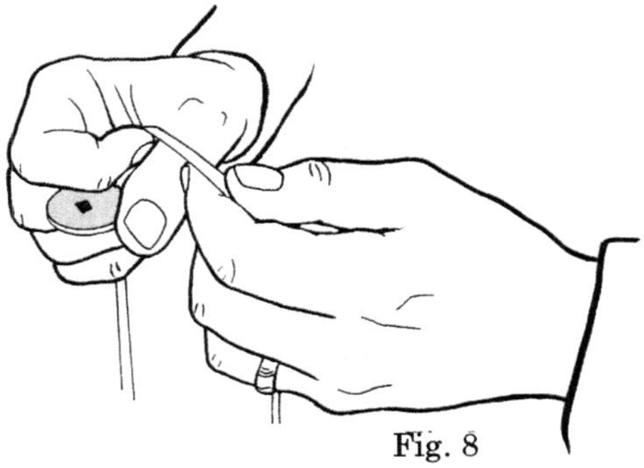

Fig. 8

Straighten your right first and second fingers, moving the coin in Back Clip proper. At the same time—**and this is critical**—the left hand carries the string to the right and over the back of the right fingers.

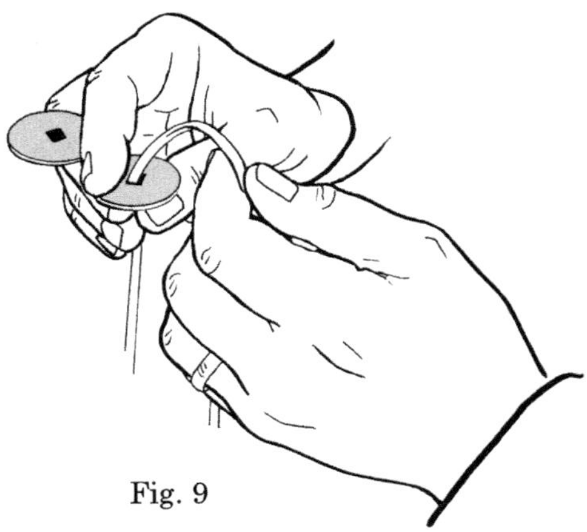

Fig. 9

It is this action of the left hand moving in front of the right hand for a split second that prevents the audience from seeing the coin going into Back Clip.

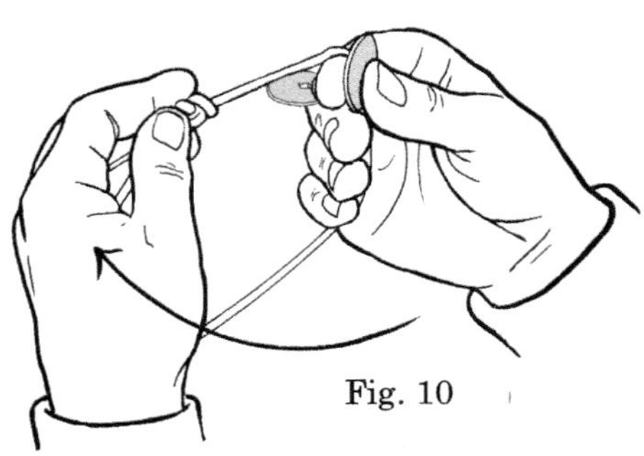

Fig. 10

This cover is only momentary and so you must have the actions of the **Back Clip Change** down cold—there can be no hesitation or fumbling. As soon as the fingers begin to straighten, the right thumb moves beneath the threaded coin and levers it into a vertical position, pressing the coin against the first and second fingers. ***The thumb covers the hole in the coin so that the audience cannot tell that it is threaded on the string.***

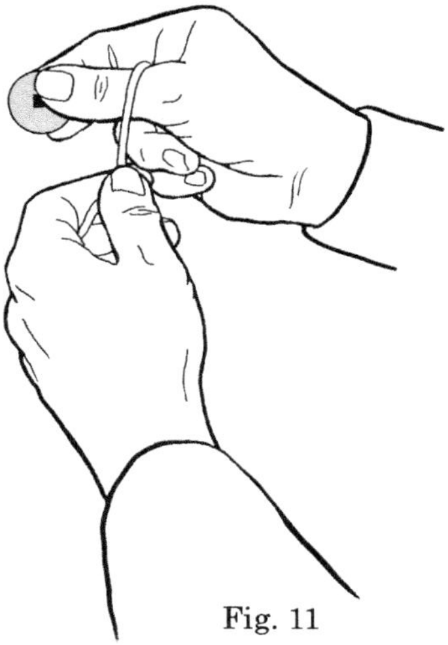
Fig. 11

Figures 11, 12 and 13 show the audience view.

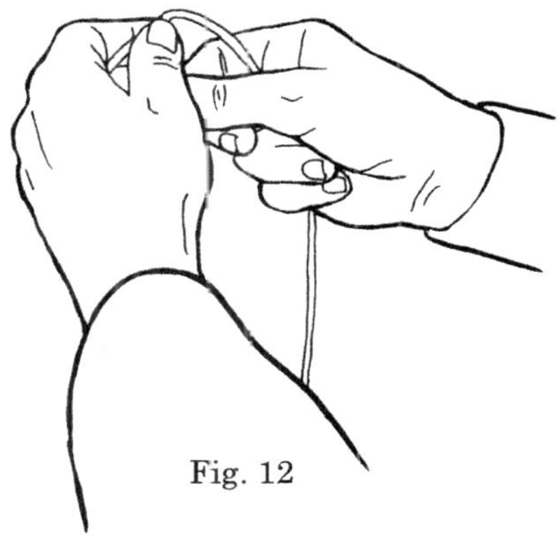
Fig. 12

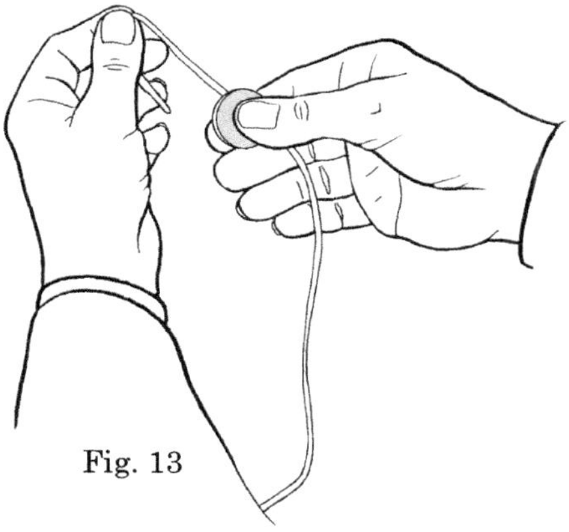
Fig. 13

The above actions take less than a second, but the illusion is perfect—it looks as if you have simply moved the string over your fingers and slightly regripped the coin. In fact, you have secretly switched the coins.

To cause the coin to penetrate onto the string, simply release the right thumb's grip. The coin falls and seems to melt through the string on its way down!

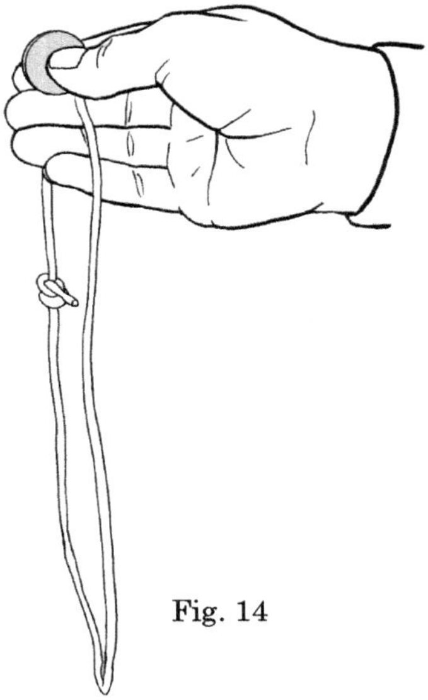

Fig. 14

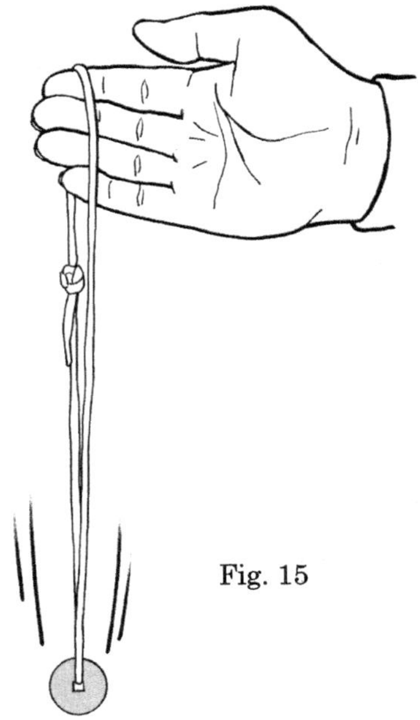

Fig. 15

Pause, so that the audience can clearly see the coin on the string. Raise your left hand behind the right and allow the Back Clipped coin to fall into left Finger Palm.

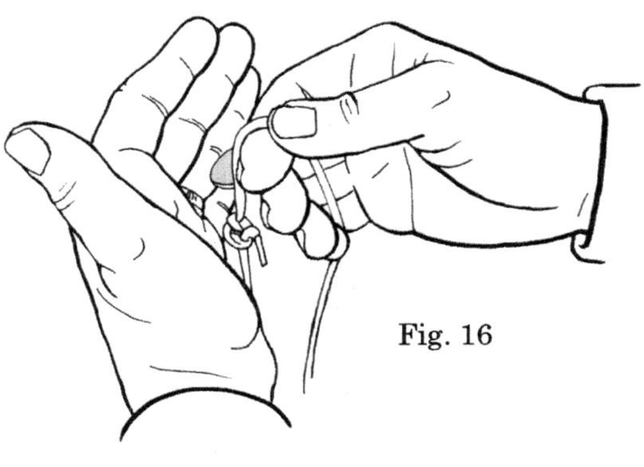

Fig. 16

In a continuing action grasp the strand of the string behind the right fingers and sweep both hands in front of you so that the backs of the fingers are toward the audience.

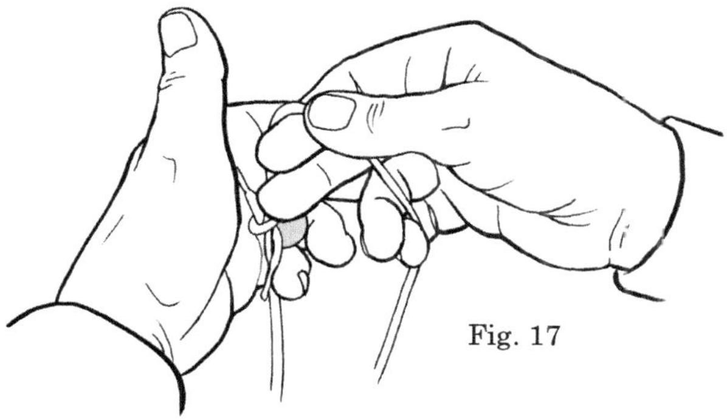

Fig. 17

Raise the string to display the coin hanging from its center. The extra coin is hidden in left-hand Finger palm. Untie the string (you can easily rotate the string to bring the knot up to your hands).

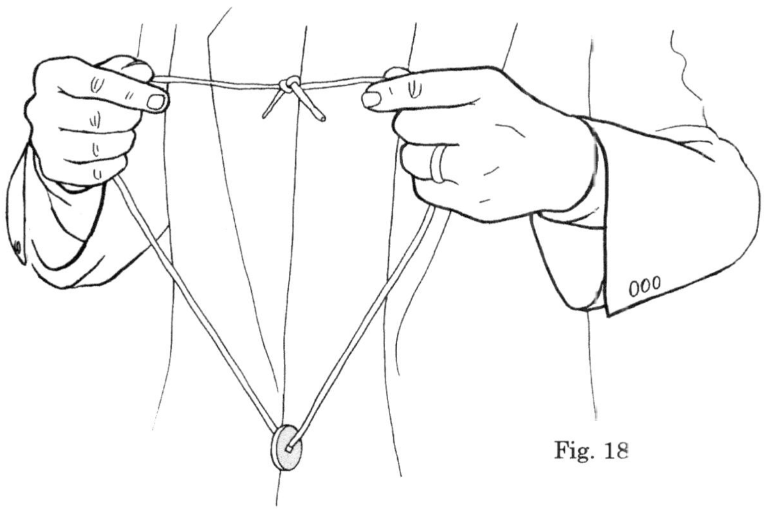

Fig. 18

I will confess that part of me says to end the routine right there—the penetration by itself is simply impossible. Sol, however, often continues by unthreading the coin and then causing it to jump back on the string while the middle of the string is in the spectator's shirt pocket...

Transfer both ends of the string with your left hand. The right hand moves down to the coin at the center of the loop and closes in a loose fist around it. The left hand drops both ends and lets them dangle. The left hand then moves into the right fist—thumb inside and fingers outside—so that the thumb presses against the threaded coin. Slide the left hand to the left, as if pulling the coin toward the end of the string.

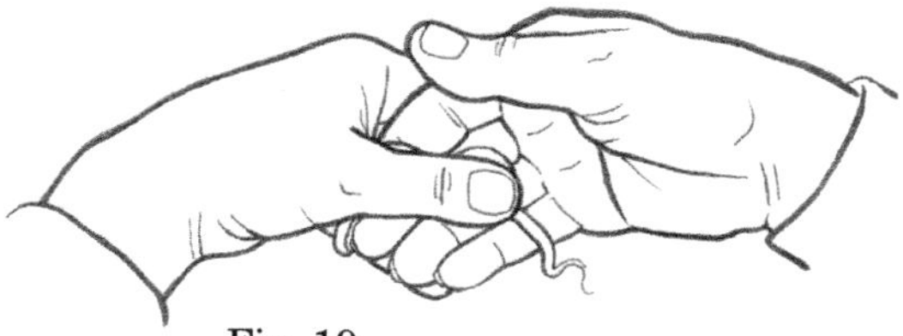

Fig. 19

In reality, the threaded coin remains in the right hand (held in place with the right thumb) while your left thumb presses the free coin against the string as it moves to the left. Continue "un-threading" the coin until it is "free" of the string.

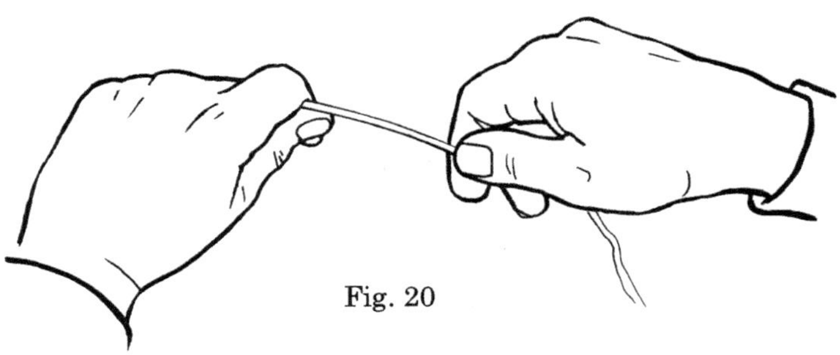

Fig. 20

As soon as the coin is free, reach out with the right hand and tuck the middle of the string into the breast pocket of the spectator's shirt or jacket. The ends of the string are free and clearly visible. Vanish the coin using the **Basic Pivot Vanish** and then have the spectator grab both ends of the string and pull. The middle of the string will pop out of his pocket with the coin threaded on it!

SIMPLE TRIPLE ONE-HAND SPELLBOUND

This relies only on **Back Clip Change Number One**. It is, in fact, the second phase of Sol's "**Advanced One-Handed Triple Spellbound**" described below, but makes an excellent sequence by itself.

You will need a copper-silver coin and a Chinese (brass) coin. Begin with the brass coin in Back Clip. The copper-silver coin begins in Back Clip Display position. It doesn't matter which direction the coin is pointing, but let's assume that the silver side is facing outward.

This is very straightforward — just execute **Back Clip Change Number One** with the **One-Two-Three Cover** two times in a row. The first time the silver coin changes into the brass coin. The second time the brass coin changes into a copper coin.

Quadruple One-Hand Spellbound

The Patriotic Poker Chip

Early in his experiments with the Back Clip, Sol wondered if it was possible to do a quadruple change. Due to the mechanics of Back Clip Change Number One, this could be easily accomplished with two double-sided coins. Unfortunately, other than the standard copper-silver gaff, there were no other double-faced coins. Sol solved the problem using double-sided poker chips that he constructed himself. He made his first set in the 1930's and still uses it today.

You will need two chips: one is red on one side and blue on the other side, the other chip is white on one side and striped red, white, and blue on the other side.

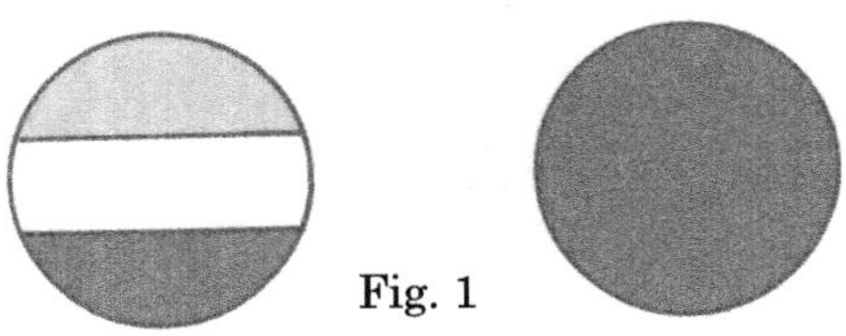

Fig. 1

Sol made his chips from inexpensive, silver-dollar size, cardboard poker chips —I will leave the construction details up to you. Just make sure that the chips are thin enough to be easily Back Clipped, but sturdy enough to stand up to the constant handling they will undergo.

Begin with the white/striped chip in Back Clip, white side uppermost. The red/blue chip is in Back Clip Display with the red side showing. Now you simply do Back Clip Change Number One with the One-Two-Three Cover three times in a row. The chip will change from red to white, white to blue, and blue to red/white/blue. Sol concludes by simply dropping the chip(s) in his pocket. That's it, both terribly easy and terribly demanding at the same time!

Advanced Triple One-Hand Spellbound

This is the routine that puts it all together. I don't know how many people will make it this far, but if you do you have entered the ranks of the elite. You will need a copper-silver coin and a brass coin. Begin with the copper-silver coin in Downs Palm, copper side up and the brass coin in Back Clip display position. Starting with the (ungaffed) brass coin showing allows you to handle this coin freely at the beginning of the routine.

***First Transformation. Brass to Silver*:** Execute **Back Clip Change Number Two** with the **One-Two-Three Cover**, changing the brass coin into a silver coin. The brass coin ends up in Back Clip and the copper-silver coin is in Back Clip Display, silver side out.

***Second and Third Transformation. Silver to Brass - Brass to Copper*:** Execute **Back Clip Change Number One** with the **One-Two Three Cover**, Back Clipping the copper silver coin and bringing the brass coin into view. Execute the Change a second time, Back Clipping the brass coin and bringing the copper silver coin into view, copper side showing.

***Fourth Transformation. Copper to Brass*:** Now execute the following sequence (which should be easy if you can do the rest of this routine). Begin by executing Change Number One up to the point where you have the brass coin pinched between your second and third fingers and the copper-silver coin pinched between your first and second fingers.

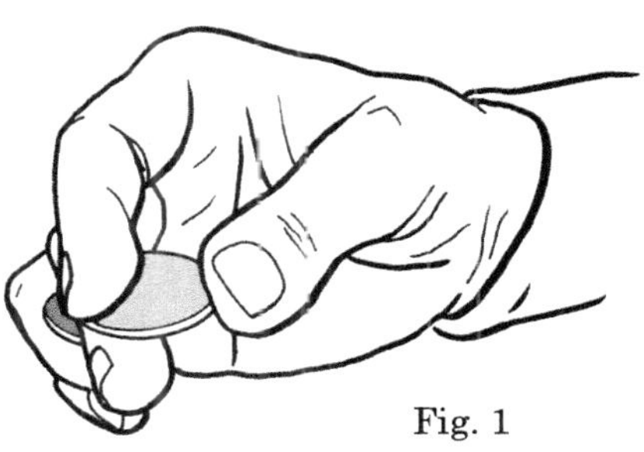

Fig. 1

Now, instead of completing the Change, curl all of your fingers inward. This delivers the copper-silver coin into Downs Palm position.

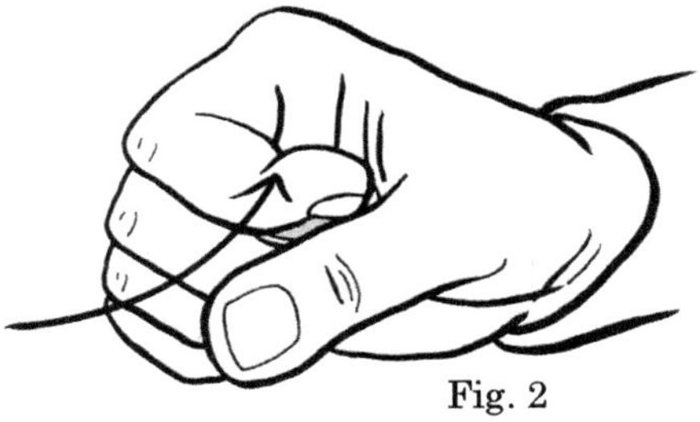

Fig. 2

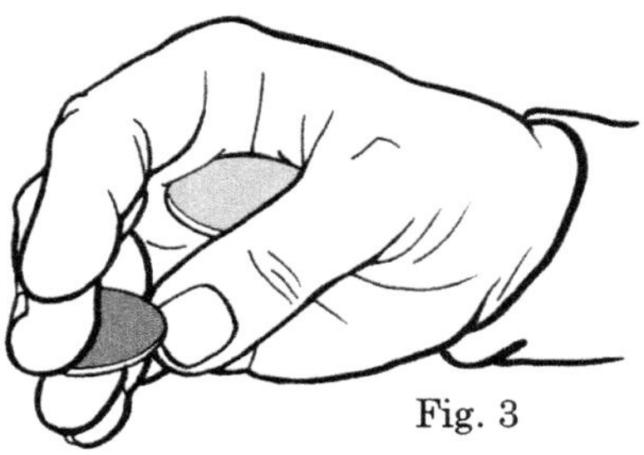

Fig. 3

Downs Palm the copper-silver coin as you straighten your fingers and move your thumb onto the exposed edge of the brass coin.

Finally, lever the brass coin up into Display Position. The entire sequence, of course, is done with the One-Two-Three Cover.

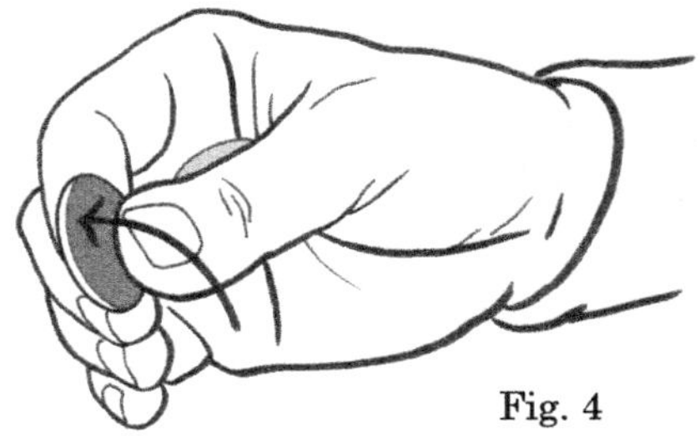

Fig. 4

That's it! Believe it or not, Sol has a handling of this routine using ungaffed coins. It requires that you hold out the extra brass coin in Classic Palm throughout the first two transformations. For details, see the Sol Stone section in **CoinMagic**.

Tenkai Pennies & Variations

Ed Balducci showed Sol the "**Tenkai Pennies**" routine in 1945. Balducci had been taught the routine by Tenkai himself, long before the routine had ever seen print. Sol taught the routine to Albert Goshman, who in turn was largely responsible for popularizing the effect in this country. In Tenkai's original handling a coin was clipped against the back of the hand by the fourth finger, and this was the method that Sol taught Goshman. Perhaps as a result, this method of concealing a coin behind the hand has become known in the United States as the **Goshman Pinch**. It is not, however, original with Goshman—who never claimed credit for it—and is more properly referred to as the **Tenkai Pinch**.

In any event, Sol loved the basic premise of the "**Tenkai Pennies**" routine but was not crazy about the **Tenkai Pinch**. Sol felt that, at close quarters, the Pinch made the hand looked awkward, cramped, and almost arthritic. Sol therefore reworked the handling using the Back Finger Clip. In his handling of the routine the **Second and Third Finger Back Clip** is used, freeing the first finger for the necessary pointing action. Martin Gardner published Sol's handling of the **Tenkai Pennies**, inadvertently neglecting to credit him, in ***Hugard's Magic Monthly***, November 1950. A description of this routine has also appeared in the ***New York Magic Symposium, Collection Two***.

Tenkai Quarters

Classic Two Coin Handling with Back Clip

Begin by borrowing two quarters. Make it clear, without actually saying so, that your hands are otherwise empty as you receive the two coins. Sol uses quarters because they are easily borrowed and because he almost always does this routine extremely close-up, with the spectator almost directly on top of him.

Each hand takes a quarter and the coins are displayed resting near the tips of the second and third fingers. The hands are palm up at about waist level in an open display position.

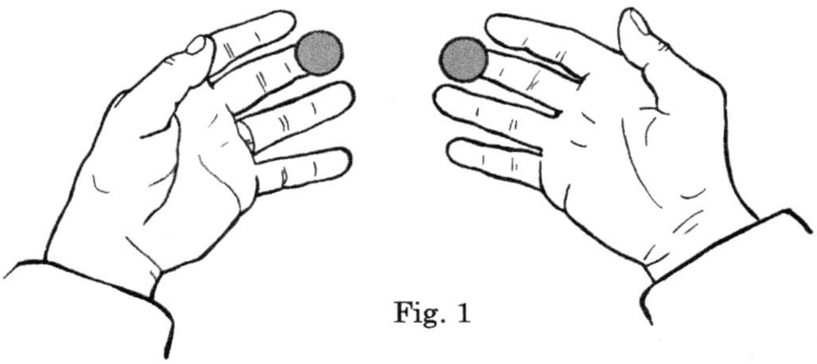

Fig. 1

As you say, "*I have two quarters. . .*" you apparently close your hands into loose fists and turn them palm down. At least that's what the audience observes. In reality, the right hand secretly **Back Clips** its coin between the second and third fingers as the hands turn palm down.

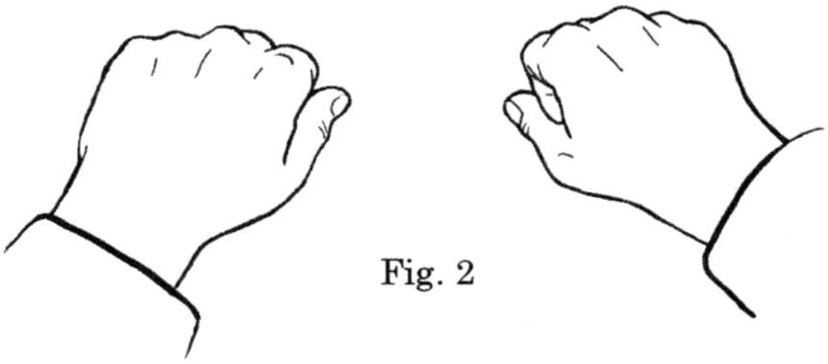

Fig. 2

The action of the Back Clip is exactly that described in the Back Finger Clip section. Cover is provided by the hands rotating inward as the fingers curl against the palm.

With the spectators looking down at your hands, the action of the move is completely concealed. You will find that you do not have to rush—once the backs of the hands are toward the audience, you can take your time (relatively speaking, of course) to position the coin in Back Clip with the thumb. As the right hand turns into a palm-down fist so does the left hand, automatically bringing its coin against the palm. For symmetries' sake, both thumbs should rest beside the fists—the right fingers and thumb finish their work by the time the right hand closes into a palm-down fist.

Now comes a carefully choreographed sequence of words and actions. Extend your left first finger and tap the back of the right fist as you say, "One quarter here."

Retract your finger. Extend your right first finger and tap the back of the left fist as you say, "And one quarter here."

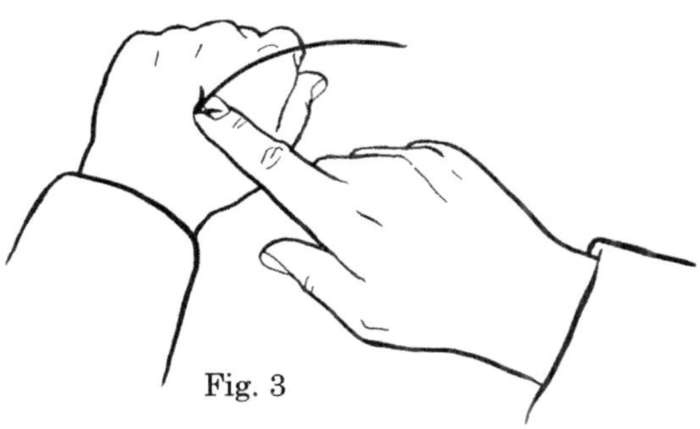

Fig. 3

This positions your right first finger directly over your left hand, in preparation for the upcoming move. (This is why the coin must be Center Back Clipped—so that you can naturally extend your right first finger.)

Turn your left hand palm up and open it, leaving the quarter on the palm of the hand. Say, "One coin here. . ."

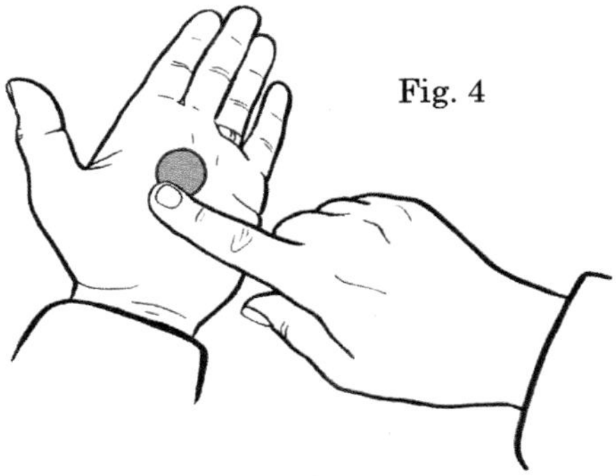

Fig. 4

The right first finger descends onto the quarter and pushes it forward, across the palm and fingers, until it rests near the tips of the left second and first fingers.

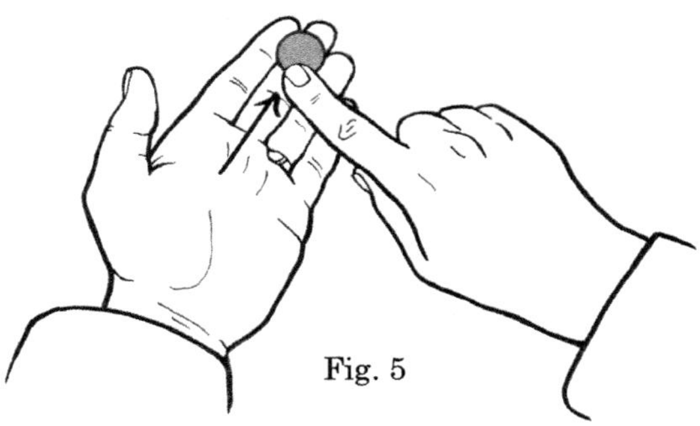

Fig. 5

Immediately retract the right first finger and begin to close the left hand. As the left hand closes, the left thumb presses down on the quarter, pinching it between the thumb and first finger.

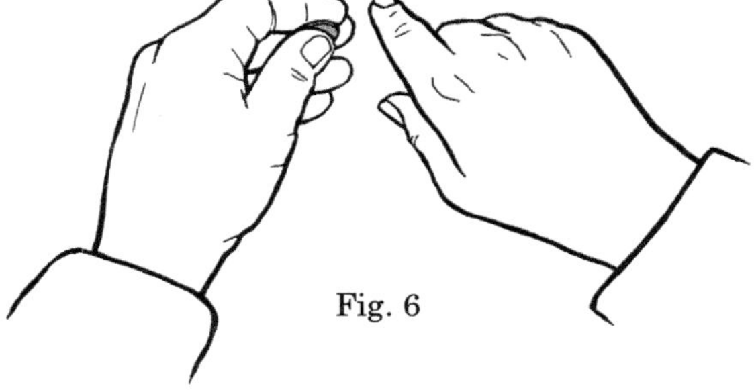

Fig. 6

In continuous action—there can be no hesitation at all—the right hand rotates palm up, turning at the wrist so that the coin in Back Clip remains concealed beneath the hand. At the same time, the left hand turns palm down, the left first finger and thumb extend (with the coin pinched between them), and the coin is placed directly onto the palm of the right hand.

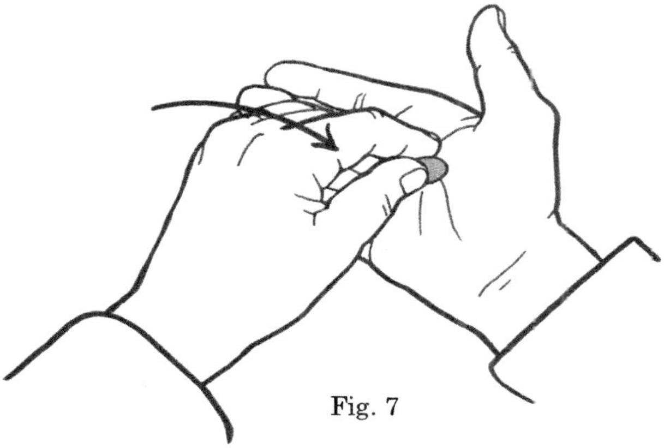

Fig. 7

There is a timing element of this move that is extremely difficult to teach on paper. It must look as if you simply open your right hand and touch the coin (that the spectators know is there) with the left fingertip. The remaining fingers of the left hand remain curled against the palm—they are supposedly holding a coin. A slight body shift from left to right will help to cover the move.

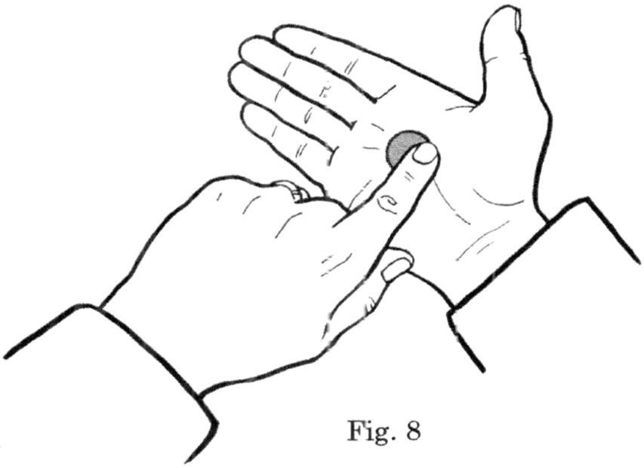

Fig. 8

As all this is taking place, say, "And one coin here."

Without pausing, the left first finger slides the coin to the right fingertips, just as was done with the coin in the left hand. This time, however, simply push the coin forward until it rests directly above the coin in Center Back Clip, absolutely concealing it from view.

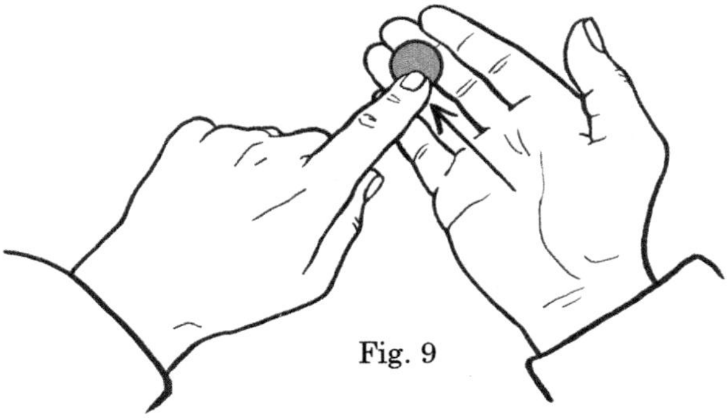

Fig. 9

The left hand withdraws and the left first finger curls against the palm. Slowly close the right hand, rotating it inwards at the wrist as you do so in order to conceal the coin in Back-Clip.

Say, "Keep your eye on this coin." Raise your left hand so that the backs of the fingers are toward the audience and pretend to slide the (now long gone) coin in the left hand to the fingertips.

Fig. 10

All of your attention is on the raised left hand. This provides ample cover for the right thumb to pull the coin from Back Clip into the right hand. There is no real "technique" to this, just pull the coin in with a minimum of fumbling and make sure the two coins in the right hand do not click together.

"The quarter in my left hand will hop up my sleeve, skip across my chest, and jump down into my right hand.. There it goes!" Follow the imaginary path of the coin with your eye, perhaps wriggling or contracting you arm and chest appropriately.

Say, "You look a little skeptical. If I showed you that the coin was gone from here, would you believe?" Open the fingers of your left hand one-by-one to show that the coin has disappeared. "But you would still want to see the other hand." Conclude by slowly opening your right hand to reveal two coins.

This is a superb routine! Best of all, the effect is completely impromptu—maximum impact is created with two borrowed coins. The only caveat is that you must practice the Tenkai Transfer until it is completely smooth and natural. There must be no hesitation or fumbling at that stage of the effect or the illusion is destroyed.

TENKAI PRELIMINARY: THE MALINI ROUTINE

In *The Dai Vernon Book of Magic* there is a routine entitled "**Malini-Vernon: 'Three from One'**" in which two extra coins are apparently "broken" off a single coin. When this was published, it reminded Al Flosso of a variant presentation of the same effect that had been shown to him by Malini. Flosso, in turn, taught this handling to Sol, who often performs it just prior to the **Tenkai Quarters** routine described above.

The only preparation is to secretly load a quarter up each sleeve. Borrow a quarter and emphatically state, "I am going to cause this coin to vanish in slow motion." As you speak, clearly let your hands be seen empty of all but the borrowed quarter. Openly and deliberately take the quarter into your left hand, close your left fingers around the coin, and focus all of your attention on the left fist. As you do so, the right hand naturally drops to the side and the coin is allowed to fall from the sleeve into the right hand, where it is Finger Palmed.

Open your left hand and act stunned that the coin has not vanished. Recover your poise and say with a shrug, "Oh well, it doesn't matter. Here, you keep this. . ." Take the visible coin with your right hand and give it back to the spectator, being careful not to flash the coin in Finger Palm. As the coin is being returned, the left hand naturally drops to the side and the coin in the sleeve is allowed to slide into the left hand. "I'll just use this one. . ." Reach out with your right hand and produce the Finger Palmed coin. "And this one." Reach out with your left hand and produce the second coin. You now have two quarters, one in each hand, and are set to proceed directly with Sol's **Tenkai Quarters** routine.

Sol likes this routine because he believes it is psychologically very strong. You start out saying you are going to vanish a coin and then fail to do so. In the wake of the disappointment that naturally follows, however, you hit the audience with two strong and unexpected productions. The whole sequence has the feeling of impromptu, yet powerful magic.

One Coin Tenkai

This is simply a "one coin across" routine which, in Sol's hands, looks exceptionally fair and above-board. Sol prefers to borrow a quarter for this effect, although you may find the vanish easier to accomplish with a fifty-cent piece. Begin by displaying the coin at the right fingertips and apparently placing it into the left hand. In reality, you must execute a false transfer that leaves the coin clipped between the right first and second finger in position to be easily Back Clipped. I will describe Sol's method for doing this.

The coin begins pinched between the right thumb and first finger. The right second finger is curled inward and rests on the lower edge of the coin.

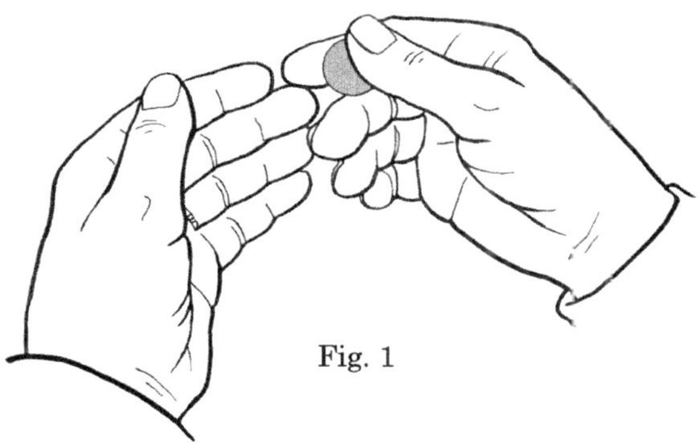

Fig. 1

As usual, you want as much of the face of the coin (on both sides) to show as possible. Display the coin by first showing its outer face and then lowering the palm-up hand to display the opposite face. From this position it is natural to turn the hand over as the coin is transferred to the left hand—which provides the necessary cover for the move.

So, the right hand rotates partially palm down and pretends to place the coin in the left hand.

As it does so, and under the additional cover of the left fingers as they curl inward, the following actions occur:

The right thumb levers the coin until it's perpendicular to the finger, the edge clipped between the first and second fingers.

Fig. 2

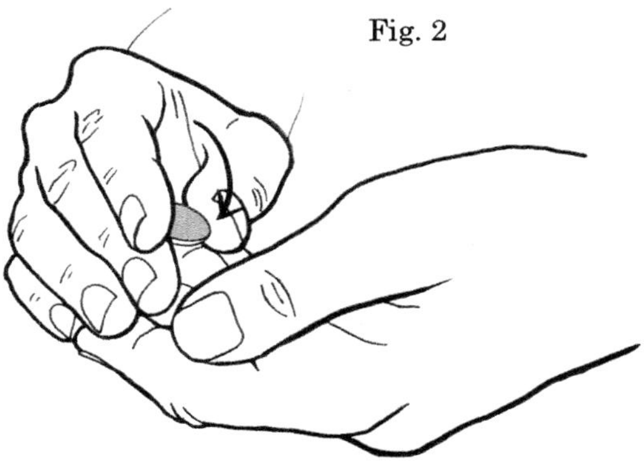

As the left fingers curl around the non-existent coin, the right hand moves away and falls casually to your side. Naturally, all these actions must blend into a seamless sequence. There is a slight knack to this vanish, but properly done it can be very illusive.

Now the coordination between your actions and words becomes important. Raise (and look at) your left hand as you say, "I will try to make the coin travel from this hand. . ." As you speak, the right hand transfers the coin from Front Clip to Back Clip. This must be accomplished almost instantly, and is done as the right hand is turning palm up and being brought into view. If you try this you will find that there is very little time to fiddle around, which is why you must use a vanish that leaves the coin in Front Clip—there is simply no time to slide the coin from, say, Finger Palm to Front Clip to Back Clip.

The right hand is turning palm up, opening, and coming into view as you say, ". . . to this hand—without my hands going near each other." The apparently empty right hand is displayed for a moment or two and then both hands curl into fists, rotating inwards at the wrists, and turn palm down.

At this point Sol extends his thumbs and just barely touches their tips against each other. Slowly turn your left hand palm up and open it to show that the coin has gone. A beat later, turn your right hand palm up, executing Back Clip Retrieval Number Two, to display the coin on the right fingers. By opening the hands one after another, instead of at the same time, you can more easily disguise the necessary action of the Back Clip Recovery.

On
The Miser's Dream

T. Nelson Downs stated that the reason he was successful with the "**Unlimited Coinage of Silver**" was because he varied the coin productions and had a great sense of humor. Although Sol never saw Downs perform, he was inspired to work on the "**Miser's Dream**" after seeing Al Flosso in a "ten-in-one" show at Coney Island. Flosso's philosophy was: "Hit 'em in the head, tie 'em in a knot, and get off!" But the truth was that Flosso could have produced coins for hours and kept people interested. When Flosso was on-stage, nobody slept! The lesson: a strong stage presence is necessary in order to put over a repetitive trick like the "Misers Dream." Sol, perhaps uncertain of matching Downs' humor and Flosso's zeal, limited himself to producing ten or twelve coins when he performed this routine at birthday parties and school shows.

Sol's Miser's Dream Sequence

Fig. 1

In this "production-toss-in-the-pail" sequence, the audience hears and sees the coins falling into the pail. It utilizes the **Basic Back Clip**, described above, and I will assume that you are familiar with this technique. You need a pail or bucket with a thin (preferably wire) handle. Sol often uses a child's sand pail (made out of tin or aluminum to maximize the noise of the coins).

You will also need a stack of five or more fifty-cent size silver coins. These begin in left-hand Finger Palm. A single coin, identical to the others, is in the right hand.

The right hand picks up the pail by its handle. The back of the left hand is toward the audience. Transfer the pail to your left hand. The arc of the handle fits snugly into the crotch of the thumb and runs diagonally across the palm of the hand. The left thumb presses down against the stack of coins and "smears" them along the second and third fingers. The coins end up in an overlapping row, held in place by the thumb and curled fingers.

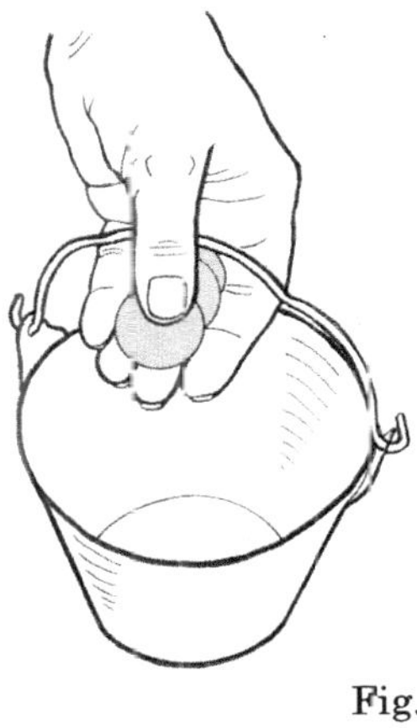

Fig. 2

The right hand has just reached out and produced its coin, which is held in Back Clip Display position.

Fig. 3

Fig. 4

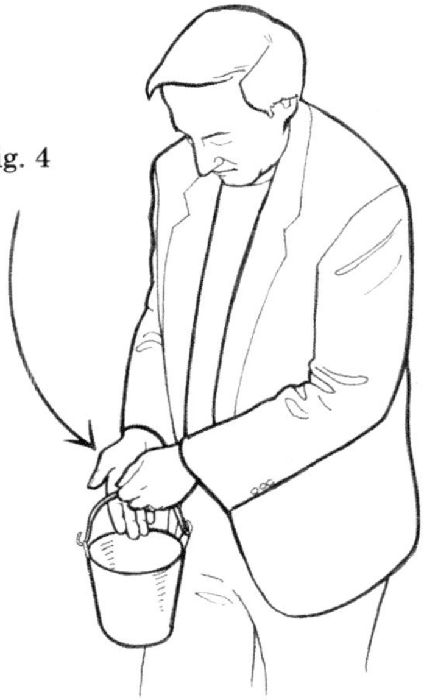

The coin is now apparently tossed into the pail. In reality, as the right hand sweeps toward the pail, the coin is secretly Back Clipped. The action of the Back Clip is concealed by the larger action of the moving hand and, to a lessor degree, by the back of the left arm and hand.

As the right hand is Back Clipping the coin, the left thumb slides one coin from the stack of coins to the left fingertips.

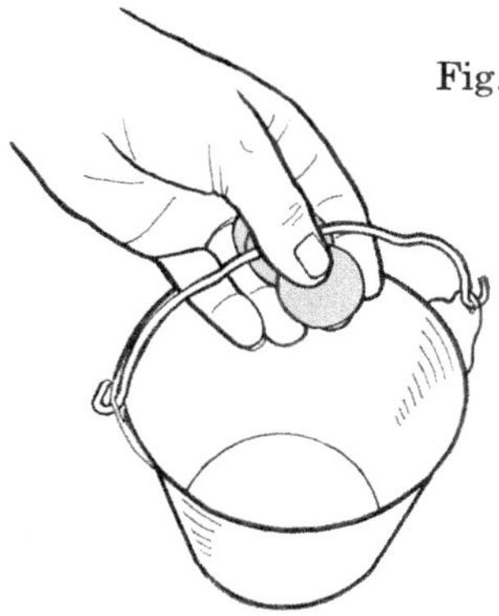

Fig. 5

Without pausing, the right hand opens so that the tips of the fingers point into the pail. The palm-up right hand should be directly above the rim of the pail and below the left fingers. Without delay, the left thumb releases the coin at the fingertips...

Fig. 6

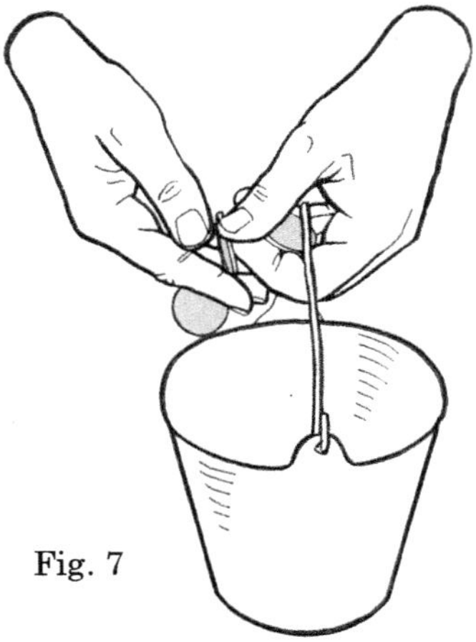

Fig. 7

...its lower edge hitting
the right fingers.

The coin flops over onto the
right fingers...

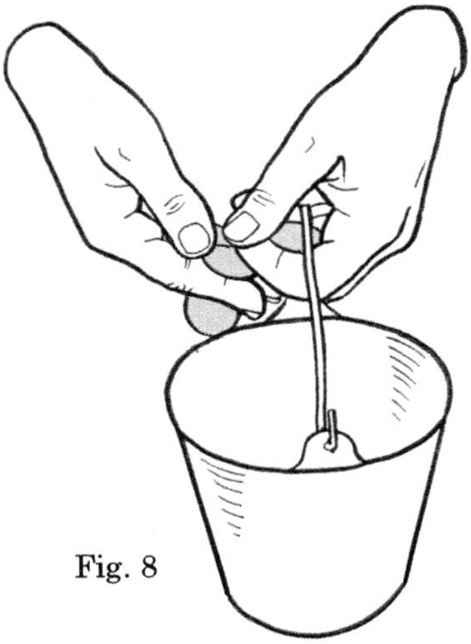

Fig. 8

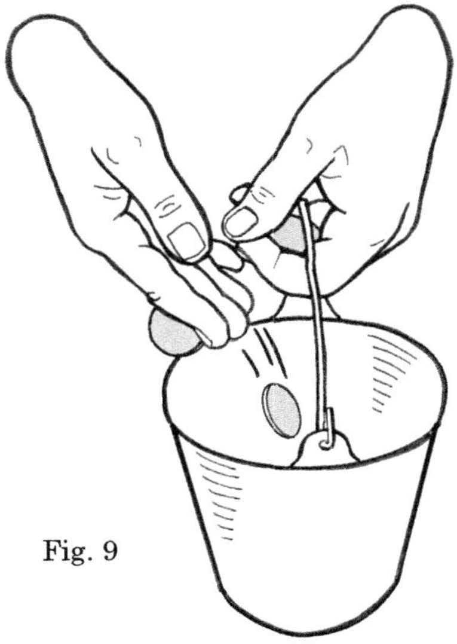

Fig. 9

...then slides off into the pail.

Timing is everything here -- as the hand opens the coin must appear on the palm. The action is similar to the classic **Han Ping Chien** technique in this regard.

After dropping the coin into the pail, the right hand reaches out and produces the Back-Clipped coin (**Recovery Number Three**) and the sequence is repeated until you run out of coins. The last coin is legitimately dropped in the pail. Naturally, the entire sequence must be carefully timed and rehearsed. Done properly, the illusion of the coin actually being tossed into the pail is perfect.

Tenkai's Miser's Dream Move

During World War II, the great Japanese magician Tenkai lived in Hawaii. To avoid unwanted harassment, he assumed an identity as a "Chinese" magician and in this guise performed frequently in U.S.O. shows for American troops.

Tenkai's **Miser's Dream Move** was shown to Sol by a serviceman returning from Hawaii shortly after the War. This individual must have seen Tenkai perform and had either been taught the move by Tenkai or was able to reconstruct his handling. Sol has kept the move to himself for all these years and it appears here in print for the first time. If this were used in conjunction with **Sol's Miser's Dream Sequence**, described above, you would have a very powerful combination indeed.

Let's assume that you are holding a champagne bucket or "coin pail" in your left hand. The pail is held by its rim, with the fingers inside holding a stack of coins against the container's side. These coins will be released as you apparently toss a coin from the right hand into the pail, creating the audible illusion of a coin being dropped in a bucket.

You have just produced, and are displaying, a coin which is held between the first and second fingertips and thumbtip of the right hand.

Fig. 1

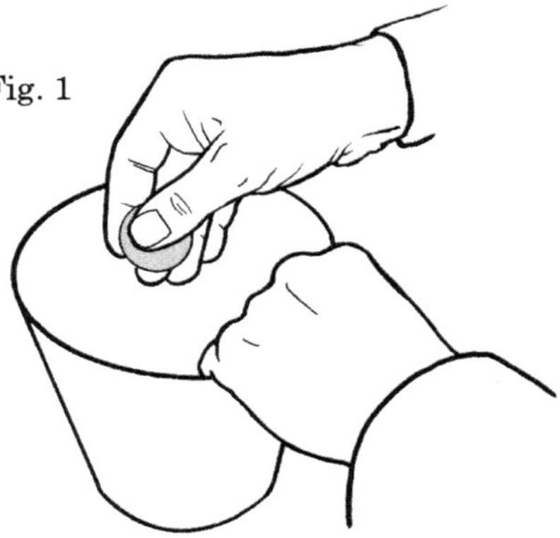

The hand is dipped inside the pail and the coin smoothly transferred to Tenkai Pinch as a coin from the left-hand stack is released. This is standard "Miser's Dream" technique, except for the Tenkai Pinch.

Getting into Tenkai Pinch is really very easy. Fig. 2 shows the starting position.

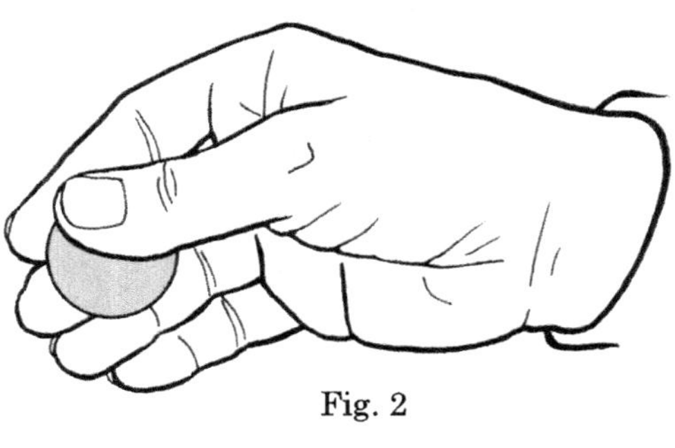

Fig. 2

While the right thumb holds the coin in place against the first and second fingers, the third dips below and in front of it. The lower edge of the coin is clipped between the third and fourth fingers and the thumb can move away. The first and second fingers hop over the upper end of the coin.

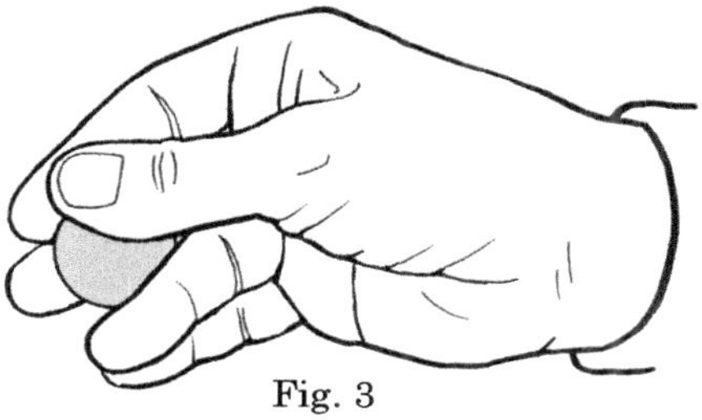

Fig. 3

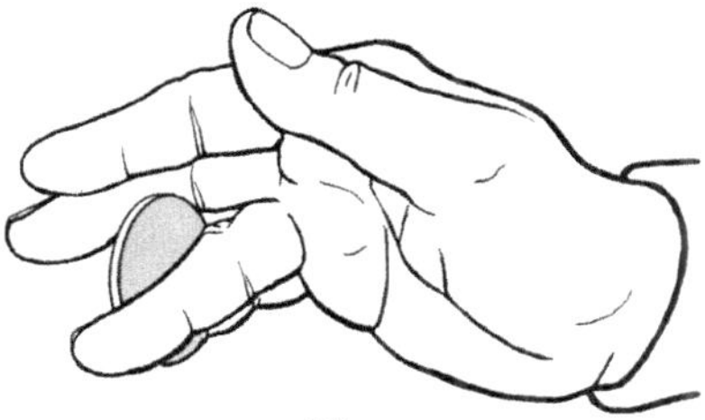

Fig. 4

The coin is clipped against the back of the third finger by the fourth finger. The coin does not lie completely flat against the hands, but protrudes at a slight angle. All this is the work of an instant.

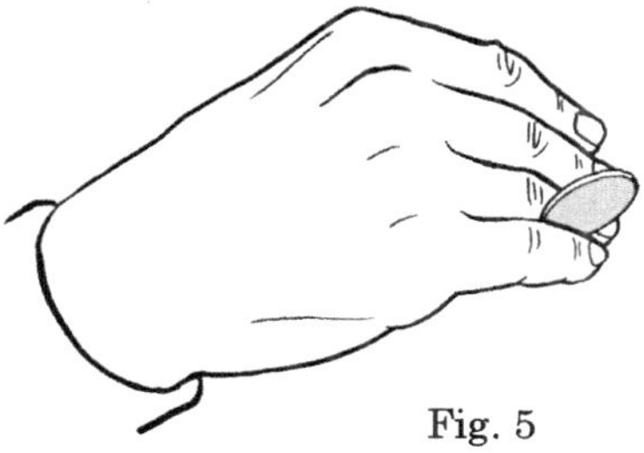

Fig. 5

As soon as the coin is in Tenkai Pinch Grip, the palm-out hand is removed from the pail. The empty palm visually confirms the fact that the coin has been tossed in the pail.

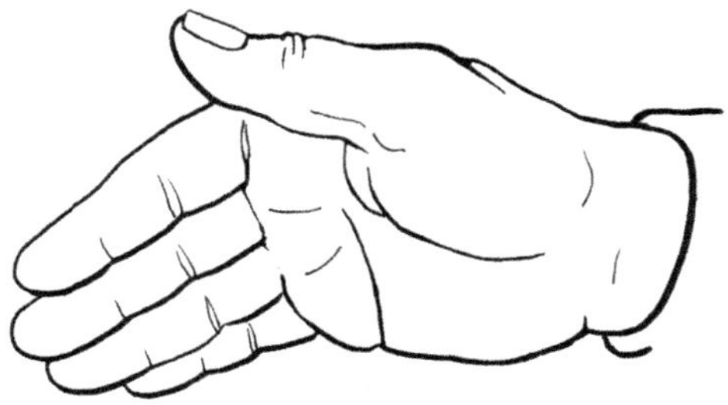

Fig. 6

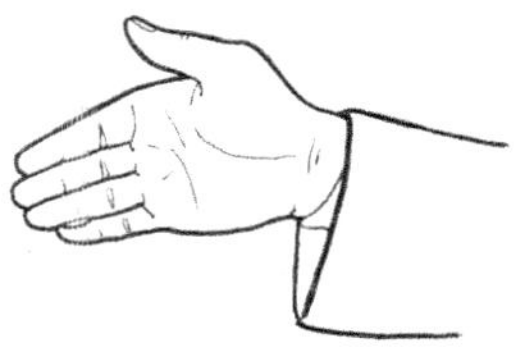

Now comes the move described to Sol. You are going to reach out with the right hand and "produce" a coin from the air. Stare ahead and pretend to "see" a coin floating a few feet in front of you. The palm of the right hand is toward the audience and the fingers are pointing in the general direction from which you intend to produce the coin.

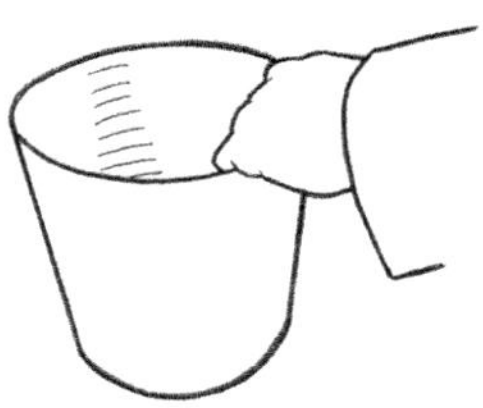

Fig. 7

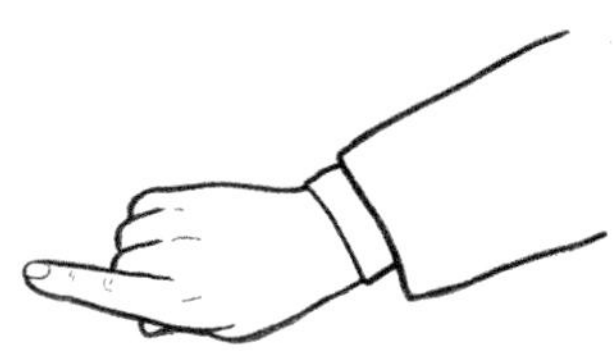

You now point to the imaginary coin with your right first finger. To do this, the second, third, and fourth fingers curl inward. At the same time, the right palm rotates away from the audience. There is only one possible way to do this—simply turn the hand so that the thumb is toward the floor.

Fig. 8

The second, third, and fourth fingers are not pressed against the palm, but are curled only partially inwards. This leaves the first finger pointing toward the imaginary coin and the back of the hand toward the audience.

Timed properly, the Tenkai-Pinched coin remains hidden from view. Better yet, the audience apparently gets a view of both the front and the back of the hand during this sequence.

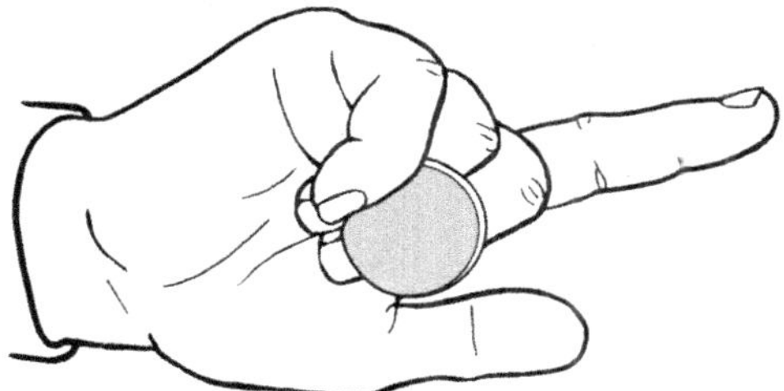

Fig. 9

The right hand now reaches and "catches" the coin. As the arm extends the thumb moves onto the face of the coin, pressing it against the back of the fingers.

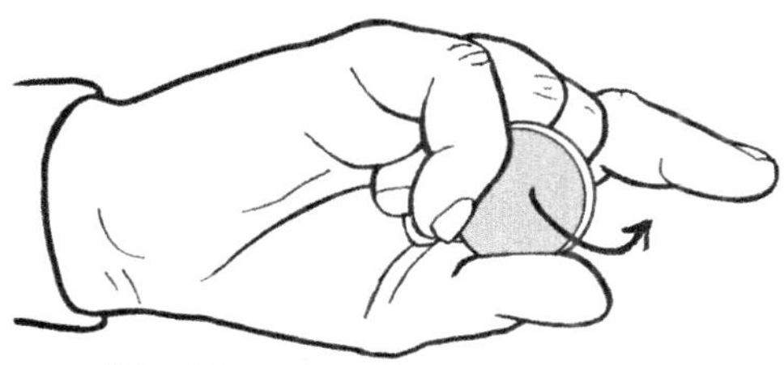

Fig. 10

The semi-curled fingers then rapidly extend, the tips moving onto the face of the coin opposite the thumb. At the same time, the palm is rotated toward the audience. This automatically brings the coin into view at the fingertips. This production can be performed rapidly or slowly with equal deceptiveness.

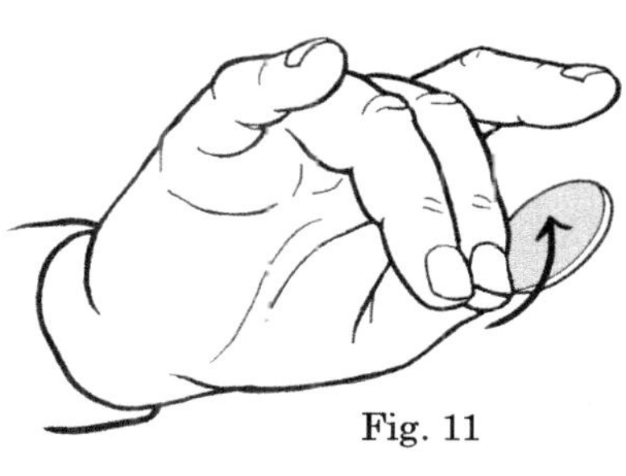

Fig. 11

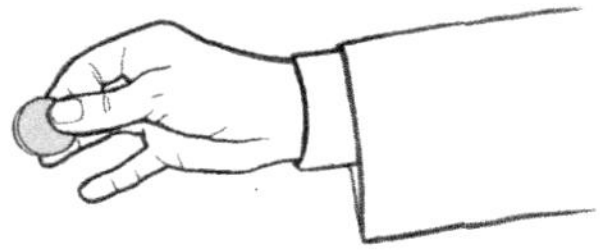

You are set to repeat the sequence: tossing the coin into the pail and producing another coin at the fingertips until you run out of coins, ideas, or time.

Fig. 12

Back Clip Vanish and Production

This is a utility sequence for vanishing two coins. Begin with one coin in the left and one coin in the right hand. Display the right hand coin in position to be Back Clipped. Make an upwards tossing action with the right hand and Back Clip the coin. You can use the **One-Two-Three Cover**, if you like, but Sol generally just rubs the tips of his thumb and fingers to cover the action.

The right hand is now palm-towards the audience, fingertips pointing upwards at about a forty-five degree angle.

The left hand comes over and openly places the second coin onto the right first and second fingertips, where it is clipped in place with the right thumb.

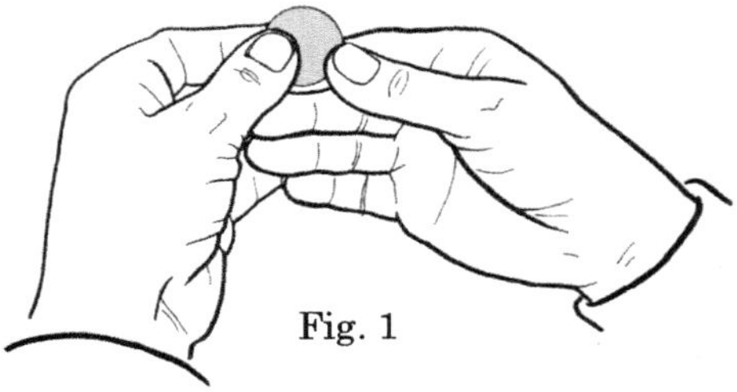

Fig. 1

At the same time, however, the Back-Clipped coin is pinched between the left second and third fingers, which have moved naturally behind the right hand.

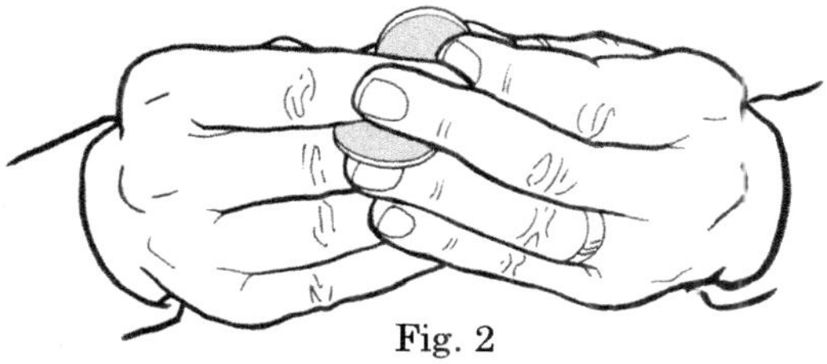

Fig. 2

As the left hand drops away, it takes the first coin with it—the left fingers curling inwards slightly to conceal the coin from view.

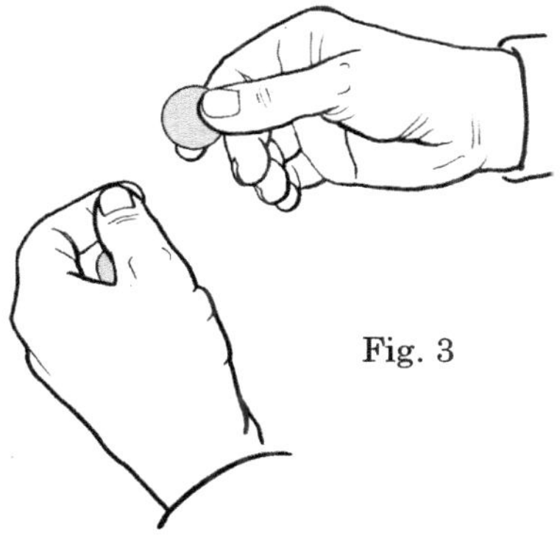

Fig. 3

The right hand now makes an upward tossing action and Back Clips the second coin, in the same manner as the first coin.

At this point you have just cleanly vanished two coins. Sol often stops here, reproducing each coin individually with the right and left hands. (See, for example, "**Fifty-One Cent Routine: Original Handling; Phase Six.**") You can, however, continue with the sequence indefinitely. Produce the coin in your left hand, place it at your right fingertips (secretly stealing the Back-Clipped coin), and then vanish this coin. Rather than just producing the left-hand coin from the air (which might give the game away), you could reach into a bucketful of coins, or your left jacket pocket, "remove" one, vanish it, and repeat—proving that it is just as easy to make the coins disappear as it is to produce them.

Impossible Links

LINKING LINKS

In this pocket effect three separate pieces of chain are apparently linked and unlinked. Sol has developed many different sequences and moves with these props, but I am just going to describe the basic routine that he usually relies upon. For more details and variations, you may want to read Harry Lorayne's description of this routine in **Best of Friends, Volume Two**.

Each piece of chain (link) is approximately an inch long. Sol uses decorative chain found in hardware stores. You will need the following: Two single links, a chain of two links, and a key link. The key link has a small gap cut at the center of one of its long sides.

Fig. 1

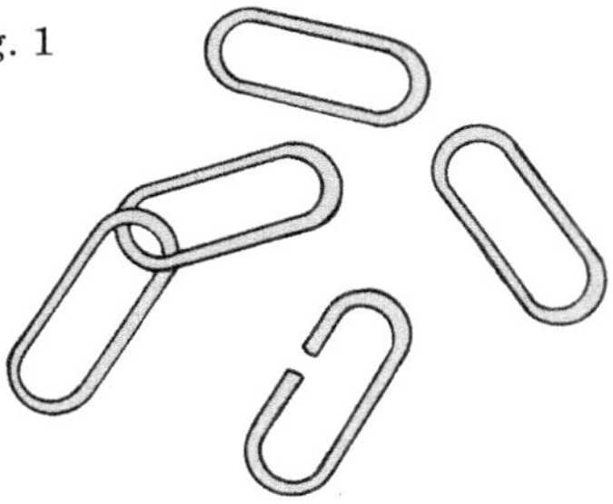

Start with the key link and a single link in your right pocket, and the chain of two and the single link in your left pocket.

Sol often begins with a little subtlety to throw off observant spectators. While performing another effect, he openly searches his pockets for some necessary prop. As he does so, both hands reach into their respective pockets and each brings out a single, ordinary link. The two links are casually set on the table as he says, "Remind me to show you something interesting with these a little later." When he finds the props he is looking for, the two links are returned to the pockets. The idea of two separate links has been established and often the spectator himself will ask to see the "trick with the links of chain."

In any event, when you are ready to perform, bring out a single link from the right pocket and hand it to a spectator. Don't ask him to examine it, just have him hold it for a moment. Reach into your left pocket and bring out the chain of two, holding it so that only one link is visible above your fingertips. The second link is concealed behind your fingers and the thumb covers the point where the two links meet.

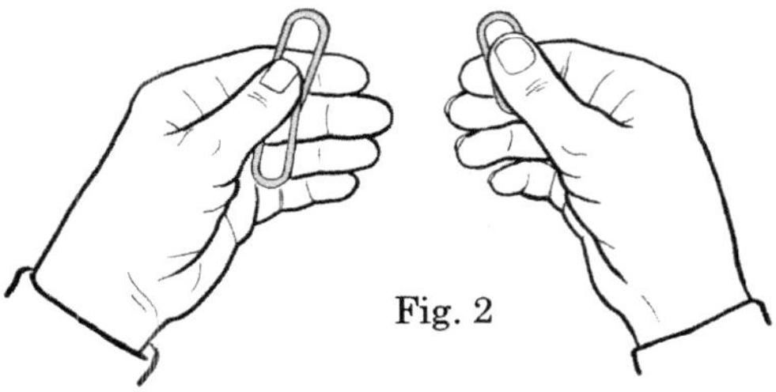

Fig. 2

Retrieve the single link in your right hand and display both links at your fingertips. To the audience it appears that you are holding two single links.

You now bring both hands sharply together and apparently link the two pieces of chain.

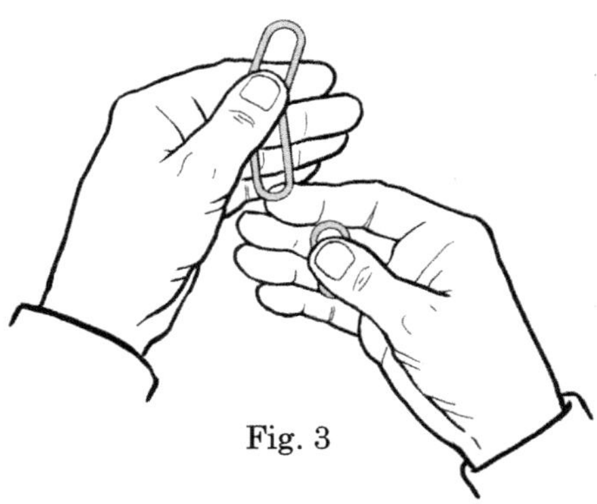

Fig. 3

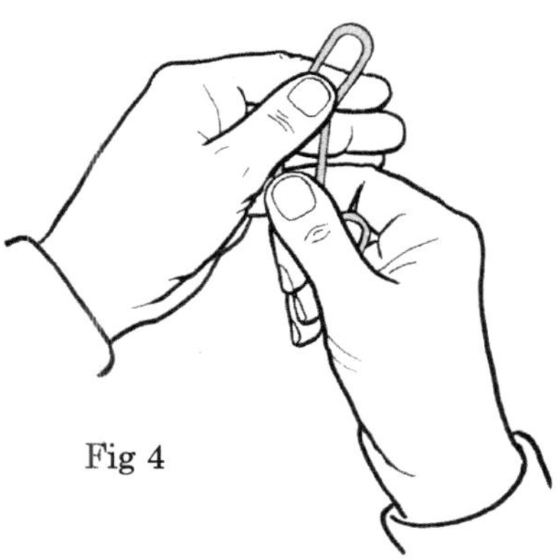

Fig 4

In reality, as the hands come together, your right thumb slides the single link down into fingerpalm.

In a continuing action, the right fingers and thumb grab the bottom link of the chain of two and pull it into view.

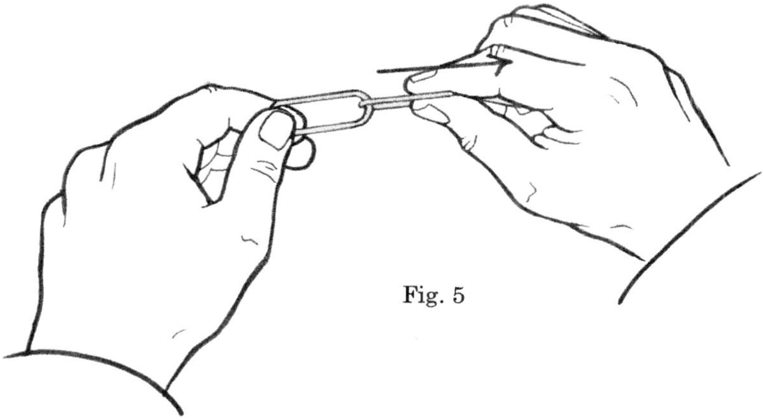

Fig. 5

Timed properly, the illusion of the two chains linking is perfect. Just as in many of Sol's coin routines, the extra link is held out in Finger Palm, concealed by the Ramsay Subtlety. Tug on the chain once or twice and then hand it out for examination.

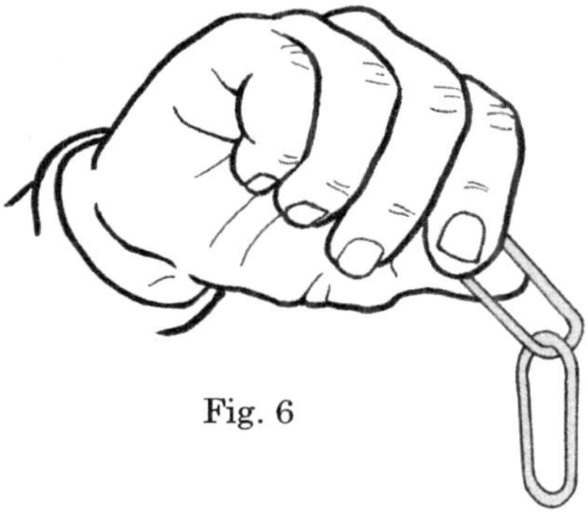

Fig. 6

As the spectators are looking at the chain, reach into your pocket with the right hand, drop the single link, and take out the key link, displaying it at the fingertips. The gap (key) is naturally concealed by the right fingers and thumb.

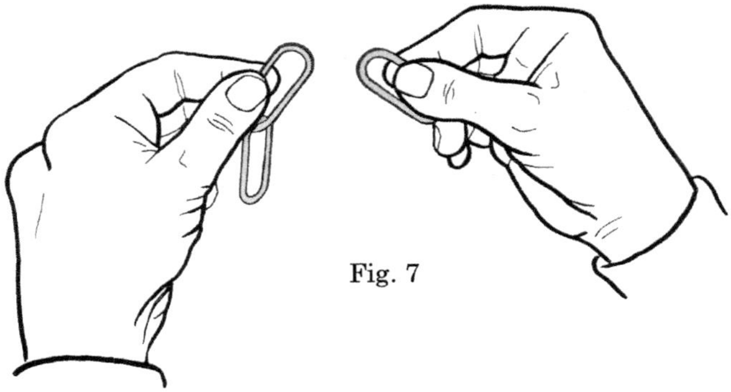

Fig. 7

Retrieve the chain of two with the left hand, holding one of the links between the first finger and thumb and letting the other link dangle from this link. Bring the hands together, linking the key link onto the upper link of the chain of two. The key link is simply passed onto the chain under cover of the right first and second fingers. There is nothing difficult about this secret linking action—just treat it as a miniature linking ring move.

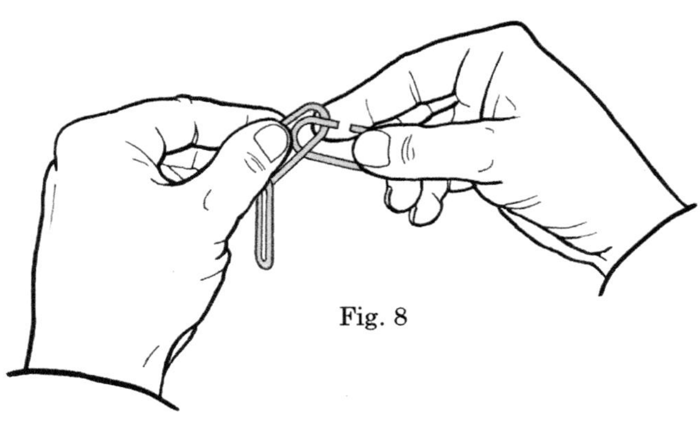

Fig. 8

Now comes a great display of the chain of three. Hold the key link in the right hand between the first finger, in front, and thumb, at the rear. The gap in the key link is hidden behind the first finger and the chain of two hangs down from the key link.

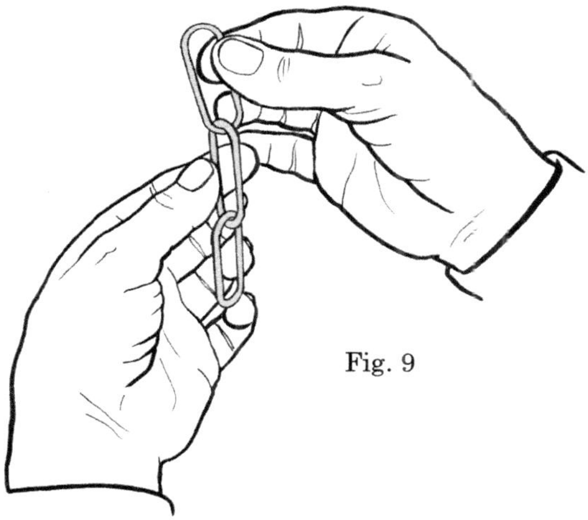

Fig. 9

Place the right first finger behind the link, directly above the thumb. Remove the thumb from the back of the link (which is momentarily clipped between the first and second fingers) and place it in front of the link directly below the second finger.

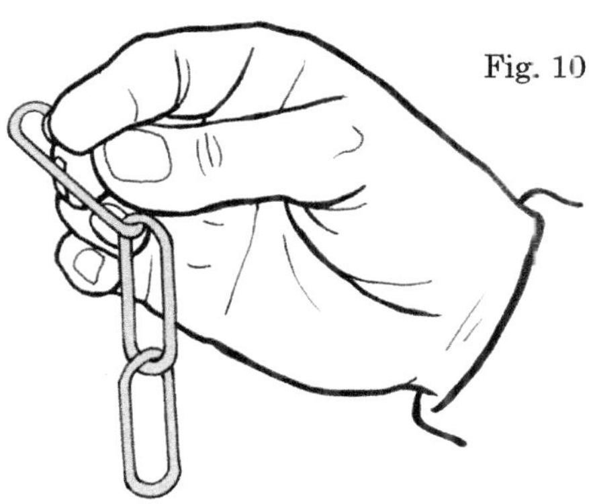

Fig. 10

Now release the second finger's grip and pivot the ring over end-for-end by squeezing the thumb upward. The chain of two will fall to the new lower end of the link as you do this.

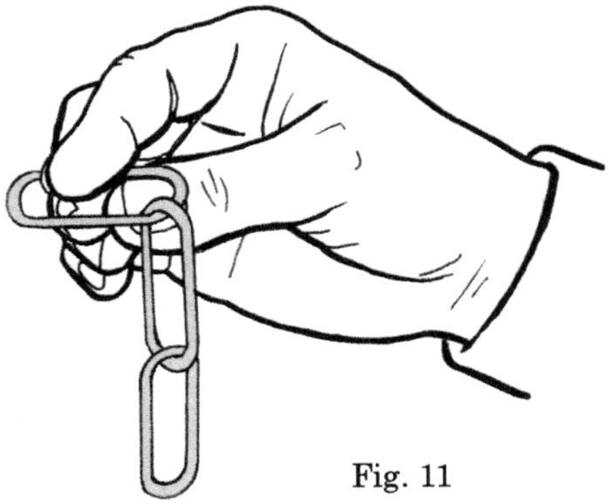

Fig. 11

The gap in the link is automatically concealed by the first finger as the link rotates. Indeed, the move is completely covered from all angles, the gap being concealed by the fingers and thumb throughout the action.

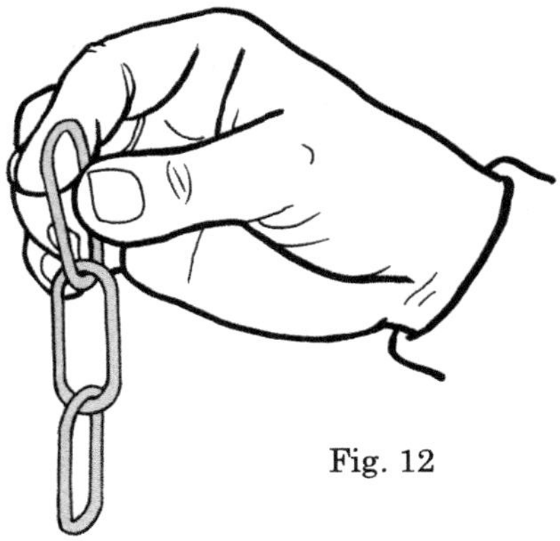

Fig. 12

Repeat this pivot display once or twice more—Sol does it very deliberately directly in front of the spectator's face. It really looks like the spectator is seeing the links from every possible angle.

Grasp the chain of two with the left hand while holding on to the key link with the right hand. Separate the hands, unlinking the key link in the process. Display the single, separate (key) link in the right hand and a chain of two in the left hand. Pretend to place the key link back in your pocket, secretly Finger Palming it as you do so. The right hand now grabs one of the chain of two and pretends to pull it free. Actually, the key link hidden in the right hand is pushed into view with the right thumb while the extra link of the chain slides behind the left fingers. This is just the reverse of the linking move done at the beginning of the routine. Display the apparently separate links and place everything in your pocket to conclude.

Ring On Pen

"On Again, Off Again"

This effect has evolved slowly over the years as Sol experimented with various moves and methods. The version you are about to read is its latest incarnation and is perhaps Sol's favorite impromptu close-up trick. This routine is the reason Sol no longer performs "Ring on Wand" or "Ring on String"—there are no props to carry and the effect can be performed anytime, anywhere. The routine has been taught by Sol to a few professional magicians who now use it regularly in their own close-up work.

The effect is divided into three phases. The first phase is Sol's, the second phase is an old bar bet, and the third phase is Oscar Weigle's. Sol obtained Weigle's move before World War II, trading the secret of the "Patriotic Poker Chip' for it. He has been using it for fifty-five years and considers it to be the most elegant method for the ring off pen that he has ever seen.

Borrow a pen and a plain gold wedding band. A ball point pen is best and the ring should have no stones or settings. Sol always carries an extra ring (I use my wedding ring) in case one can't be borrowed, but it is obviously better to borrow the props. Sol generally performs this while standing, directly opposite from a spectator who is also standing.

First Phase:

Hold the pen in the palm-up right hand so that it rests across the fingers with the bulk of the pen protruding past the first finger. If the pen has a clip or cap, it should be at the first finger side of the hand. The opposite end of the pen must not lie beyond the fourth finger. Let's call the writing end of the pen the "tip" and the opposite end of the pen the "clip end."

Fig. 1

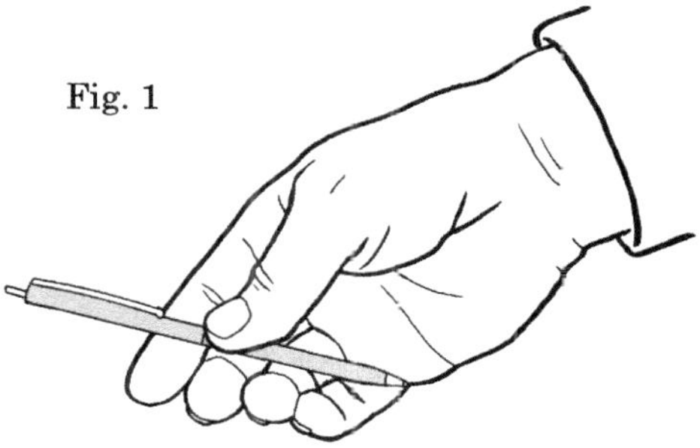

Take the ring and place it directly on top of the pen so that it rests above the first and second fingers. Lower your thumb onto the ring, holding it in place.

Fig. 2

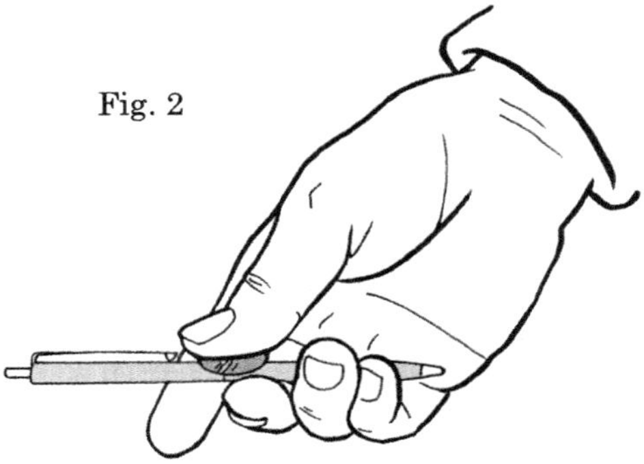

Casually display the pen and ring. This is not a move, just a displaying action. Sol verbally emphasizes that the ring is "on top of the pen."

Now comes the critical moment. You will apparently close the right hand around the pen and ring and, in the process, secretly thread the ring onto the pen. Here is the action, broken into steps --

First, the right hand turns palm down. As this occurs, the thumb begins to slide the ring towards the tip of the pen.

Fig. 3

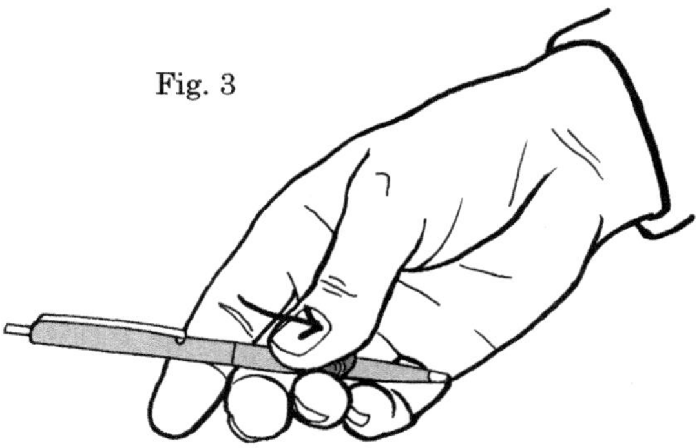

The left hand then grasps the clip end of the pen, which should now be pointing to the left, and both hands move upward for about six inches and then outward toward the spectator.

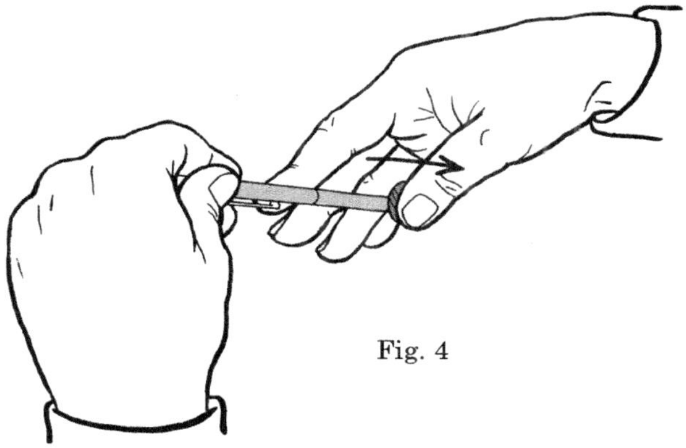

Fig. 4

Under cover of this larger action, the right thumb slides the ring to the very tip of the pen—to do this smoothly the left hand assists by pulling the pen half an inch or so to the left). There is absolutely no pause in the action. Firm pressure against the ring by the thumb causes the ring to snap around and onto the end of the pen.

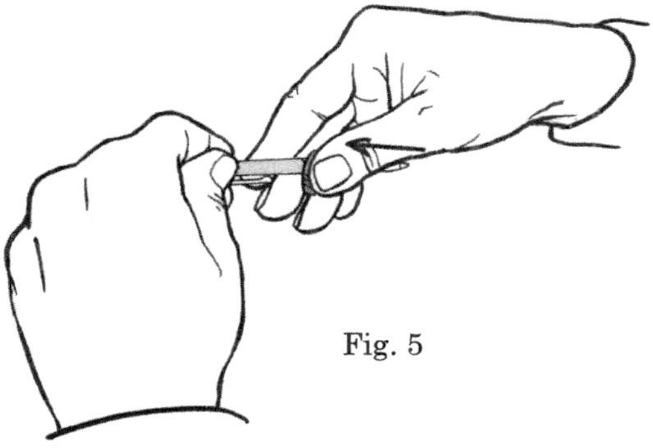

Fig. 5

The right hand then slides to the center of the pen, carrying the ring (now threaded on the pen) with it. As soon as the right hand is in position at the center of the pen, the left hand releases its grip on the pen.

The back of the right fingers conceal the fact that the ring is on the pen and both ends of the pen are visible.

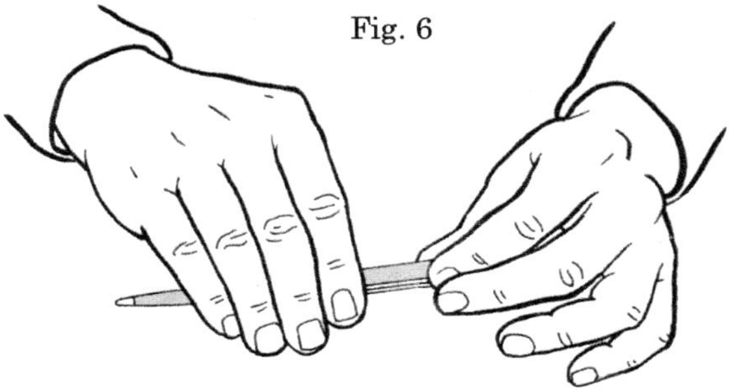
Fig. 6

This entire sequence must be rehearsed until it is smooth and invisible. In Sol's hands, there is absolutely no hint that the ring ever came near the tip of the pen. Indeed, it appears as if the right hand never moved from its position at the pen's mid-point.

The sleight is further covered by your looking at the spectator and saying: "Please hold this end in your right hand and this end in your left hand." Have the spectator grasp the end of the pen with his left finger and thumb as shown in Figure 6 above.

Keep your right hand over the ring, hiding the fact that it is on the pen. As soon as the spectator has a good grip on the pen, say "Watch!" Pull the right hand sharply away, leaving the ring behind, spinning on the pen. You will know if you have done the move correctly if the spectator does a "double-take" at this point.

***Second Phase*:** No magic happens in this phase; instead a gag is used to put the spectators off their guard and to set up the final phase of the routine.

The spectator is still holding the pen by both ends as you say, "You look like a good sport. If we met at a party and I said that I could take that ring off the pen without moving your hands, unscrewing the pen, or breaking the ring, would you bet me a beer that I couldn't do it? Of course you would. Well, we won't bet a beer, but I am going to teach you how to drink free for the rest of your life."

Pause and then say, "The ring is on the pen. Watch closely." Grip the ring between your first and second fingers dramatically lift it slightly up so that it no longer rests on the pen and say, "The ring is off the pen!"

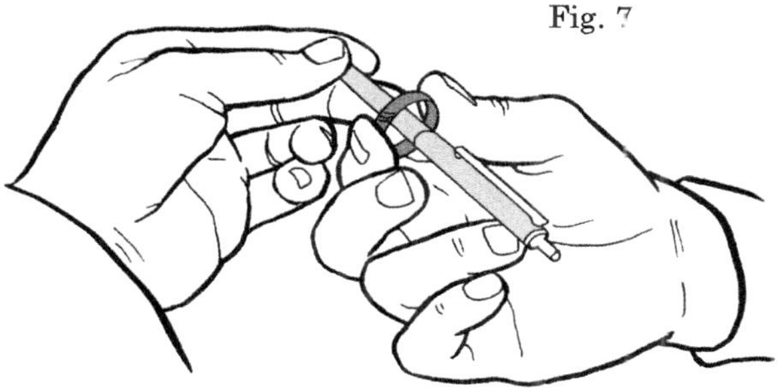

Fig. 7

This gets a laugh as the spectators realize that they have been conned. In Sol's words, this phase is a "clearing of the palate after one dish and before another."

Third Phase : Say, "What you were expecting was magic, and what I just showed you was tragic." As you speak, gently take the pen from the spectator. Hold it by the clip end in the left hand and remove the ring with the right hand, briefly display it, and then put it back on the pen, sliding it to the middle. Spin the ring on the pen. These actions are a fake, designed to condition the spectators to the upcoming move. They should mimic, therefore, the actions described in the next paragraph.

"I don't want to disappoint you, so let's do it again." As you speak, remove the ring with the right hand, and hold the pen in the left hand by its clip end. Rest the ring on the tips of your right second and third fingers.

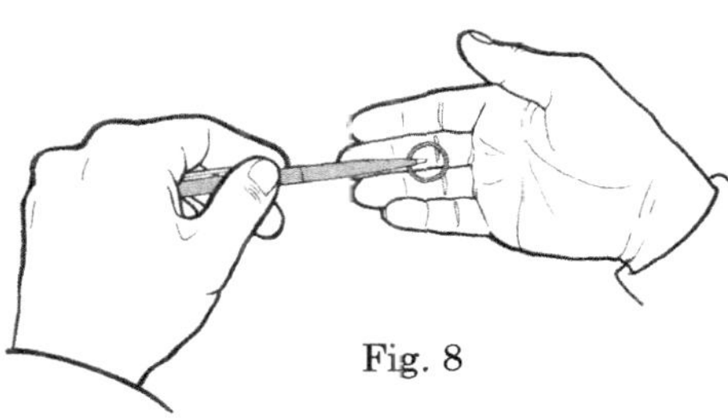

Fig. 8

The tips of the fingers point toward the left, while the tip of the pen points toward the right. With the tip of the pen, press down on the left side of the ring, causing it to lever upwards.

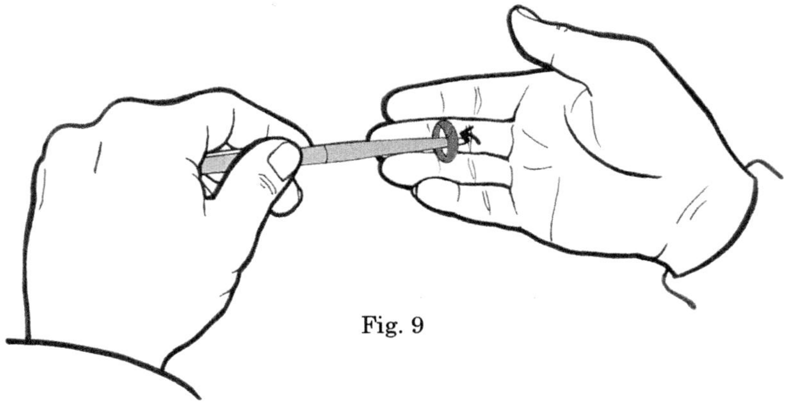

Fig. 9

The right hand begins to turn palm down and, at the same time, the right thumb comes down against the upper side of the ring, so that the ring is pinched between the thumb and second finger.

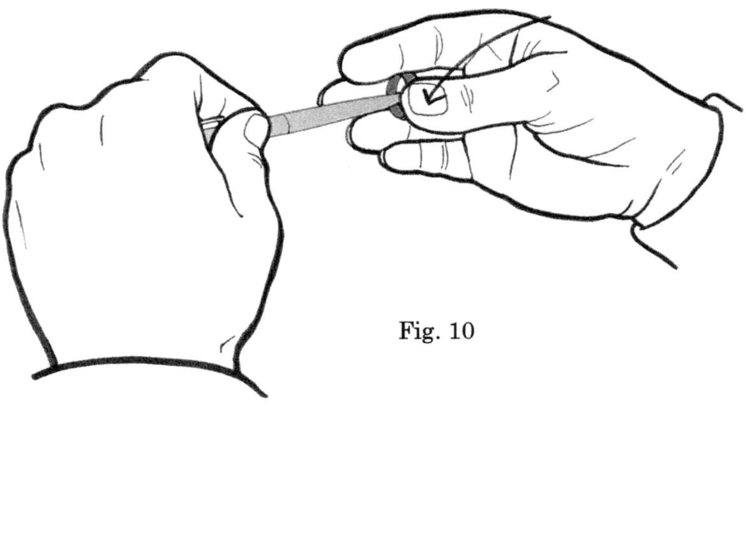

Fig. 10

As the right hand continues to turn palm down, the ring is automatically rotated off the end of the pen.

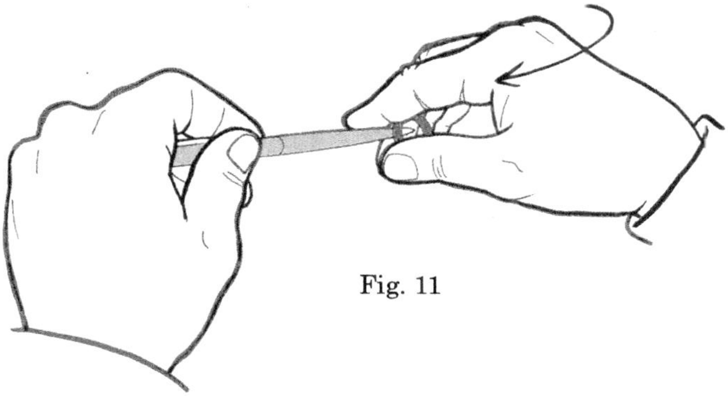

Fig. 11

In a continuing action, slide the right hand to the center of the pen, acting as if the ring was on the pen.

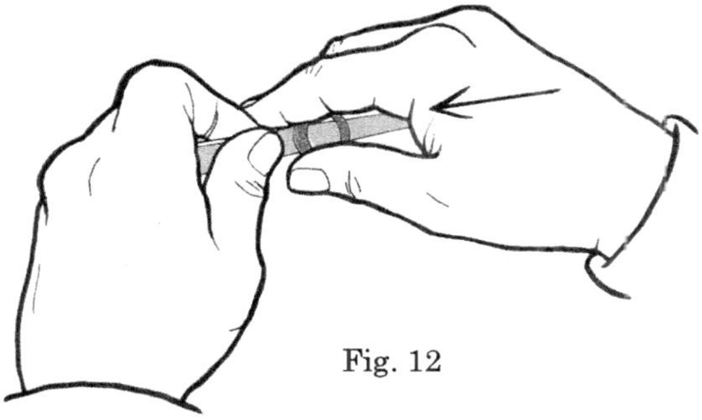

Fig. 12

Have a spectator hold both ends of the pen as before and say, "The ring is on the pen, now it is off!" Pull the ring sharply away with the right hand and display the ring at the fingertips. The borrowed ring has apparently melted through a borrowed pen.

The purpose of the second phase is to lull the spectators into thinking that the trick is over and therefore to observe your actions less closely. You are not trying to hide the move in the third phase—which is invisible—but make them forget that the pen ever left their hands.

Odds & Ends

The Ultimate Imp Bottle

The dealer's item known as the "**Imp Bottle**" would seem to offer little room for improvement or variation. Sol, however, has a completely different approach to this standard item that will fool even those who are aware of the traditional secret.

You will need two imp bottles—the small, thin-necked plastic bottles that sell for a few dollars at your local magic dealer.

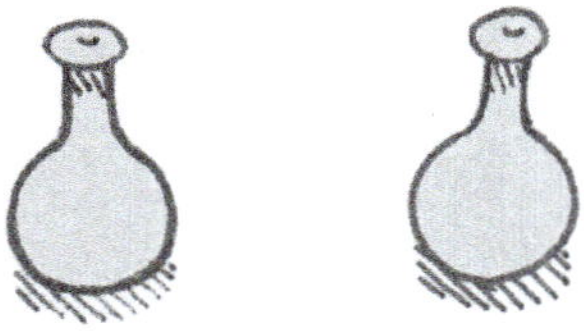

Fig. 1

Remove the weights (the modus operandi) from both bottles and discard them, leaving you with two identical bottles. (Alternatively, you can openly remove the weights in front of magicians as you "explain" how the trick is done and then proceed to perform the effect anyway.)

You will also need an **Avery "Press Dot**." These are small dots of rubber cement that come in sheet form. Before the performance, secretly remove one of the dots and press it firmly on the table in a convenient position in front of you. When the dot is in place, it becomes invisible—you must therefore place it in a known and locatable position. If the table top has some sort of pattern or design on it, this can be used to locate the dot.

If the table is bereft of overt markings, place the dot next to some small blemish or imperfection that is noticeable only to you.The bottom line is that you must be able to locate the dot without hesitating or obviously searching for it. If you want, you can place another press dot at a different position on the table.

The course of the trick is now obvious. Introduce the two Imp Bottles and allow a spectator to examine them. Place both bottles on the table and allow the spectator to choose which one he wants to use. Have him tilt the bottle so that its lip touches the table and then to remove his hand. Of course, the bottle immediately springs upright. At the same time you lower your bottle to a horizontal position, secretly pressing the lip onto the press dot.

Fig. 2

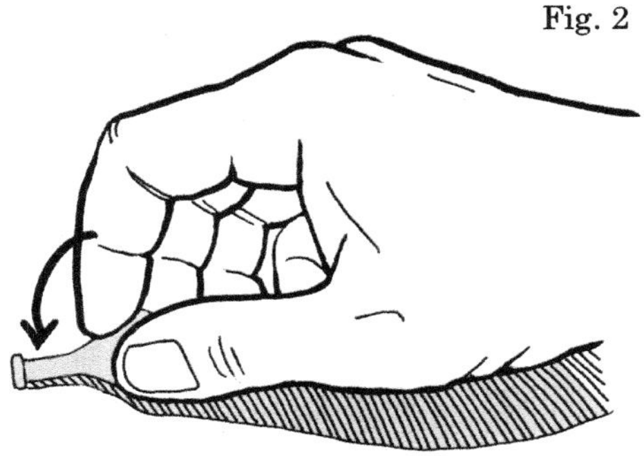

When you release your hand, the bottle remains in position.

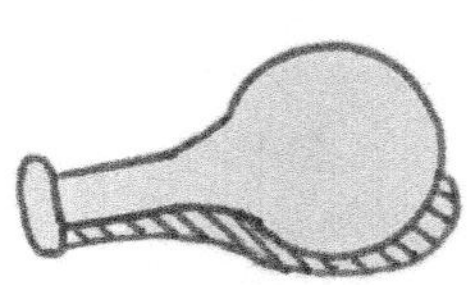

Fig. 3

Once the situation has sunk in, pick up your bottle and offer to trade with the spectator. Repeat to prove that your bottle always stays down while the spectator's bottle always pops upright. Three or four repetitions are more than sufficient to prove the point, although if you are performing for magicians you may find yourself doing this quite a few more times as they try to puzzle it out.

FINGER THROUGH JACKET

I'm not sure who invented the gag of apparently pushing your thumb through a spectator's sleeve or shirt, but its a great "bit."Sol has a slightly different handling, that utilizes a Finger rather than a Thumb Tip, which I would like to share with you.

You will need a realistic looking plastic Finger Tip, available from most magic dealers. The Finger Tip begins in left-hand Finger Palm with the opening pointing toward the thumb. Ideally, the nail side of the Finger Tip lies against the fingers, but this is not crucial.

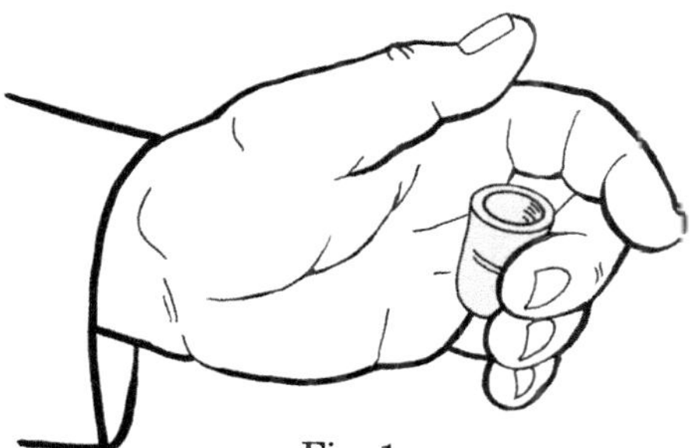

Fig. 1

Begin by approaching a spectator and asking permission to touch his shirt. This is important—don't just run up and grab the spectator's clothes! Many different types of clothing are suitable—the edge of a T-shirt, a thin sweater, or a shirt sleeve are all ideal. You must, however, be able to reach under the cloth with your right hand and it helps if there is some slack or give to the material. Let's assume you are working with the spectator's shirt sleeve.

Say: "*It looks like you have a little hole right here.*"

As you speak, your right fingers slide into the sleeve (under the cloth) while the right thumb slides above the sleeve.

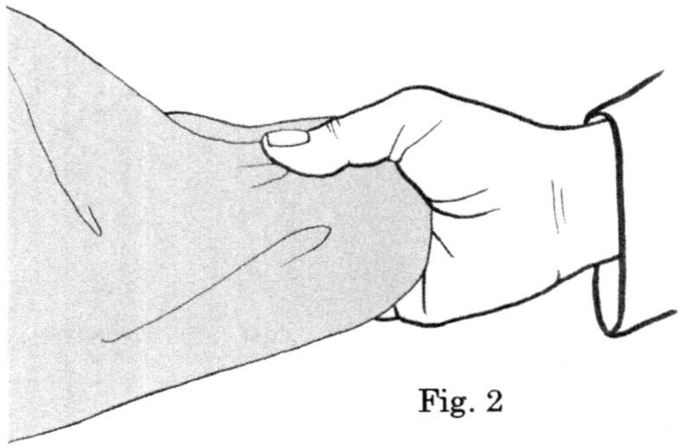

Fig. 2

A moment later, the palm-down left hand moves over the sleeve and the thumb and first finger pinch a small bit of cloth just in front of the right first finger.

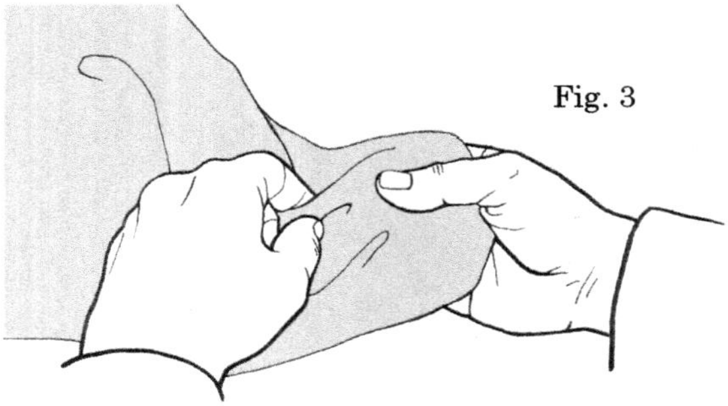

Fig. 3

The right first finger is now pushed forward, into the left thumb hole, carrying a portion of the sleeve with it. The finger (and portion of sleeve) is pushed directly into the Finger Tip. This action is screened by the back of the left hand. (**Figure 4 is an x-ray view**).

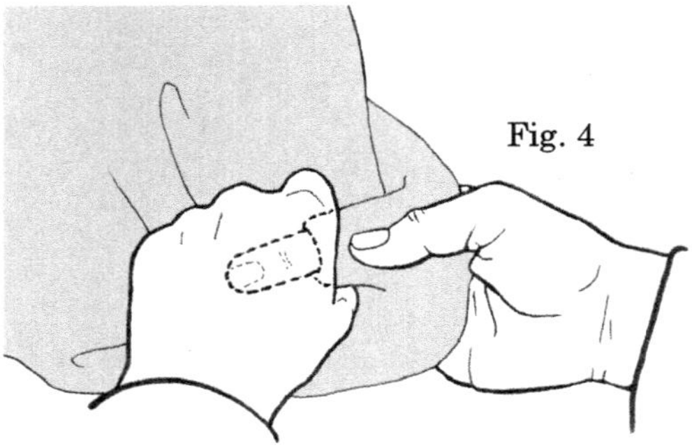

Fig. 4

Without pausing, curl the right finger inward, bringing the tip out from behind the left hand and into view. It's fine if the spectators see the cloth coming out of the bottom of the Finger Tip—in fact, that helps to sell the illusion that the finger has been pushed through the cloth.

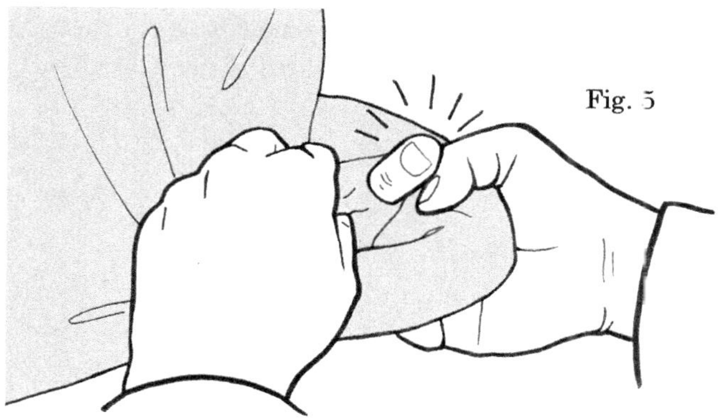

Fig. 5

Wag the Finger Tip back and forth once, twice, and then immediately straighten it out behind the left fingers. The sudden appearance of your finger sticking through the cloth is shocking, but you don't want to linger at this point.

The Finger Tip is left behind in left-hand Finger Palm as the right first finger straightens out. Say, "*Don't worry, I think we can fix that magically.*" Remove your right hand from beneath the sleeve and massage the cloth at the point of penetration between the first fingers and thumbs of both hands. After a second or two, retract your hands and let them fall to a relaxed position at your sides. As the spectator is examining his sleeve for holes, casually unload the Finger Tip into a convenient pocket.

The New York Jumping Knot

The genesis of this effect lies in a little-known Paul Rosini routine. He would introduce two silk handkerchiefs and borrow a gentleman's handkerchief. He would stretch one silk between his hands, have the spectator throw his handkerchief over the middle of the silk, and then have the spectator hold both ends of the silk. Taking the second silk, Rosini would tie a knot in it. A wave of his hand and the knot would vanish. The handkerchief was removed from the first silk and a knot was then seen tied in its center.

Sol liked the Rosini effect very much. When he entered the army, however, carrying silk handkerchiefs around was simply not an option. Sol therefore replaced the silks with two lengths of parachute cord. He then had the inspired idea of eliminating the extra handkerchief by throwing the rope over the spectator's neck. Now the routine became eminently practical—it was easy to carry (or to find the necessary props) and could be performed under almost any condition.

Here is the basic structure of the routine: Sol introduces two pieces of rope, each about thirty inches long, and has a spectator hold one piece in each hand. The spectator is asked to select one piece of rope and give it to Sol. Taking this rope, and holding an end in each hand, Sol throws the center of the rope over the spectator's head so that the two ends fall over the shoulders and onto her chest.

The ends of the rope are clearly visible to the spectator. Taking the second piece of rope, Sol ties a knot in its center. Sol holds the knot in his hand and has the spectator hold the two ends of the rope. After a magical gesture, Sol slowly opens his hand to reveal that the knot has vanished.

Taking the rope from the spectator, Sol steps back a pace or two. Finally, the spectator herself pulls the rope from around her neck to find that it now has a knot in the middle.

Obviously, the routine breaks down into two problems: how to get the knot on rope number one and the false knot tied on rope number two. Sol uses two techniques that can be found in Stewart James's ***Encyclopedia of Rope Tricks for Magicians***. In both cases, however, Sol was familiar with the techniques before they were described in this book. While I am not a "rope magic" expert, it would seem that both techniques are fairly ancient.

"The Lightning Knot" : This is the name that Stewart James used; Sol knew this as "**The Fastest Knot in the World**." In fact, most magicians are probably already familiar with this technique—it can often be seen in many rope routines. Almost without exception, however, it is used openly as a flourish or fancy display. The interesting thing about Sol's handling is that the sleight is done secretly.

Hold the rope in the right hand so that the backs of the fingers are toward the audience, the tips of the fingers point to the left, and there is about three inches of rope protruding above the first finger. The left hand grasps the rope just below the right hand, backs of the fingers toward the audience and tips of the fingers pointing to the right.

Slide the left hand down the rope until there is about three inches of rope protruding from beneath the fourth finger. Move your hands until the knuckles are opposite each other and about two inches apart.

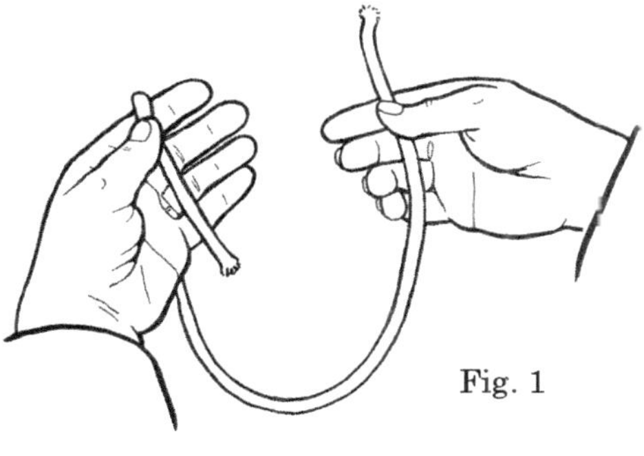

Fig. 1

Have a spectator stand facing you. You are going to form the knot as the center of the rope goes out of sight over the spectator's head. Figure 2 shows the starting position.

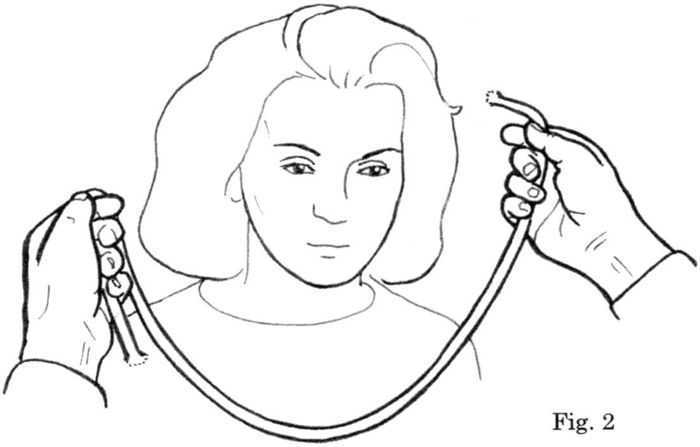

Fig. 2

Use the thumbs to pinch each end of the rope in place against the upper side of the first fingers and then open all the fingers of both hands, the left hand slightly in front of the right.

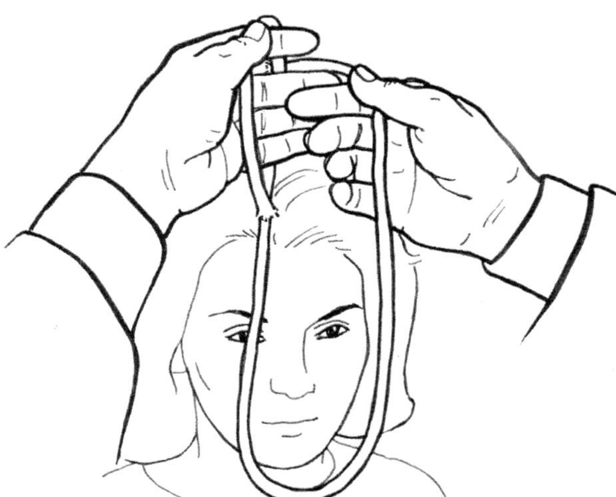

Fig. 3

You will find that the first and second fingers of the left hand are in position to clip the *right* end of the rope between them, while the same fingers of the right hand are in position to clip the *left* end of the rope.

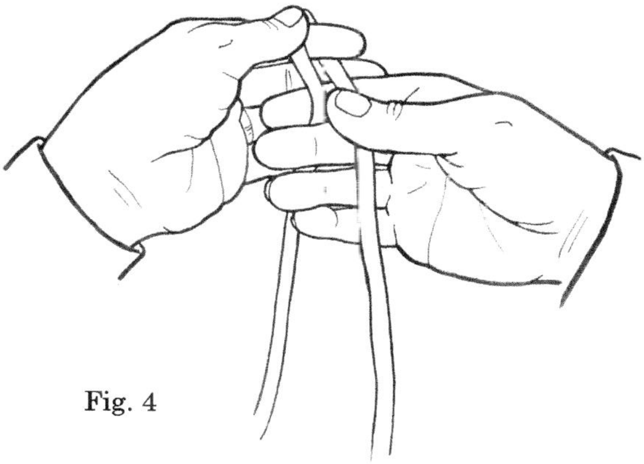

Fig. 4

So, clip the rope between your respective fingers and draw your hands apart. A knot forms in the middle of the rope. Lay the rope loosely around the back of the spectator's neck and bring the ends forward onto the shoulders.

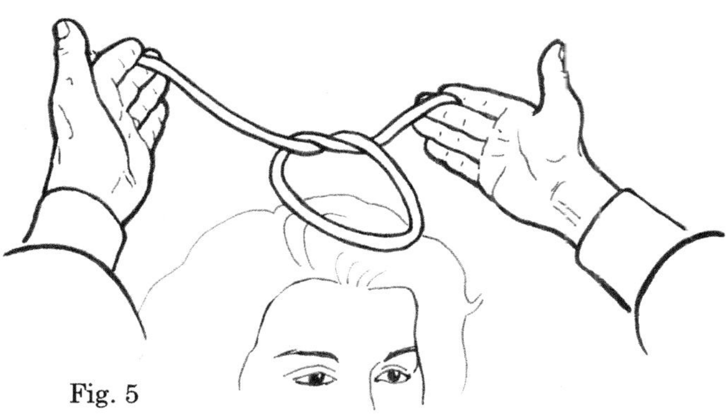

Fig. 5

In performance, the action must be smooth, unhesitating, and quite fast. You are helped, however, by several factors. First, and most importantly, you are executing the move as you are placing the rope over the spectators head.

If you keep your hands apart until they are above the spectator's eye level (out of her line of sight) and then tie the Lightning Knot as you drape the rope over her shoulders, the action is completely invisible. **Figures 6, 7, 8 & 9 show the sequence.**

Fig. 6

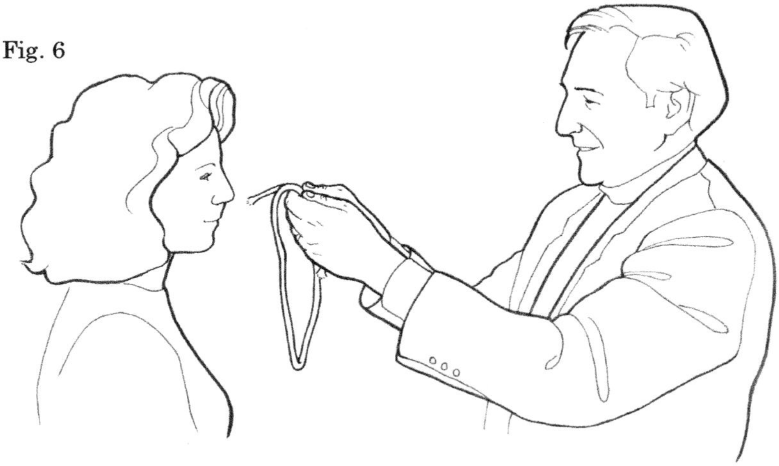

Fig. 7

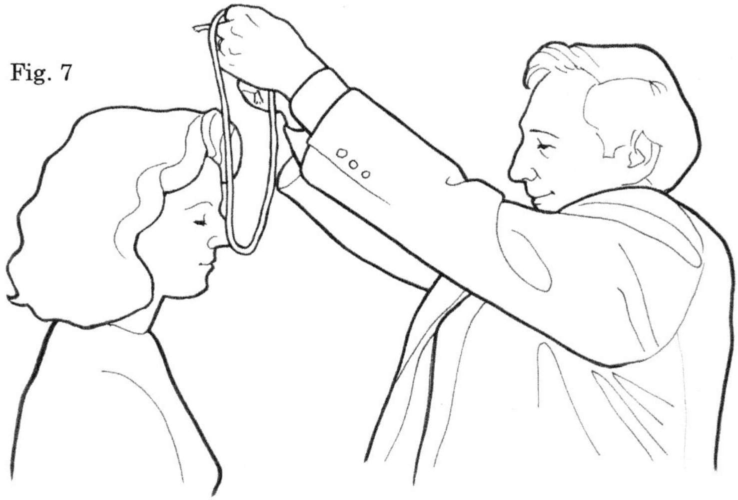

Fig. 8

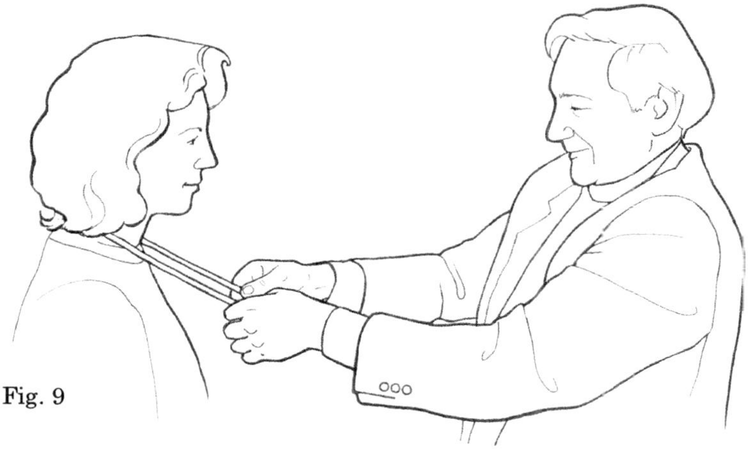

Fig. 9

In this regard, smoothness is perhaps more important than speed; there must be no sense that you are doing anything other than placing the rope around the spectator's neck. Sol has another small throw-off. He asks the spectator to "look at the ropes, choose one, and hand it to him." This, of course, is a meaningless choice, as the ropes are identical, but it gives the spectator something to think about. By the time she is done asking herself, "What's so special about that rope?" you have already placed it over her head. Finally, the fact that the spectator can see both ends of the rope resting on her chest after it is in position strongly suggests that "nothing tricky could have been done to the rope."

***Ralph Hull's Famous Vanishing Knot*:** Again, this is the title given by Stewart James; Sol knew this as the **Ghost Knot**. I am also told that it is related to the **G. W. Hunter False Knot**. Whatever its name and origins, it is a beautiful and deceptive false knot that is worth learning.

Begin with the rope in the right hand. The backs of the fingers are toward the audience and the tips of the fingers point to the left. About a third of the rope protrudes above the first finger. (The amount of rope protruding from above the hand will help determine where the knot falls on the rope. This, however, will also vary with the size of your hand and the manner in which you "tighten" the knot. Practice and experimentation will teach you exactly where to position your right hand on the rope.)

The left hand grasps the rope just below the right hand. The tips of the fingers point to the right but the palm of the hand points toward the audience. Slide the left hand down the rope until about a third of the rope is protruding from beneath the first finger. Lower the right hand at the wrist only, so that the portion of rope stretching across the right fingers is roughly horizontal.

Fig. 10

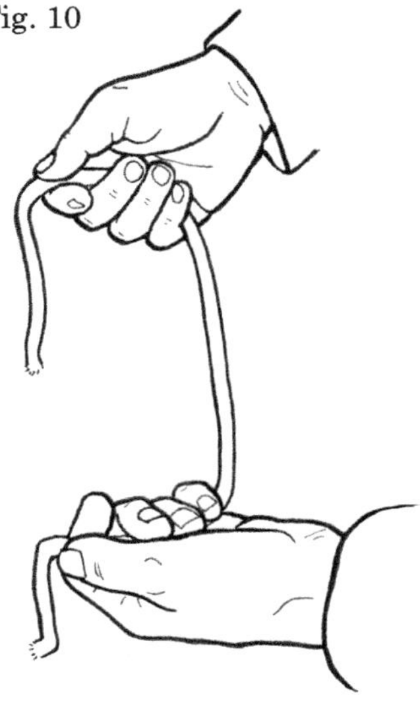

Now comes the first crucial moment. Curl the left hand inward, bringing the length of the rope below the left hand into the right hand so that it rests across the right fingers alongside the length of rope already there. This creates a circle, or loop, in the rope.

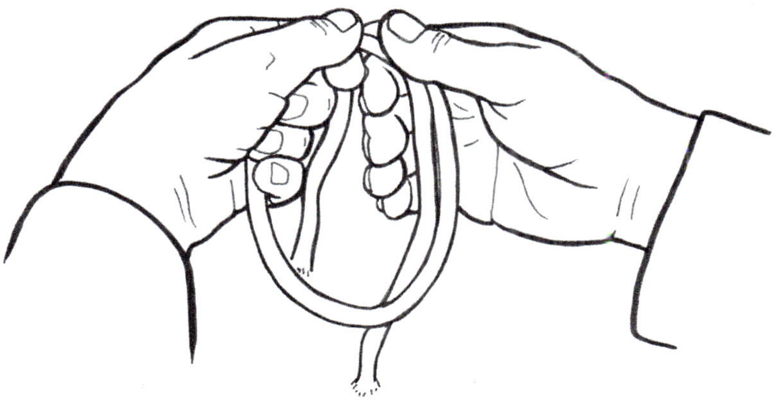

Fig. 11

Important: the left side of the rope must not cross or overlap the right side of the rope—the two lengths simply rest next to each other. **(Figure 11 is an exposed view.)**

In reality, the right second, third, and fourth fingers curl around the two lengths of rope, holding them in place. The left hand maintains a similar grip on its single strand of rope.

There is an end of rope hanging over the right first finger. With the aid of the right first finger, flick this length up and over so that it lies across the circle you have created in the rope. With your left first and second finger, reach up through the circle and clip this strand of rope.

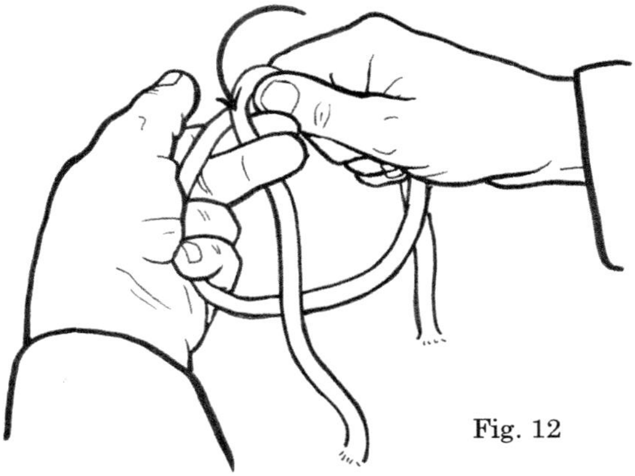

Fig. 12

Draw the strand through the circle, releasing the rest of the left-hand grip on the rope and move the hand forward.

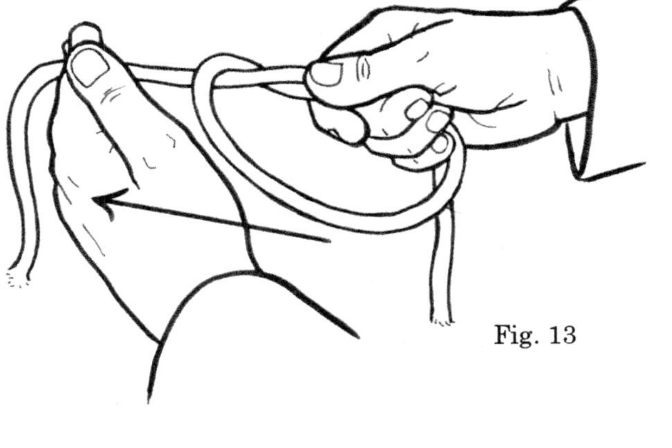

Fig. 13

As this takes place, the right thumb presses down on the double strand of ropes running through the right hand, holding them in position. You have apparently created a simple overhand knot in the rope.

You will now apparently tighten the knot, which really helps to sell the illusion. The right thumb presses the double strand against the right first finger. The right hand remains stationary while the left hand pulls its end away from the body. As the left hand moves away, the shaded strand remains stationary, while the single strand to its right is allowed to slide underneath the right thumb. The knot gradually "tightens."

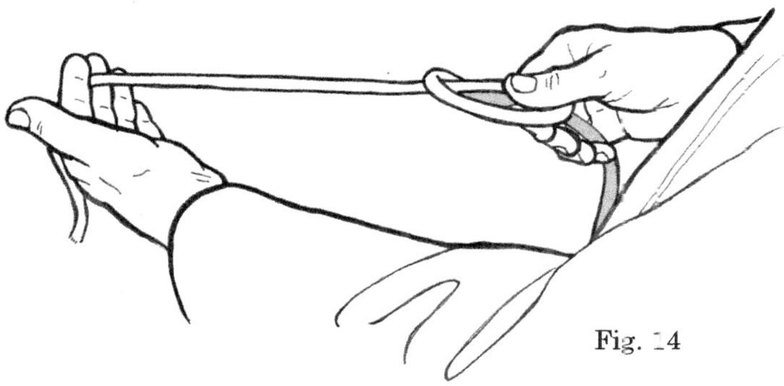

Fig. 14

When the diameter of the circle has been reduced to about two inches, stop pulling the rope. Release the left hand and regrip the end that is protruding from below the right hand. Slowly pull this end toward your body. This time, however, the pressure from the right thumb changes.

The strand to the right of the shaded portion is pressed against first finger and held stationary while the shaded portion is allowed to slide underneath the thumb. In this manner, the knot can be tightened all the way down.

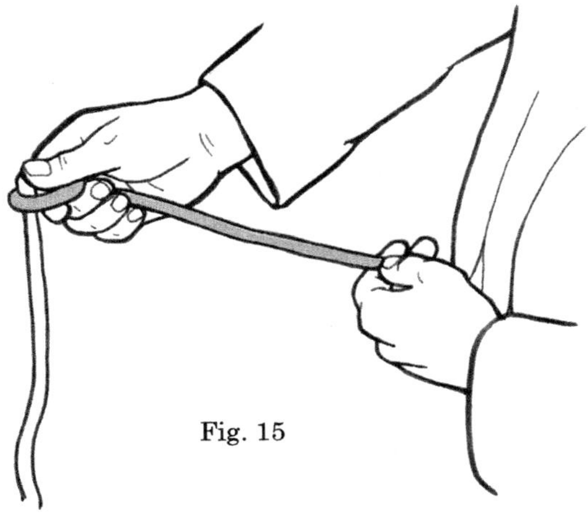

Fig. 15

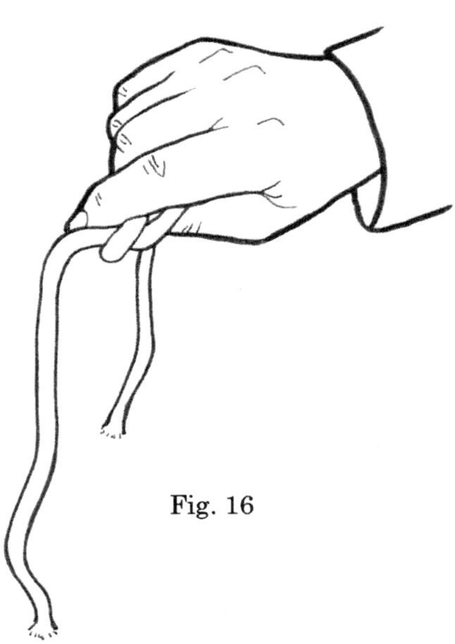

Fig. 16

You can't, of course, let go of the knot. It must be grasped or pinched between the right thumb and first finger, which both hold it in position and mask the fact that the knot is not properly intertwined. You obviously do not want to remain in this position for too long. So briefly display the knot and then place it in the left hand which closes in a fist around it. To conclude, have the spectator grasp both ends of the rope; make a magical gesture and open your left hand to show that the knot has vanished.

The Bornstein Floating Bill

Mike Bornstein taught Sol his floating bill trick many years ago. Sol liked it so much that he has carried it in his wallet ever since. Fred Kaps and Philippe Fialho were surprised and delighted when Sol performed it for them and insisted on personal instruction. Mike gave Sol permission to publish this effect.

You will need two relatively stiff bills of the same denomination. In addition, you will need a rectangular piece of thin acetate. In length the acetate should be two-eighths of an inch less than the length of the bill; in width, one-eighth of an inch less than half the bill's width. Place a piece of transparent tape across the width of the acetate at mid-point. Now stick the acetate on the back of the bill so that one of its long sides lies an eighth of an inch in from one long side of the bill and each of its short ends are an eighth of an inch from the short sides of the bill.

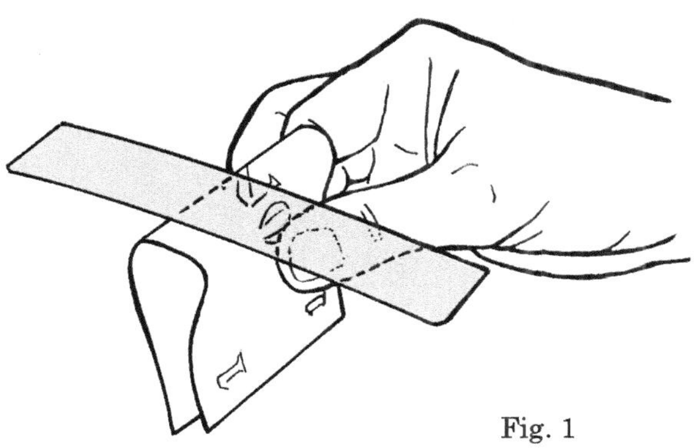

Fig. 1

Figure 1 shows the bill, the relative dimensions of the acetate, and the correct placement of the acetate on the bill.

Fig. 2

Figure 2 shows the bill flat. The acetate will be attached to the side of the bill that is showing here.

You must remember the orientation of the strip of acetate in relation to the bills. For this reason, Sol always places the acetate strip on the back of the bill underneath the *upper half* of the portrait. Place the gaffed bill on top of the ungaffed bill so that both bills face the same direction and place both in a long, flat wallet (for obvious reasons, the bills can't be bent).

When you are ready to perform, remove the bills and set the wallet aside. Hold the bills in your palm-up left hand, thumb above and fingers below. The portrait should be upright from the spectator's perspective and the strip of acetate lies nearest to you on the underside of the top of the bill.

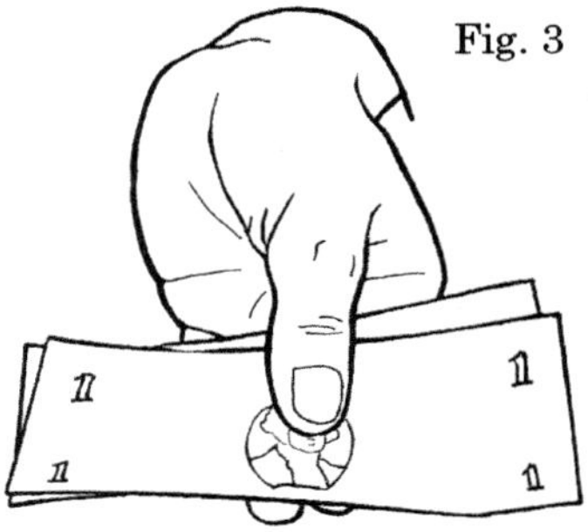

Fig. 3

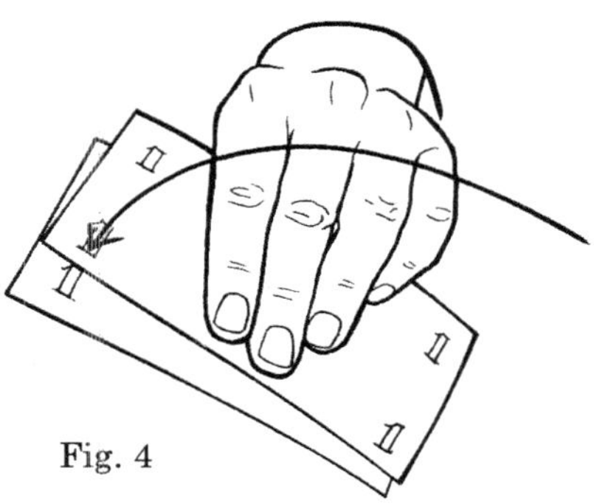

Fig. 4

Casually show the reverse side of the bills by turning your hand palm down and, at the same time, sliding the gaffed bill toward the spectators for half its width. The strip of acetate remains hidden behind the ungaffed bill.

Turn the hand palm up, leaving the gaffed bill jogged off the ungaffed bill. Take both bills in the right hand's fingertips.

You now slide the gaffed bill onto the left palm so that it lies diagonally across the thumb and fingers. The strip of acetate must end up on the underside of the bill, nearest to you. This is easy, because it already is on your side—just allow the gaffed bill to slide off the ungaffed bill onto the left palm.

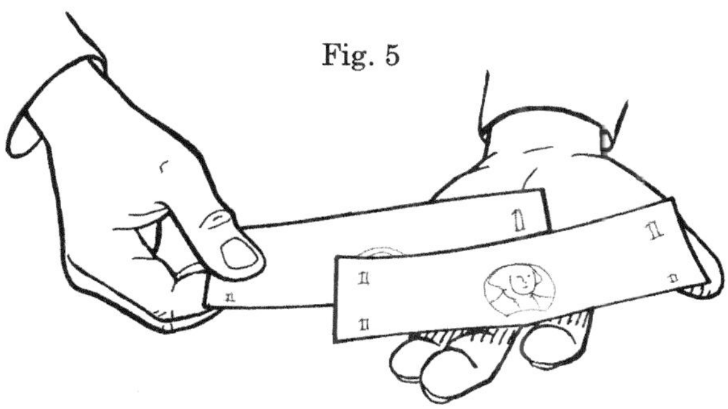

Fig. 5

The left thumb should naturally contact one short end of the acetate strip, while the left fourth finger contacts the opposite end of the strip.

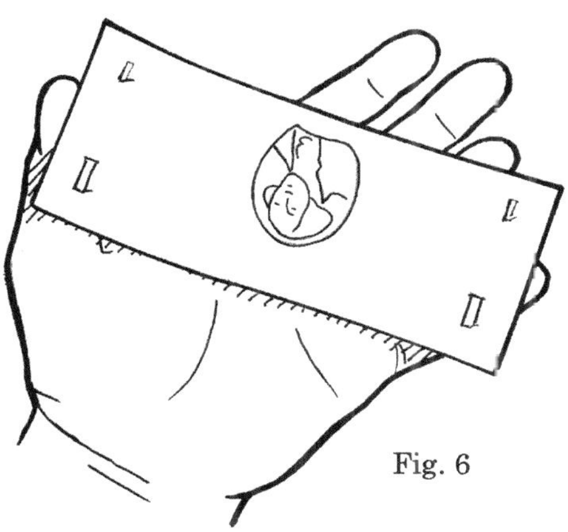

Fig. 6

At this point, Sol generally patters about how stage magicians accomplish their illusions with living people, but as a close-up magician he will simply use an image of a person as seen on the bill. He then pretends to generate "a little static electricity" by rubbing the ungaffed bill against his arm. Holding the ungaffed bill at one short end, he slowly waves it a few inches above the gaffed bill.

As this is taking place, the left thumb and fourth finger gently press together. The acetate strip arches, causing the bill to rise in a very eerie manner. **(Figure 7 shows an audience view of the rise while Figure 8 is an exposed view.)**

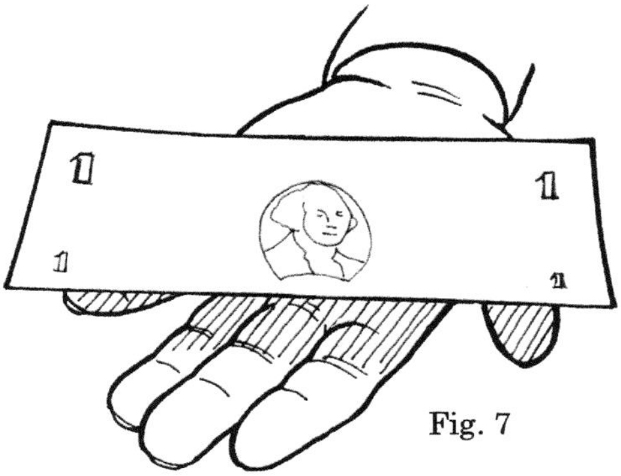

Fig. 7

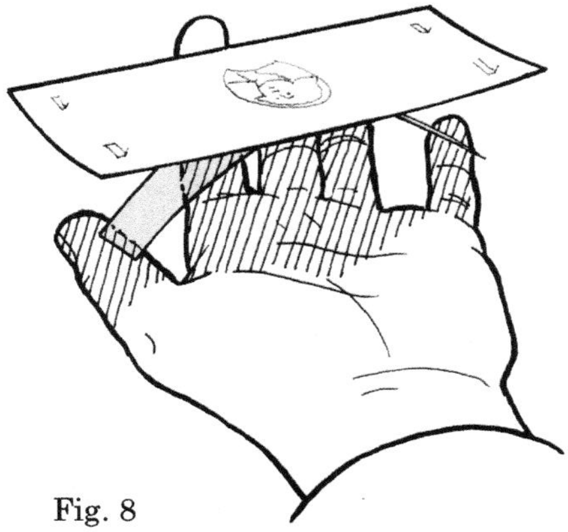

Fig. 8

Two things are worth mentioning: First, the reason for using stiff bills is now evident. Because the bill is only supported at mid-point, only a stiff bill remains horizontal for its entire length. Second, the acetate must be on your side of the bill, where it is completely screened from view. If the acetate is on the other side of the bill, it will almost certainly flash.

With the bill still in the raised position, you can slide the ungaffed bill underneath it—apparently proving the lack of any support. Simply turn the ungaffed bill perpendicular to the gaffed bill and push it through the arch created by the raised acetate, entering from the side nearest you.

Fig. 9

Pull the bill out from the opposite side of the hand and drop it on top of the floating bill. As soon as the two bills touch, release the pressure from the left thumb and fourth finger—both bills fall flat on the hand. Finally, use the ungaffed bill to scoop up the gaffed bill, casually flash the backs of the bills as was done at the beginning of the routine, and put the bills away.

Two Classics

The Chaperone

Sol admits that the patter for this "**Three in the Pocket, One in the Hand**" routine may seem a little dated. Remember, however, that Sol worked at a college for more than thirty years. When he talks about a "fraternity man, a sorority woman, and a house mother" or a "boy, a girl, and the world's greatest chaperone" it makes sense. Actually, this is one of the very few "Three Ball" routines that has any sort of presentation at all. Another nice aspect of this routine is that it uses three different colored balls. Each ball represents a different person in the story. The idea of using different colored balls is not original with Sol. Sol's inspiration was a similar routine performed by Dr. Daley.

You will need four small rubber balls: one blue (the "boy"), one red (the "girl"), and two yellow (the "house mother" or "chaperone"). Sol performs this routine in many circumstances—sometimes standing, sometimes over a table, sometimes onto a glass plate (like the one used in "**Cointemplate**"), sometimes over a handkerchief held by two spectators. Let's assume that you are using the glass plate. Three balls, one of each color, are resting on the plate. The extra yellow ball is secretly Finger Palmed in the right hand. You should be wearing a jacket or pants with easily accessible front pockets.

***Phase One*:** Pick up each ball, display it, and replace it on the plate as you say, "*Boy* (blue), *girl* (red), *and the chaperone* (yellow)." Don't name the colors, just indicate which ball is associated with which color.

Continue, "*Boy goes into the living room.*" Pick up the blue ball with the right hand and toss it into the left hand, immediately closing the hand into a fist. "*Girl goes into the living room.*" Pick up the red ball and toss it into the left hand, at the same time secretly tossing the extra yellow ball with it. Close the hand into a fist around all three balls. "*Chaperone goes into the kitchen.*"

Pick up the yellow ball with the right hand, casually letting it be seen that the hand is empty, and place the ball into the right jacket pocket. The yellow ball is secretly retained in Finger Palm and the hand removed from the pocket. "*As soon as the boy and girl embrace, the chaperone suddenly appears.*" Open the left hand to show the three balls at the base of the fingers.

The blue ball is between the first and second fingers, the red ball between the second and third fingers, and the yellow ball between the third and fourth fingers.

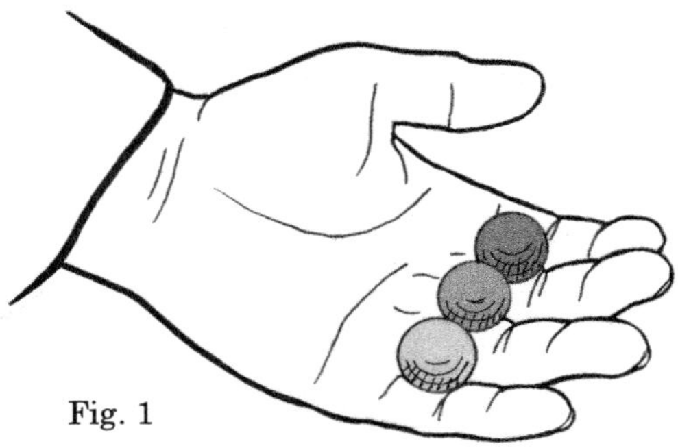

Fig. 1

The extra yellow ball is secretly concealed in the right hand at the base of the third and fourth fingers.

Phase Two **:** Sol now performs a "Shuttle Take" instead of a "Shuttle Pass" as the three balls are apparently transferred to the right hand. The palm-down right hand comes over the left hand and picks up the blue and red balls between the right thumb and first two fingers.

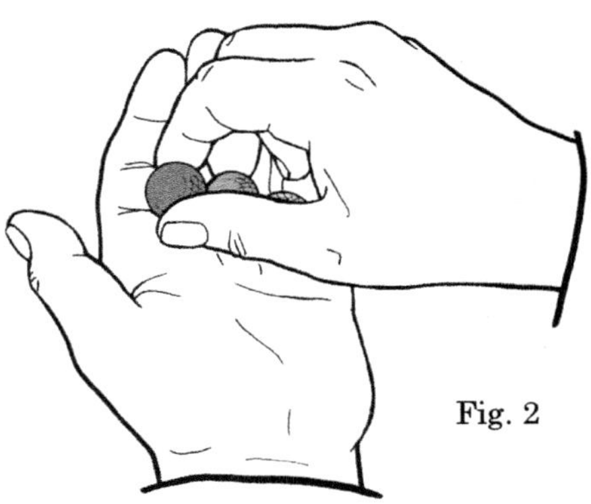

Fig. 2

Both hands immediately turn over—the right hand turns palm up to display three balls, blue, red, and yellow; the left hand turns palm down, concealing the extra ball in finger palm.

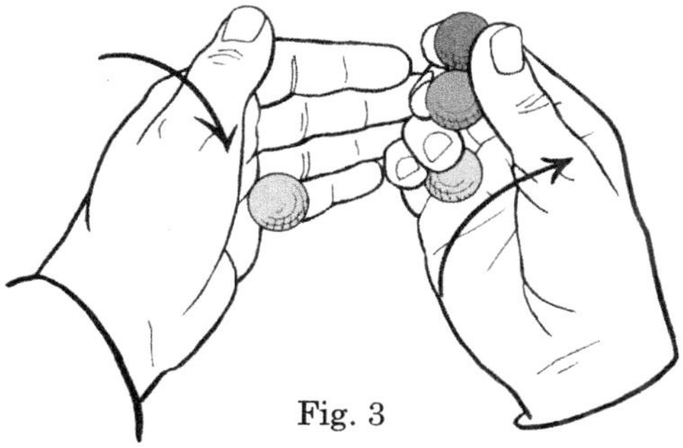

Fig. 3

Note that the balls in the right hand are displayed in the same color order as they were in the left hand.

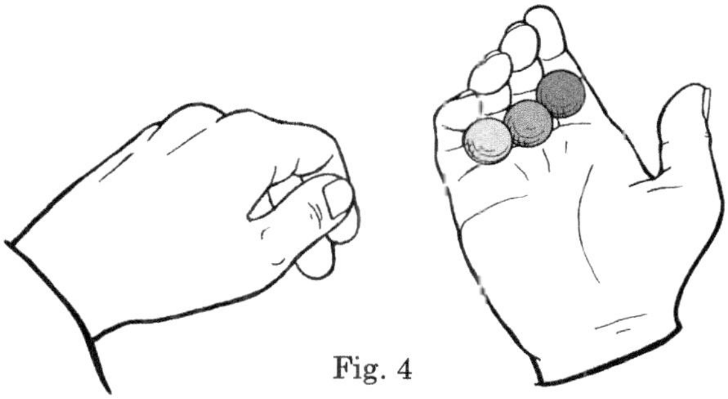

Fig. 4

Say, "*Boy goes out to the porch.*" Close the left hand into a fist, with the thumb hole pointing upward. Place the blue ball on top of the fist, display it, and let it sink into the hand.

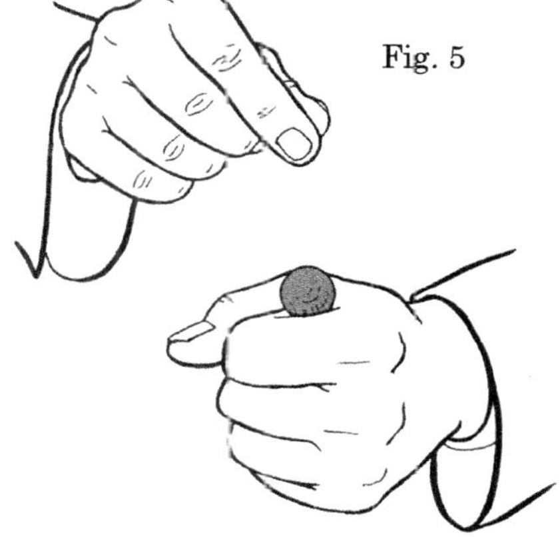

Fig. 5

"*Girl goes out to the porch.*" Place the red ball on top of the left fist and let it sink in to join the other balls. "*Chaperone goes down into the basement.*" Place the yellow ball into the pocket and leave it there. Remove your hand and casually let it be seen empty. "*As soon as the boy and the girl embrace, the chaperone suddenly appears.*" The balls are counted onto the plate as they are named.

Phase Three**:** Say, "*Boy goes into the basement.*" Pick up the blue ball with the right hand and place it into your pocket. "*Chaperone is on the porch.*" Pick up the yellow ball with the right hand, display it at the right fingertips, and then pretend to take it with the left hand.

Actually, execute a **French Drop**, pretending to take the ball with the left hand but really allowing it to fall into right-hand Finger Palm. The left hand closes into a fist around the (imaginary) yellow ball. "*Girl sneaks into the basement.*" Pick up the red ball with the right hand and place it into your pocket, leaving both balls (red and yellow) behind. "*But as soon as the boy and the girl embrace. . .*" Clap hands together, showing that the yellow ball has vanished. "*The chaperone suddenly vanishes from the porch and joins them in the basement.*"

Sol simply taps his pocket to indicate the location of the three balls. By now, the audience *knows* the yellow ball has joined the blue and red balls!

$1,000 Dice Routine

Sol is normally very generous with his magic, willingly sharing his ideas and routines with both newcomers and professionals. This routine may be the solitary exception—Sol has had it under wraps for years, sharing it with no one and declining to release it for print. Sol was actually offered $1000 dollars for the secret to this trick by two businessmen who believed that he really could "push spots through the die" and who thought they could use the secret to win money at craps. Naturally, Sol declined their offer. When it came time to describe this routine, I could sense Sol's reluctance to part with the secret. If you take the time to gather the necessary props, you too will want to keep the secret to yourself.

In Sol's words, "This has all the visual impact of routines that use two dice, without the confusion." Only one die is used at a time and no calculations are required on the part of the spectator in order to understand the effect. The rather diabolical secret lies in two special dice. For years Sol had performed a version of the Dr. Theodore Sack's routine with two dice. One Saturday, he was talking with John Scarne and Audley Walsh and the subject of mis-spotted dice came up. Sol realized that he could greatly simplify his dice routine through the use of a "trick" die. Some time later, he discovered the subtle differences between American and European dice and gradually the entire routine evolved into its present form.

The die used in the first phase of the routine is simply mis-spotted. You need to find or have made a die that fits the following specifications. Two opposite sides of the die have one spots in the center. Two other opposite sides have six spots. The remaining two sides of the die have two different sets of spots, say a three and a four. (Actually, because these two sides of the die never come into play they can have any combination of spots that you like.

Sol's die has two fives—they are never seen and go completely unnoticed.) Because dice are cubes, the two six spots will always be next to the two one spots. Moreover, because the one spot is always "right-side-up" the orientation of the six spots relative to the one spots is never an issue.

The third phase of the routine relies on a difference between European and American dice. The relative positions of the two and three spots on European dice are arranged differently from American dice. On American dice, if the three spot goes diagonally from the upper left to the lower right, then the two spot will go from the lower left to the upper right. On European dice, however, if the three spot goes from the upper left to the lower right, the two spot will also go from the upper left to the lower right. The difference between the two dice is shown in Figure 1.

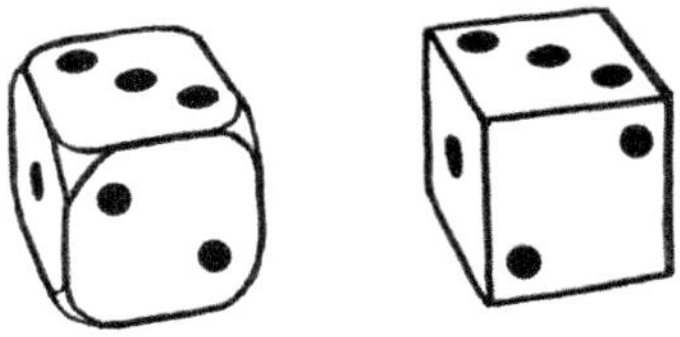

Fig. 1

In other respects the dice are normal—the two and three spots are adjacent to each other and the opposite sides of the dice always add up to seven. How Sol noticed this difference, I'll never know. It is unclear whether every European die is made this way, but many are and this little known difference is subtly exploited in the final phase of the routine.

The basic sleight used throughout the routine is the classic Paddle Move. I'm sure this is familiar to most readers and I am not going to describe it in detail. I do, however, want to make sure our terminology is clear before we begin.

Hold a regular die between the tips of the thumb and first finger of your right hand. The palm is pointing toward the floor and the tips of the fingers point to the right so that the audience can clearly see the front of the die. This is the "starting position."

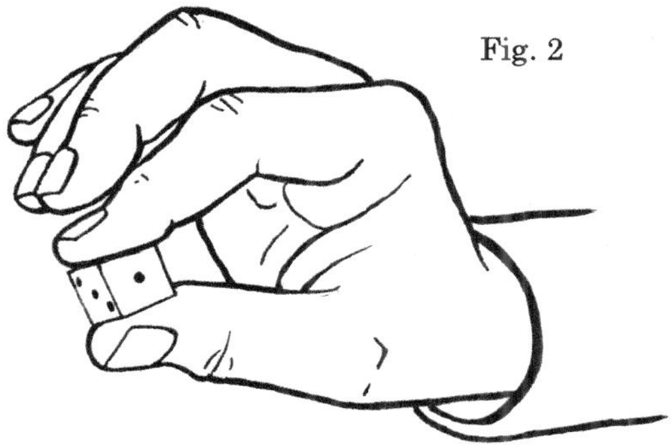

Fig. 2

For explanatory purposes, let's assume that the one is facing front and that the two is under your first finger. If you simply turn your hand over at the wrist, so that the palm points upward, the six spot on the back of the die will be brought into view.

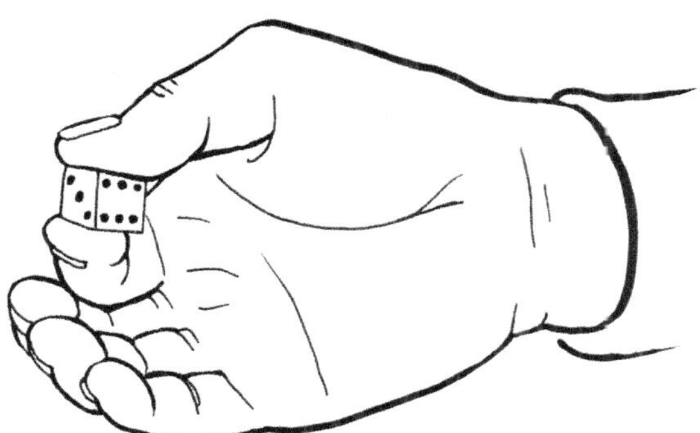

Fig. 3

This will always be described in the following way: "Turn your hand over (no move) to show the back of the die."

Turning your hand palm down at the wrist brings the one back into view. This will always be described as: "Returning the hand to starting position (no move)."

Now, turn your hand palm up, at the same time giving the die a quarter turn between your thumb and first finger. This brings the one spot beneath the tip of the first finger and displays the two spot on the back of the die. This is the basic "Paddle Move."

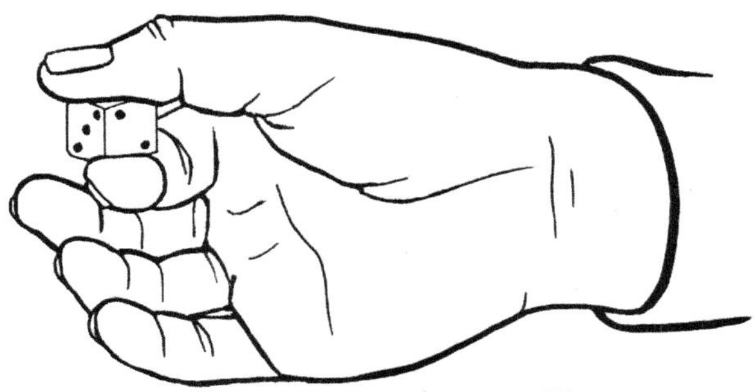

Fig. 4

Return your hand to the starting position, at the same time giving the die a quarter turn in the opposite direction from the Paddle Move.

This brings the one spot back into view at the front of the die (the two spot is again under your first finger). This is the "Undo Move."

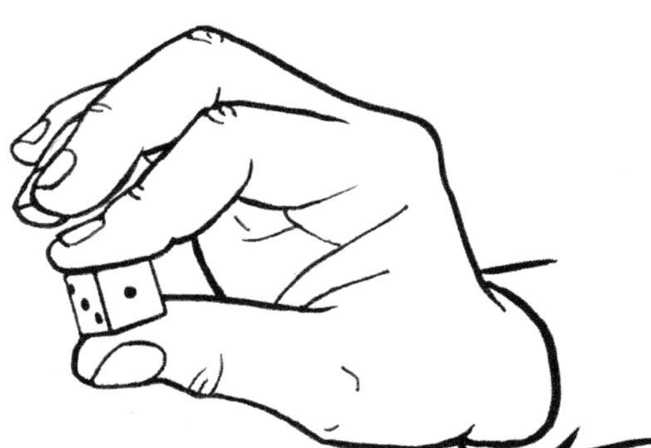

Fig. 5

Turn your hand palm up (no move). Now return your hand to the starting position, at the same time giving the die a quarter turn so that the five is brought into view at the front and the one moves underneath the first finger. This is the "Reverse Paddle Move."

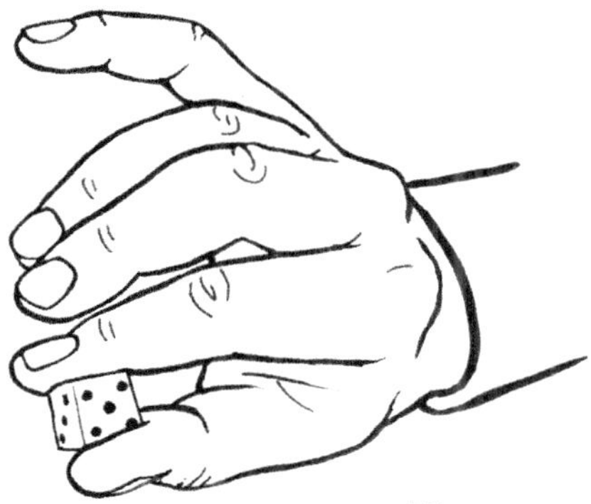

Fig. 6

All this sounds confusing, but is actually quite simple. Just remember that the Paddle Move is always done as the hand turns palm up. The Undo Move is the exact opposite of the Paddle Move and is always done as the hand turns palm down. The Reverse Paddle Move actually accomplishes the same thing as the Paddle Move (in terms of rotating the die) but is always done as you return the palm up hand to starting position. Now, on with the routine...

Begin by taking both dice out of your pocket and casually displaying them. At this point, Sol explains how all dice are manufactured so that the opposite sides always add up to seven. He does this by asking if any of the spectators play board games or gamble. "*Even people who play board games or gamble sometimes don't know that the opposite sides of a die add up to seven. Look, here we have a six on this side and a one on this side, for a total of seven. Similarly, on this side we have a three and on the other side we have a four, for a total of seven. That leaves the five and the two, for a total of seven.*"

Sol uses the European die to demonstrate his point as he talks—the opposite sides of this die add up to seven as they are supposed to. Sometimes a spectator will say that he knows about the "rule of seven" in which case Sol says, "*Good, this will be easy for you to follow.*" If they don't know about the "rule of seven" he says, "*Don't worry, this will be educational as well as entertaining.*" Drop both dice into your left hand and pick up the gaffed die with your right hand.

***First Phase*:** Place the gaffed die in the starting position so that a six is showing and a one is under the first finger. Without calling attention to the action, turn your hand over, executing the Paddle Move, to display a one on the bottom of the die. Say, "*Now that you know that both sides always add up to seven, if you see a one on this side what is on the other side?*" The spectator will say "six." Return your hand to the starting position, executing the Undo Move, to show a six on the front of the die as you say, "*Correct.*"

"*But if I rub the back of the die, the one becomes the six and the six becomes the one.*" Rub the die with your left second finger and then slowly turn your hand over (no Paddle Move) to show a six on the bottom of the die.

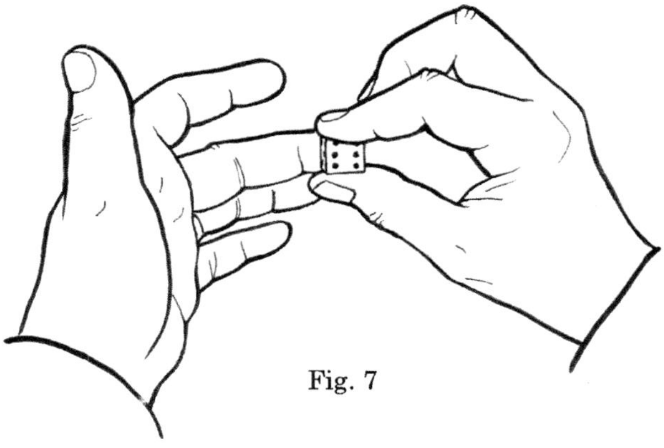

Fig. 7

Then return your hand to the start position, executing the Reverse Paddle Move to show that the one has jumped to the front.

"If I shake the die, the one becomes the six and the six becomes the one." Shake your hand rapidly up and down, moving it no more than a few inches, and under this cover rotate the die back to its starting position.

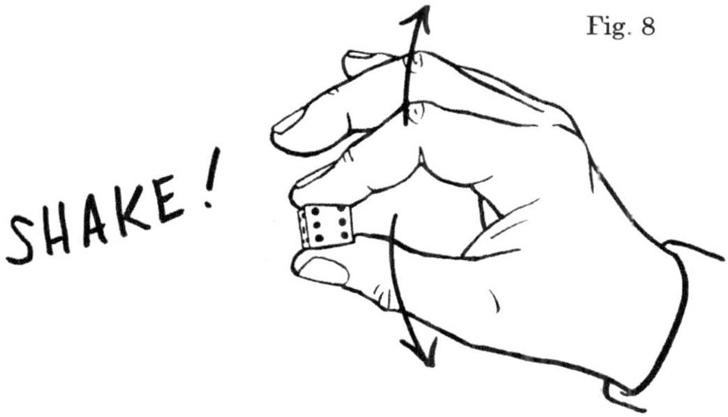

Fig. 8

This will cause the one to visibly transform itself into a six. Slowly turn your hand over, executing the Paddle Move, to show that the one has returned to the back of the die.

The tempo now picks up a bit. "*Some people think they see a six on this side and a six on this side.*" Return the hand to the starting position, executing the Undo Move. This brings a six to the front. Turn the hand over (no Paddle Move) to show that there is also a six on the back of the die.

The tempo gets faster. "*Some people swear they see a one on this side and a one on this side.*" Return your hand to the starting position, doing the Reverse Paddle Move. This brings a one to the front. Turn your hand over (no Paddle Move) to show a one on the back of the die.

The tempo slows down as the phase draws to a close. "*But you and I know that there is a six this side and a one on this side.*" Return to your hand to the starting position, executing the Undo Move, to show a six on the front. Turn your hand over, doing the Paddle Move to show a one on the back.

The first phase is over. It can, of course, stand alone, but Sol almost always continues with the following two phases.

During the transition between the phases, relax and casually drop the gaffed die into a convenient pocket as you say, "*Would you like to know how that is done?*" The spectators always say yes. "*Well, every Saturday afternoon at 2:15 I explain how this is done, so you're in luck!.*" Here you fill in the current day and time.

"*I add spots, subtract spots, and push spots from one side of the die to the other.*" By this time you should have the European die in position to commence the second phase. This casual exchange of the dice always goes unnoticed.

Second Phase : Hold the European die in starting position with the three facing front and the five under the first finger (this will automatically place the four at the rear of the die). Repeat your last words, "*Remember—add, subtract, and push.*"

Reach out and pretend to pull a black spot off of the sleeve of an audience member with your left thumb and forefinger. Say, "*We have a three on this side and a four on this side.*" Turn your hand over showing the four on the reverse side of the die.

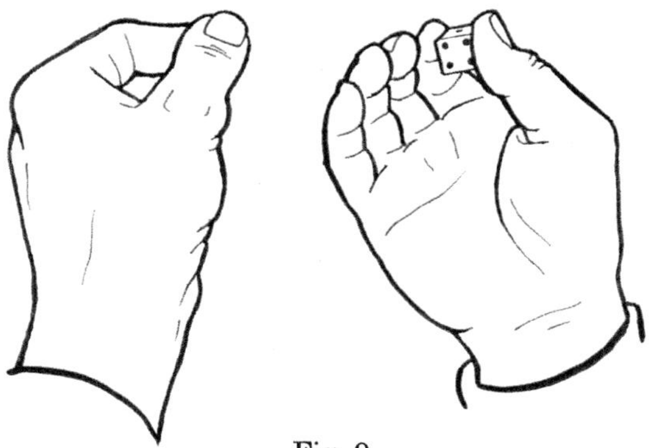

Fig. 9

Return the hand to starting position and pretend to place the imaginary spot on the back of the die (i.e., on to the four).

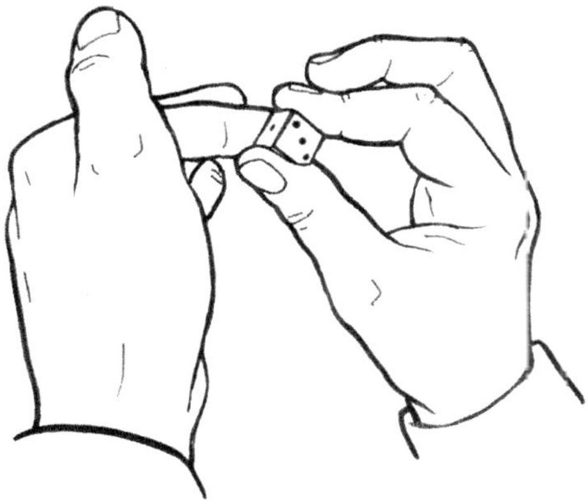

Fig. 10

"*When I add the spot to the four, it becomes a five.*" Turn the hand over, doing the Paddle Move, to show that the four has become a five.

Fig. 11

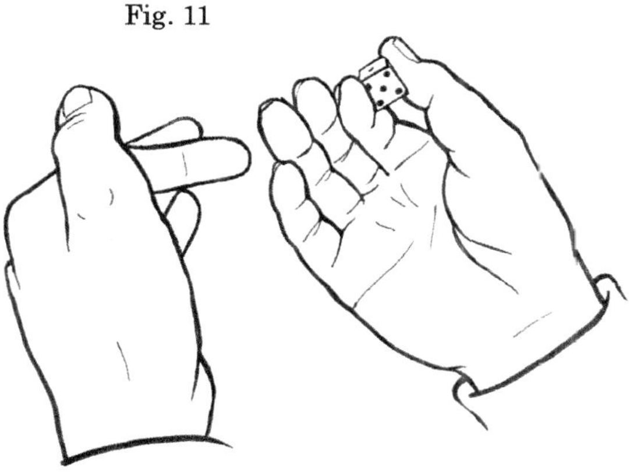

Return your hand to the starting position, executing the Undo Move. Pretend to remove the spot from the back of the die as you say, "*I take the spot away and it becomes a four.*" Slowly turn your hand over to show that the four spot has returned.

Repeat the actions of the previous two paragraphs fairly rapidly, saying, "*Add and it becomes a five, subtract and it becomes a four.*" When you are done, pretend to replace the spot on the spectator's shirt.

Third phase **:** Say, "*I've just shown you addition and subtraction, now let me show you how to push spots from one side of the die to the other. If you squeeze the center spot on the three between your thumb and forefinger, it will go right through the die and come out here.*" As you talk, lightly squeeze the front and back of the die between your first finger and thumb then turn your hand over and point to the center of the four by way of illustration. Say, "*Give it a good hard squeeze.*" Have the spectator squeeze the front and back of the die between his thumb and first finger.

The following actions must be closely timed to your words:
1) Say, "*It's beginning to fade.*" Display the three on the front of the die.

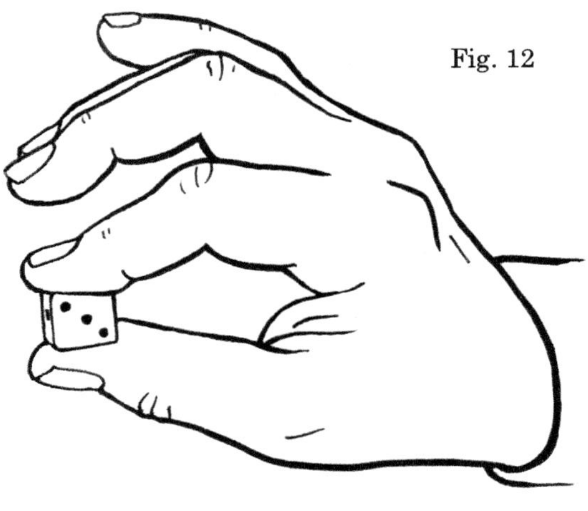

Fig. 12

2) "*It's about half way through.*" Turn hand over (no move) showing the four on the bottom.

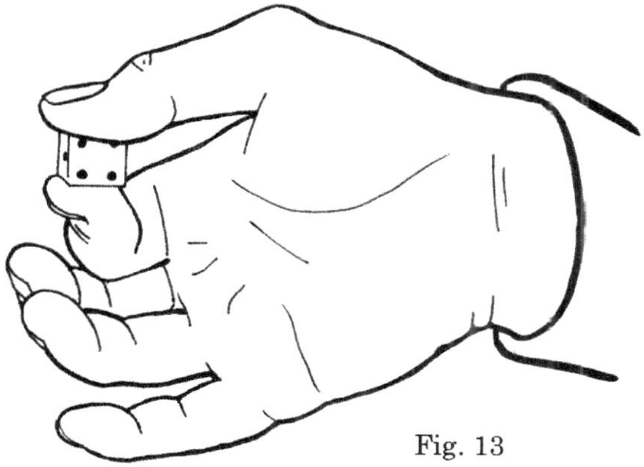

Fig. 13

3) "*It's all gone!*" Return your hand to the starting position, doing the Reverse Paddle Move, to show the two on the top of the die.

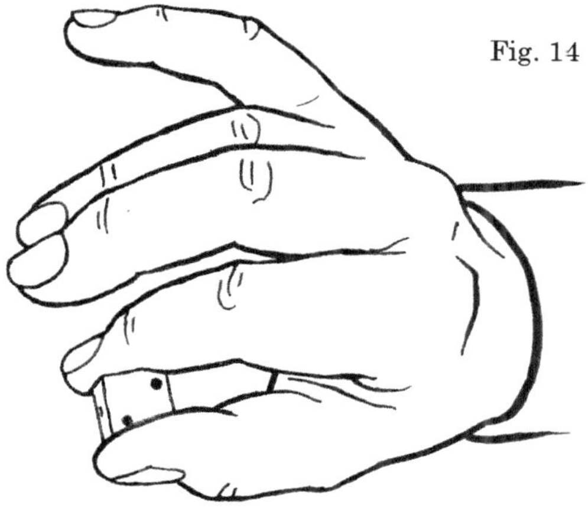

Fig. 14

4) "*And here it is!*" Turn hand over (no move) to show the five on the bottom of the die.

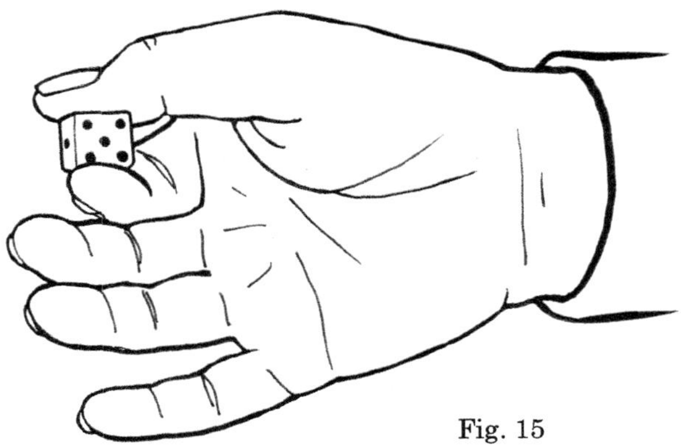

Fig. 15

Note that in step three of this sequence the two spot points along the same diagonal as the three spot did in step one. This creates a very strong illusion that the middle spot has simply melted away. If you are using an American die, however, the two spot will suddenly change direction from the way in which the three spot was pointing. You can do the routine with such a die, but it is not quite as effective.

Conclude by dropping the die into the spectator's hand and letting them examine it to their heart's content. All sides of the die add up to seven and nobody will ever notice the unique orientation of the two and three spots.

APPENDIX
SOL STONE IN PRINT

Apocalypse, Lorayne & Kaufman (1978), Lorayne (1979 - present).

“The Jarred Coin.”*
“Cointemplate.”*
“One to Five.”*
“One-Coin Tenkai.”*
“The Strung Coin.”*
“Two-Timing Transpo.”*
“A Very Pretty Thing.”*
“In Your Hands.*
“Sweet and Low.”*
“Soft Sleeve.”*
“A Beautiful Vanish or Change.”*
“Soft Sleeve Cover.”*
“A Bird in the Hand.”*
“Clipped Again.”*
“On-Off Again.”*
“The Chaperone.”*

“Knives-Knives-Knives.” (Gonzalez, Kaufman, Stone) Vol. 3, No. 5, p. 342 (May 1980).
“Flip-Over-View.” (Krenzel, Sabatino, Badet, Weigle, Lorayne, Stone) Vol. 4, No. 6, p. 495 (June 1981).
“Flip-Side Up.” Vol. 6, No. 5, p. 772 (May 1983).
“Flip-Side Split.” Vol. 8, No. 1, p.1013 (Jan. 1985).
“Penetrating Transposition.” Vol. 10, No. 4, p.1340 (April 1987).
“Split Secoined.” Vol. 10, No. 7, p.1374 (July 1987)
“Hot Potato Transpo.” Vol. 10, No. 10, p. 1411 (Oct. 1987).
“Pretty Interlude.” Vol. 11, No. 8, p. 1531 (Aug. 1988).
“Arithmagic.” Vol. 12, No. 1, p. 1587 (Jan. 1989).
“Six Bits.” Vol. 13, No. 1, p 1733 (Jan. 1990).
“Through and Through Again.” Vol. 13, No. 6, p. 1796 (June 1990).
“Snap-Press.” Vol. 14, No. 1, p. 1875 (Jan. 1991).
“Click Through.” Vol. 14, No. 1, p. 1867 (Jan 1991).
“No Propellant.” Vol. 15, No. 3, p. 2043 (March 1992).

* These items were reprinted in a set of lecture notes entitled *The Magic of Sol Stone from Harry Lorayne's Apocalypse.* The notes were published in October of 1993 and limited to seventy-five copies.

"A Very Pretty Thing." Vol. 16, No. 1, p. 2166 (Jan. 1993).
"More Coin-Fusion." Vol. 18, No. 3, p. 2479 (March 1995).

CoinMagic, Kaufman (Kaufman and Greenberg, 1981)
"Turnover Vanish."
"Ramsay Vanish Refined."
"One-Hand Spectator Sleeve Change."
"Tumble Switch/Change."
"One-Hand Triple Spellbound No. 1."
"One-Hand Triple Spellbound No. 2."
"Hung Coin."
"Pulling Silver."
"Double Twist."
"Half and Half."
"Silver Hole Switcheroo."

The Tarbell Course of Magic, Volume VII, Lorayne (Tannen, 1972)
"Sol Stone's Changing Chips."
"Sol Stone's Visual Copper Silver."
"Continuous Coin Production and Vanish."
"Sol Stone's Miser's Dream Move."

Best of Friends, Volume Two, Lorayne (Lorayne, 1985)
"Linking Links."
"Inflation."

New York Magic Symposium Collection Two, Kaufman (1983)
"Tenkai Pennies Perpetuated."

New York Magic Symposium Collection Three, Minch (1984)
"The Laced Coin."

Tannen's Magic Manuscript
"The Invisible Touch (March/April 1987)."

Patter Punches, Stone (Abbott, 1947)

Index

INDEX (cont'd)

INDEX (cont'd)

INDEX (cont'd)

INDEX (cont'd)

INDEX (cont'd)

INDEX (cont'd)

INDEX (cont'd)

T

INDEX (cont'd)

INDEX (cont'd)

PATTER PUNCHES

Price $1.00

An Abbott Publication

INTRODUCTION

Patter Punches was Sol Stone's first book. It was a comedy book for magicians that came out in 1947.

How did one of the most influential sleight-of-hand artists and coin magicians in the world end up writing a book about one-liners for magicians? I once asked Sol that question and here is what he explained.

To make his magic more entertaining he started collecting and writing jokes and one-liners in hopes of eventually integrating them within routines. Lou Tannen found out about it and offered to put the collection out in booklet form. One of Sol's friends who did the same, offered Sol his joke file which was incorporated into this booklet.

By the time the booklet was written Lou changed his mind about publishing it. Coincidentally next door to Tannen's at the time was Abbott Magic's New York store which was run by Ken Allen who convinced Percy Abbott to publish it.

I thought that it would be nice to include that book here as a bonus thus incorporating all of Sol's writings in one place and making this book even more essential. I phoned my friend Greg Bordner who owns Abbott Magic and pitched him the idea and he enthusiastically agreed to let me reprint it here.

Humor is very subjective, and tastes change over time making jokes less relevant and funny as time goes on. Many of the following jokes were written in the 1930s and 1940s and capture a moment in time. That time was more than three-quarters of a century ago. I decided to include all the jokes and not edit any of them. Most jokes are still viable if you change the targets and keep the premise.

I really enjoyed going through them and I hope you will too.

Meir Yedid
Fair Lawn, New Jersey
November 2021

PATTER PUNCHES

By Sol Stone

The purpose of this booklet is to provide the performer with a wealth of laugh tested material, suggested patter routines and hints on presentation.

No attempt has been made to write the complete patter for anyone effect. The author feels, that in all too many cases, this causes the performer to use material not in keeping with his personality.

Every effort has been made to include only clean humor. A particularly filthy gag might get a laugh, but your audience will be laughing more at your brashness than at the quality of your Material. Do not risk offend a single member of your audience. It is bad business.

Above all, remember that you are first and foremost an entertainer. Masterly technique is desirable. A smooth-flowing line of breezy, entertaining patter is essential. Fortunate is the performer who possesses both, for the customers will be pleased, the management will be pleased, and what is even more important from a financial point of view, the agents will be pleased.

Sol Stone
Brooklyn, New York
1947

ALIBIS

If a trick or gag falls flat as they occasionally do, make a rapid recovery with:

This microphone is A.C., my voice is D.C.

You can't blame my writers ... they've been dead for thirty years.

Nothing like new material ... I wish I had some.

That was a throw out gag . . . I should have thrown it out before the show. Hurry up and laugh. . the spotlight's fading my new suit.

Did you hear that splash? Well, it wasn't the weather.

Ten more like that and I'll have an even dozen.

That gag, ladies and gentlemen, was written for posterity ... it's just your tough luck you had to hear it now.

APARTMENTS

I live in a honey of an apartment ... but who wants to spend his life in a beehive?

To get from the kitchen to the living-room you just stand where you are. Next year we expect to add plumbing and wiring.

When we bought the house, the real-estate agent told us that on a clear day we could see the Atlantic. He forgot to tell us that on a windy day we'd be in it!

We just rented a new apartment. It's on Vaysmere Boulevard overlooking the rent. It has a raised terrace and a sunken mother-in-law.

I wanted the landlord to include a clause in the lease stating that if he doesn't ask me for the rent ... I won't ask him for a receipt.

There isn't a single mouse in the place ... they're all married.

We've been living in the same apartment for 12 years and it looks like we'll be living there another 12 years. My mother is a very honest woman. She wants to leave the place just like she found it. Do you know where I can get hold of 17,000 cockroaches in a hurry?

APPLAUSE AND LAUGHTER

Don't applaud ... if you like it, just throw cigarettes.

Don't applaud ... if you like it, just nod.

No scattered applause, please ... all together or none at all.

See? ... and you thought you wouldn't catch on.

Go ahead and laugh ... tomorrow you'll hate yourself for it.

They laughed at Fulton but he went ahead anyway and invented a fish market.

How can you look so clean and laugh so dirty?

You aren't laughing ... whatsa matter, you wash your face in cement?

ARMY

I was in the Army and my outfit was so tough, even the chaplain went over the hill.

There's so much red tape in the Army, you can't burp without doing it in triplicate.

The war is really over ... a civilian won a quiz contest.

I know a second lieutenant who wasn't born ... he was issued.

I know a GI who designed his own hats so beautifully, they gave him a commission in the WAC.

I know what the Big Three means ... they're my points.

I'm a little jumpy ... my nerves were shot from the war ... I thought I was going to be drafted.

He was classified 4F ... in the Campfire Girls.

My draft board warned me not to start reading any continued stories.

AUTOMOBILES

With the automobile situation the way it is today, these gags will get laughs.

My car wouldn't start this morning . . . the carburetor is probably clogged up with pedestrians.

I installed a cute little gadget in my car. When you see a woman driver coming your way, you simply press a button on your dashboard ... the car collapses and hides in the bushes till she passes.

There's a new gadget that keeps the inside of a car quiet ... it fits over her mouth.

I had an accident yesterday ... the motor fell out of my car. I'll never use that cheap adhesive tape again.

I had my car painted red on one side and yellow on the other side so I could have fun listening to the witnesses contradict each other.

One of those New York to Los Angeles bus rides is a good way to kill a few years. One couple in our bus were married in Pittsburgh ... they had a baby in Chicago ... in Denver, they celebrated their golden anniversary.

What traffic! I drove three miles before I discovered my motor had been stolen.

This woman driver signaled all three ways ... then went straight up.

I couldn't afford to have my car painted so I had it wall-papered.

I don't like lady drivers ... they knit while they drive. They knot one, purl two, hit three ...

CHILDHOOD

My mother is mad about children ... she'd have given anything if I'd have been one.

Even as a boy I had to scrimp and scrape ... I saved every cent I stole.

When I was three, my folks helped me to leave home.

Was I tough! At five I was head repaint man for a hot tricycle ring.

He was such an ugly baby his mother didn't know whether to buy him a crib or a cage.

He's very talented. When he was twelve years old, he was already playing the piano and the horses.

I remember when I was a boy singing in a choir. My voice was so high, I had to sing with the girls. But when I was old enough to enjoy it, my voice changed.

CIGARS AND CIGARETTES

Build your cigarette productions or manipulations around this little story and watch the fun. Produce a comedy lit cigar or a pipe immediately after the punch line. It's a natural!

It's funny how I broke myself of the smoking habit. It was difficult at first, but I finally won out ... just by perseverance ... just by sticking to it. I triumphed and now I limit myself to one cigarette after each meal ... and I eat only seventeen meals a day!

Hmmm, a real Havana cigar. You smoke it in New York and smell it in Havana.

You and that cigar! You ought to rent yourself out as a smudge-pot.

When I smoke a cigar, I look more high-class than the guy who threw it away.

CITIES AND STATES

Ah, Boston ... the town with crooked streets and straight politicians.

The Pentagon is Texas with washrooms.

Our next war will be with Mexico to force her to take Texas back.

Ah, Miami! After a week there you feel good enough to go back to work and poor enough to have to.

Philly! What a town! There, they lock you up for breathing on Sunday.

CLOTHES

The clothing shortage is real bad. A friend of mine who was just discharged from the Navy had to join the Army to get a suit.

That's a nice dress ... you must wear it sometime.

Is that a suit you have on or are you dancing with someone?

That's a lovely gownless evening strap you have on.

On seeing a girl in a revealing dress: I'm just trying to decide whether that's a low neckline or a high hem.

How do you like my new suit? Do you think the style will ever come back?

I bought a suit with built-in gravy stains.

This is the kind of suit that retains its shapelessness after dry cleaning.

The pants remind me of two French towns ... Toolong and Tooloose.

I just bought a new suit ... a two-piece rag with a three-way sag. When I stand, the suit sits. When I sit, the suit stands. Maybe we ought to get together, huh?

He looked so well in his cutaway coat and his torn away pants.

His clothes fit perfectly ... but who?

I put on the coat and went outside to see what it looked like in the daylight. People stopped and stared ... little boys laughed ... women screamed ... then the clerk brought out the pants.

I had a girl who wore a sealskin coat, sealskin shoes, and a sealskin hat. When she said she was hungry, I threw her a fish.

I'm ashamed to be wearing last year's suit. I was ashamed to wear it last year, too.

She wore an amber dress with a white collar ... like a short beer with legs.

An Adams hat? It looks like Adam wore it.

COINS

I'm not feeling very well ... I had a bad day at the market ... there were no more chickens left.

I've been losing so much at gin rummy, I'm getting fan mail from a guy named Schneider. (Localize).

I'm looking for a girl with a beautiful figure ... about a million dollars.

I don't want to be a millionaire ... I just want to live like one.

The stock market decline didn't hurt me any. All my money was tied up ... in a handkerchief.

Rich or poor, it's good to have money.

He has a wonderful hobby ... he collects money.

Money can't buy you friends, but it can get you a better class of enemies.

I lit my cigarette with a ten-dollar bill ... it came from the grocer.

I'm so short ... I'm practically a midget.

You can't buy love with money, but it certainly puts you in a swell bargaining position.

Running into debt doesn't bother me ... it's running into my creditors that's so upsetting.

I get paid weekly ... very weakly!

He's very rich ... land was discovered on his property.

All I am or ever hope to be ... I owe!

Poverty is SO monotonous!

His salary comes to four figures ... three chorus girls and a fan dancer.

DANCING

I've been dancing the rhumba ever since I was a kid ... my bicycle had a loose seat.

You know what the rhumba is? It's waving goodbye without using your hands.

We danced cheek to cheek ... from head to toe.

I wanted to dance with his girl and he said, "Over my dead body!" It worked out fine after I put some wax on his chest.

My girl and I danced for two hours in a jitterbug contest. We were doing okay but suddenly I was disqualified ... one of my feet touched the floor.

Ah, Roseland (name local dance hall) ... that's like a night in Central Park, (localize), only you have to keep moving.

The dance hall was so crowded I fainted and had to dance around four times before I could fall.

DOUBLE GAGS

She: Who was that girl I saw you with last night? He: That was no girl, that was my brother ... he just walks that way.

She: Will you love me when my hair is gray? He: Why not? I loved you when it was every other color.

He: Is that coffee I smell? She: It is and you do.

She: What has Lana Turner got that I haven't got? He: Well, the raw materials are the same but the assembly job's a lot better.

He: Goodness, what beautiful diamonds. She: Goodness had nothing to do with it.

She: You're a one-woman man and I'm a one-man woman. He: Maybe the four of us should get together for bridge tonight.

DRINKING

If not overacted, a drunk act can be highly amusing. The performer should assume the role of a slightly inebriated, happy young man-about-town in a confidential mood. Everything he does should amaze him as much as it does his audience. His voice should not be too thick. A good opening for a routine of this nature ' is to produce a shot glass of liquor and say, "Well! Civilian plasma!" I've used this gag for the past four years in the Army and it has always gotten a big laugh.

Have you tried that new drink ... the Cuba Leibowitz?

That man can really hold his liquor. I saw him drink two quarts of Southern Comfort at the Zanzibar last night and he didn't even stagger. Stagger? ... he couldn't even move.

I've got an absent-minded grandmother ... the family can never find her glasses ... she just leaves them where she empties them.

My Pop drank so much, his ulcers were bonded.

And then came the sad day when Pop read that advertisement, "Drink Canada Dry ..." and left for Canada.

Don't worry about the walls having ears ... because the walls are plastered and wouldn't hear it straight anyway.

I saw a bear ... took a couple of shots ... then I saw two bears.

Not only does he like to drink Zombies ... he married one.

I had one rye after another ... I must have had ten slices.

He'll either have to give up drinking or get his knees half-soled.

I walked out of the saloon and keeled over from fresh-air poisoning.

He's been under the table so much, he's going steady with the face on the barroom floor.

He's so anemic, when he has a hangover only one eye gets bloodshot.

That stuff was powerful ... I took one sip and then drew a picture of an auto on the wall. My girl took one sip, jumped into the auto and drove away.

He's been drinking too much. You know that white line that runs down the middle of Broadway? (localize) Well, this morning I found him trying to roll it up on a spool.

EYES

Do you see spots before your eyes? Well, use Goldberg's eyelash dye and see them in technicolor.

She's got patriotic eyes ... blue with red whites.

Carrots are wonderful for the eyes. Did you ever see a rabbit wearing glasses?

FOOD

The food situation is so bad that nowadays when a man bites a dog it isn't news ... it's lunch.

The bread situation is so tough that in Ruben's (local restaurant) they're serving a salami sandwich between two shots of rye.

I ate at the Astor (localize) this morning ... one of those breakfasts where they give you all you can eat for $30.

The bread shortage is so bad, that when I ordered a corned beef sandwich in Lindy's (localize) the waiter asked, "You want it on apple pie or raisin cake?"

GAMES

Mah-Jong the new yentatainment.

Did you ever play post office? At my house we play pony express. That's post office with a little more horsing around.

When I feel like exercising, I just lie down until the feeling passes away.

He was quite an athlete ... he played right mudguard for Chrysler.

GENERAL

This material should be used to fill in those awkward pauses that sometimes arise during a show and to keep your own act flowing nicely along.

If an act is delayed, say: He got stuck in the scenery and we can't get him out.

Calling up child, say: I've known this man for the past thirty years.

Come up here ... you look easy enough to fool.

Ask assistant if he drinks and if the answer is 'Yes', pass him a handful of straws.

I'm worried about my Dad ... he'd kill me if he knew I was doing this for a living ... he thinks I'm still selling dope.

Words fail me so I'll use letters ... P.U.

I bought two rabbits last year ... today I've still got two rabbits ... I finally discovered they are brothers.

If performer is wearing a bandage, say: I was living the life of Reilly ... last night Reilly came home.

Call to someone off-stage: Now Lana put down that gun ... you'll just have to make up your mind to forget me!

May I have the sexy spotlight, please?

The last word in aviation ... Jump!

We've got a show here this week that'll pack the Roxy.

You've no doubt seen Broadway shows, Roxy, Paramount ... wait till you see ours and you'll see the difference.

Let me tell you about myself ... got an hour?

He's a moth-eaten wolf. He got that way hiding in closets.

GIRDLES

Try this material at your next church performance or childrens' show.

You don't have to do Magic for a living ... you can always starve to death.

Good evening, ladies and gentlemen. The management of this theater has requested me to announce that the proceeds from this evening's entertainment will be contributed to a fund to help the destitute girdle manufacturers.

Ladies, are you lumpy, bumpy and dumpy? Does your girdle hitch-hike? Does your two-way stretch, stretch three ways? Then use Madame Myrtle's form fit girdles. Reinforced seats for skiing, skating and flagpole sitting. They are washable, wearable and repairable. So girls, don't have a figure like a turtle's, use Madame Myrtle's form fit girdles.

She has a figure that's out of this world ... but if she put a girdle on she might be able to get it back in again.

HAIR

Additional material will be found under "Hecklers."

My hair is getting thin ... and anyway who likes fat hair.

My doctor gave me a prescription to regain my eyesight. It read ... "Get a haircut."

I'd like a lock of your hair, honey ... I'm stuffing a mattress.

She dyes her hair so often, she's got technicolored dandruff.

HECKLERS

There is a definite way to squelch a heckler without antagonizing your audience. Overlook his first and even his second interruption. This will give the customers time to become aware of the pest. Then look direcly at him and wither him with one of the following remarks:

You remind me of a window ... easy to see through ... hard to shut ... and strictly a pain.

Run along before I knock you down with an ad lib.

Why don't you crawl back into your nightmare?

I think with a little encouragement we could get him to shut up.

Happy heart attack!

Why don't you go outside and brush up on your ignorance?

Why don't you rent out your head to block hats?

I don't know what I'd do without you, but I'd rather.

You better watch out how you talk to me. I'll have John L. Lewis brush you off with one of his eyebrows.

Are you still gargling with Draino?

I don't know what makes you so stupid, but whatever it is, it works.

He was arrested four times for impersonating a human being.

Lassie, go home!

How did the voice of the turtle get in here?

Now there's a living scallion if I ever saw one!

He wasn't born ... he was caught in a rat-trap.

You notice I don't give him a second thought ... he wouldn't know what to do with it.

What does your brain want to be when it grows up?

You keep on with those jokes and someday you'll be the life of the breadline.

Did it ever occur to you that you'd make a wonderful stranger?

Pay no attention to him ... he's just something left over from lend lease.

He would make a terrific companion in a suicide pact.

Is your family happy or do you go home at night?

Why don't you quit now while it's still up to you?

Imagine that poor little mind all alone in that great big head.

If he's stout: He's lost weight, but he was once the biggest jerk in town.

You look like a model for slip covers.

He carries himself well ... only he's so fat, he has to use both hands to do it.

Some people grow up and spread good cheer ... you just grew up and spread.

Ah, Jowls Boyer. He has so many double chins, he looks like he's looking over a Venetian blind.

She looks like Miss America ... and half of South America too.

If he's bald: The next time you order a toupee, get one with brains.

Are you using the new hair tonic, Staybald?

Put your fingers in your ears and they can use you for a bowling ball.

This is the first time I ever saw a part with ears.

My God! A honey dew melon with ears.

What do you do, comb your hair with a sponge?

Didn't I shoot you in the side pocket last night?

If she's pretty: Did you get that coat to keep you warm or keep you quiet?

She talks so much that when she goes to Miami she spreads sunburn lotion on her tongue.

If he or she is homely: You ought to work for a butcher ... you'd look so natural in the window with an apple in your mouth.

She's got the kind of face you don't want to remember and can't forget.

She's so ugly that when she sucks a lemon, the lemon makes a face.

Your mother should have thrown you away and kept the stork.

Is she ugly! You know, when the stork brought her, he circled the zoo for three days before they could talk him out of it.

Is that your lower lip or are you wearing a turtle neck sweater?

I call her my Melancholy Baby ... she has a head like a melon and a face like a collie.

Are those your own ears or are you breaking them in for a jackass?

He loves nature ... in spite of what she did to him.

I'm going to name my next nervous breakdown after him.

Who brought you in? It couldn't be Frank Buck ... he brings them back alive.

Do you always talk like that or are you wearing fuzzy underwear?

I live alone and like it. He lives alone and looks it.

I never forget a face, but in your case, I'll remember both of them.

If you keep on making me laugh like that, I'll be happy and live to be as old as you look.

Why don't you go home ... your cage must be cleaned out by now.

Have you got a chip on your shoulder or is that your head?

You can't help having a face like that, but you could at least stay at home and hide it.

If he's smaller than you: You now have 32 teeth ... would you like to try for none?

After bludgeoning the heckler with some of the foregoing material, administer the coup de grace with: If I said anything to insult you ... believe me!

Please remember that jumping on a heckler too soon will cause those members of your audience who are not yet fully aware of him to think that you are a poor sport.

HOLLYWOOD AND THE MOVIES

I don't mind the Hollywood climate ... it's the weather that bothers me.

Lana Turner had a horrible dream last night and woke up in a cold sweater.

Last night I had a date with Ingrid Bergman's sister ... Ingra Toenail.

I just made a new movie, a three-dimensional film. You'll be able to see it, hear it and smell it.

Did you hear about the Hollywood producer who likes his new wife so much, he's holding her over a second week?

I went to a movie but got on a nylon line by mistake. I wanted Greer and they gave me sheer.

A box of nylons has been found. Will the woman who lost it please form a double line in the outer lobby.

MGM kept calling and calling but I wouldn't answer ... I didn't like what they were calling me.

My next movie will be 'Blood and Sand' or 'Hemorrhage on the Beach'. Then I'll star in, 'Henry Aldrich Smokes a Reefer', and after that, 'Easy to Wed' or 'The Life of Tommy Manville'.

I just heard a rumor that Butch Jenkins divorced Margaret O'Brien and the alimony will be three lollipops a week.

Hollywood! Where else could you have breakfast with Lana Turner, lunch with Betty Grable, dinner with Bacall ... not that I did all that, but where else could it happen?

The Hershey chocolate people are trying to keep me in pictures. When I'm on the screen, more people come out in the lobby and buy Hershey bars than for any other actor.

The trouble with the movies is that they shoot too much film and not enough actors.

I once starred in a film, and do you know, Warner Brothers got a letter from three Eskimos stating it was the best film they ever ate.

It was a wonderful picture, so refreshing ... I felt like a new man when I woke up.

I passed the Roxy (local theatre) last night and heard the doorman shout,

"Step right in folks ... a short wait for no seats."

I took my girl to the Paramount (localize) last night and we couldn't get seats in the balcony so there was nothing else to do but see the picture.

I like that great actress Choo Choo Rabinowitz. The critics say her latest picture is a must. That makes two for her ... she mussed up the last one, too.

They're advertising a double feature at our neighborhood theater ... 'A Tree Grows In Brooklyn' and 'Lassie Comes Home'.

He played in the picture entitled, 'Love Letters'. He licked the stamps.

I've done some screen work myself. I fixed the two on our kitchen windows last summer.

I went to the movies with my girl last week. We saw a very romantic picture. I held her hand, then I cuddled close and finally I kissed her. Suddenly I remembered that we didn't get two seats together.

HORSES

The horse-racing enthusiasts in your audience might enjoy some of the following material:

My friend always makes money at the race track ... he sells hot-dogs there.

He's so crazy about horses that if his wife ever gave birth to triplets, it wouldn't surprise me any if he named them Win, Place, and Show.

I beat the horses today. I beat them in the first seven races and if I'da had any money left I'da beat them in the eighth race too.

The horse I bet on was so slow ... the jockey carried K-rations.

He bet so much on the ponies, he's walking around with feed-bags under his eyes.

The horse I bet on was so late, it tiptoed back into the stable.

Maybe you don't know it, but this is dumb animal week and every dollar I make I'm going to give to the horses.

He was voted the Bookie of the month.

My grandmother broke an arm ... it slipped off the two dollar window at Aqueduct.

My horse ran a steady race ... last all the way.

Last week I bet on a horse at 20 to 1 ... he came in 20 after 4.

He was the only horse I ever saw that started from a kneeling position.

I follow the horses, and the horses I follow, follow the horses.

One of Bing Crosby's horses looked good to me, so I went out and had my eyes examined.

The last horse I bet on came in five lengths behind the jockey.

My wife threatened to leave me if I didn't stop playing the horses ... gee, I'm gonna miss her.

HOTELS

At my hotel they change the sheets every day ... from one room to another.

I asked the hotel clerk for a five-dollar suite and he handed me a Hershey bar.

Last week I stopped at a hotel with a golf course. Every room was a hole.

This hotel has so many flies, MGM wants to give it a screen test.

There's no heat, but every hour a bellhop comes in and reads a chapter of 'Forever Amber'.

A sign in the room read ... Don't turn off the electric fan, it's holding up the walls!

Mrs. Katz is a very nice lady. She gave me a wonderful room with a private towel. The only trouble was that all night long people came in to wash their hands.

The bed was very comfortable. They even turned the water off at night. When I woke up in the morning my face was flushed.

We had a room with an adjoining house detective.

They had a room to fit every pocketbook, and some rooms were even larger.

My room was so small, people used to put pennies in the keyhole, turn the door knob and wait for the gum to drop out.

We had one lovely closet overlooking a moth.

Instead of a wash basin they installed a dixie cup. In two days I was talking with a southern accent.

I spent the week-end in a swell hotel. I was there three days and $5 went just like that. (Snap your fingers.) Next time I'll go alone.

INTRODUCTIONS

Magical M.C.'s are becoming increasingly popular with agents since they can kill two birds with one pay check. Therefore this collection of varied introductions has been included.

Good evening, Ladies and Gentlemen. I just returned from Hollywood where I made quite a name for myself ... I can't repeat it but believe me it was some name.

You know, it really thrills me to be working before so many people again. At the last show I gave, my audience was so small that after the performance it got up and went home together in a taxicab. But don't get the wrong idea ... I don't mind when my audience gets up and starts to leave ... it's when they start walking towards me that I begin to worry.

A funny thing happened at the theater last night. I was half-way through my act before I discovered they had forgotten to raise the curtain. When I left the stage, the crowd went wild with applause ... that's because they knew I wasn't coming back anymore. That was the night they presented me with the house ... a brick at a time. However, the real reason I wanted to be here tonight was that I read tomorrow's paper and saw I was a big hit.

I didn't expect to be called on, so I'm only here with a four-piece band.

I've just been signed by Warner's ... they want new faces on the picket line. Not very long ago I was making personal appearances in the subways.

I just graduated from college and I hope I forget everything I learned there ... you can't make a living necking.

Sorry to be late but I was just conferring with two dictators ... my wife and my mother-in-law.

I was late getting to the theater. I met my old commanding officer and he let me off at the wrong floor.

If you think crime doesn't pay you ought to see my act ... and I'm working steady.

General: He's been in pictures and now he's making a personal appearance to apologize.

He's all tired out ... last night he dreamed he was working.

He's at that in-between age ... too old for Castoria and too young for Serutan.

He's done quite a bit of radio work ... he fixed four sets last week.

Introducing the man who made B O what it is today ...

I would now like you to meet Hop-along Cassidy's uncle ... Drag-along Schwartz.

The curtain rises ... against its better judgment and we bring you ...

He's not himself tonight, folks ... can you notice the improvement?

She's very well reared and looks good in front too.

He's a first grade comic ... that being as far as he went in school.

He kills the people in every city except Boston ... they have air conditioning there!

Dancers: You heard of the famous dancing girl Salome? This is her younger sister Salami!

Just watch their feet and you'll see they're as light as zephyrs ... Lincoln Zephyrs!

These boys have a lot of polish. They'll sell it to you right after the show.

Instrumental: He's a musician in a fish market ... he scrapes the scales.

My pawnbroker had my violin so much, he plays it better than I do.

He was about to give a recital last week and the crowd cheered and cheered ... the piano was locked.

He loves music. In fact, he used to go to the opera every week ... whether he needed sleep or not.

Singers: Nelson Eddy once told this lad that his voice had a very fine range ... it kills at thirty feet!

He won an audition at the Metropolitan ... and has already sold two policies.

Recently his singing has improved ... his friends are now putting cotton in only one ear!

Before he starts singing, I must warn you that he is very temperamental. As soon as anybody starts shooting at the stage ... he leaves.

He will now sing, "I'm dancing with tears in my eyes, 'cause the girl in my arms is a boy."

He sang in a choir for a year and 400 people changed their religion.

It takes the mike an hour to cool off after she sings into it. She's hot! Every time I pass her, the water on my knee percolates.

INVENTIONS

I just invented a new communications instrument, much faster than telephone or telegraph ... the tele-woman.

I just invented a new roach trap. You lure a roach up a rope, then you start cutting the rope and when the roach climbs down, he falls into a plate of ice cream and catches pneumonia.

Reconversion is coming along fast. I just bought a quart of milk with a built-in radar set for hunting the cream.

My brother is also an inventor. He invented a time stretcher. When the time is almost up, you press a button and all the clocks stop until you're through.

I've invented an insomnia machine retailing at $490. It provides 12 sheep and a picket fence for them to jump over.

I just invented a new fountain pen. You fill it with water and it writes under ink.

JOBS

He's got a new job ... decoy for a dog catcher.

He made a career out of collecting unemployment insurance.

He has a new job at the UNO ... he opens the door when the Russians walk out.

He works for a lawyer ... he's a professional hideous corpus.

He saw a sign in the Post Office, "Murderer Wanted!" so he went in and applied for the job.

I left school to sell nylons in Macy's. One day a beautiful girl asked me to put the stockings on her. "Why, Miss," I told her, "if I did a thing like that I'd lose my job." And so after, I lost my job.

LOOKS

Additional material will be found under "Hecklers."

She just won second prize in a beauty contest. Dracula beat her out of first prize.

He has a nice open face ... it's open most of the time.

She has a heavenly face ... eyes like stars and a nose like the Big Dipper.

She's so well built, even her dandruff is sexy.

He's the only guy I know who has a cauliflower face.

I saw a circus elephant this morning that looked better than you do.

She's demure, like Ingrid Bergman. By that I mean, demure you look at her, demure you like Ingrid Bergman.

Next time somebody tells you that you look like some movie star, say, "Yeah, I forgot to wash tonight." I dare you!

She's so healthy she wears vitamin pills for earrings.

She was in a terrible accident ... she was having her face lifted and the derrick broke.

She has a nice profile ... all the way down.

Handsome or ugly ... it's nice to have a face.

LOVE

Unless you like your vice, versa, you ought to enjoy these gags.

Would you like to know how to attract the opposite sex? Simply send your name and address and ten cents for our little booklet entitled, "How To Make Love," written by the night watchman in Central Park.

You know Central Park ... that's a famous battle ground around here.

You should see the lovers lanes ... the girls think midnight to dawn are the "oui" hours. In the Spring a young man's fancy turns at almost anything that passes.

I'm getting lazy ... today I gave up after only ten blocks.

June is a romantic month ... even Lassie won't come home.

I'm the caveman type of lover ... one kiss and I cave in.

MEDICAL

I went to my doctor's office and saw a sign on the door, 11 to 1, so I went home ... I want better odds on my life.

My brother isn't exactly a doctor, but he got arrested for performing an illegal operation ... splitting a man's head with a hatchet.

He's a painless dentist. When he works on you ... it doesn't hurt him a bit.

I've got that new ailment ... sacroiliac of the head.

MEN

He's a character ... that's a jerk with personality.

He's going out of his mind and his mind is glad he's leaving.

He's a man of letters ... he eats alphabet soup.

Jail food is home cooking to that guy.

Over there sits a lucky man ... he has a wife and a cigarette lighter and they both work.

He's so inquisitive ... he wanted to take his nose apart to find out what made it run.

He's the living proof that man can live without a brain.

He takes his bad breaks just like a man ... blames them on his wife.

He's a taxicab wolf ... the original Paw-Knee Bill.

NEWSPAPERS AND BOOKS

I have a 93-year-old grandmother who has better circulation than that newspaper.

He writes a gossip column, "In the Know with Cock-Eyed Joe." He's the only reporter who can peek, through a key-hole with both eyes at the same time.

I can't read the news ... the printing is too close to the paper.

I read a funny thing in the want ad column this morning ... Beautiful girl would like to meet Nelson Eddy. Object ... Shortnin' Bread .

My uncle was an old newspaper man, but he decided to give it up ... there was no money to be made in old newspapers. My father was a newspaper man, too ... he ran a stand on 42nd Street and Broadway. It runs in our family. Even I once owned a newspaper, but I left it on the subway. It was one of those tabloids ... you know, a screamlined newspaper with a permanent crime wave.

I just heard about a nightgown made of newsprint ... good for husbands who read in bed. Imagine a husband after finishing the news stories telling his wife, "Now turn over so's I can read the funnies."

I finally wrote something a magazine accepted ... a check for a subscription.

My mother writes me ... "Just reminding you that you will be 28 this week. If your father hadn't stuttered, you'd have been 29."

I just finished my latest novel, "Life in California" or "Two Years Before the Mist." I called the one before that, "Interesting Places to Visit for People Who Walk in Their Sleep."

He got the idea for his latest book from the movie based on the radio adaptation of his first one.

He reads just enough to keep himself misinformed.

NIGHT CLUBS

Audiences enjoy an entertainer who pokes fun at the management. This stems from a suppressed desire to do so themselves. So remember, for hearty bellylaughs, kid the management.

We now have an eight-course meal for two dollars ... a piece of seven-layer cake and a glass of milk.

There's no cover, no minimum, and no ventilation. It's one of those exclusive spots where nobody's allowed in.

Before they close up they always make sure the customers are piled up neatly on the sidewalk.

This joint is very exclusive. In order to get in, you have to push the door open.

There's a dime cover charge to keep out the riffraff.

The tables are $5 and $10. With the $10 ones, you get a chair.

Their food is wonderful. They specialize in stews ... the place is always full of them.

They have a new show every Monday ... a new management every Thursday and a new address every month.

And what decorations! It's furnished throughout with antiques ... including the chorus.

One fellow ordered demi-tasse and the waiter brought him coffee, but he didn't know the difference.

There's no charge for hat check ... you just don't get your hat back.

There's no cover charge either ... just a $3 rental item for each chair.

Sometimes they have trouble because of the bobbysocks ... you know, Bobby socks Betty, then Betty socks Bobby ... from there on you're on your own!

It's a little crowded there. I reached over to scratch my back and a guy five tables away said, "Ah-h-h!"

This joint's so far underground, you'll get the bends if you leave too fast.

The waiters here are tip top. If you don't tip them, they blow their top.

ORCHESTRA

Make good tonight, boys. Remember, we can easily be replaced by a juke box.

You sound like something that was caught in Jessica's Dragonet.

They don't have to work for a living. They play at Tommy Manville's weddings. The pay's not big, but the work is steady.

Music by Sid Suds and his three-piece band ... they know only three pieces.

It's a swell orchestra ... they go out together, they live together, they eat together ... now if they could only finish together.

I'd like you to meet some of the best musicians in the country. In the city I don't know, but in the country they're wonderful.

To orchestra leader: Listen, if you're a conductor, I want a transfer.

He's so rich, he changes suits for each show. First show: Blue jacket and gray pants. Second show: Gray jacket and blue pants. He keeps that up all day.

RADIO

Tune in again next week, folks. Same station, same time, same jokes.

Men, when you get up in the morning, do you regret it?

Grow a mustache, remember, Fuzz does everything.

Morning exercise: 1-2, 1-2, ... and now the other eyelid.

Calling Dr. Kildare! Dr. Kildare is opening a new case ... bring your own ginger ale!

I am now sponsored by Ginsberg's Sausage, the sausage with the skin you love to touch.

This is Pan-America Day, folks, when South Americans pan America.

This is the Peachy Toffee Company ... the only toffee with the two-way stretch. Presenting Dr. B.O.

I've got an old radio set folks and the tubes are getting very weak. The other day it took ten minutes for "John's Other Wife" to warm up.

An analysis: Mr. Churchill has made one thing clear tonight. What it is I do not know.

RESTAURANTS

Everybody comes to Sam's Delicatessen (localize) ... everybody but the Board of Health.

After you eat there, you'll probably never live to regret it.

I ate at Lindy's with my brother-in-law, 'yesterday. I picked up the check and he picked up the tip.

We ate at a clip-joint, yesterday. When the waiter brought me the check I told him there must be some mistake ... I have more money in my pocket than that.

SCHOOL DAYS

In high school, I was a wonderful athlete ... in fact, I was a three-letter man ... an R-A-T.

I can't forget my first day in school. Everybody looked so nice in new clothes, but my family was poor and couldn't afford to buy me shoes ... so I painted my feet brown and laced my toes.

I was as smart as the next fellow. The only trouble was that the next fellow was always an idiot.

But I got good marks in school. Me and the kid in front never got less than 98. He got 90 and I got 8.

I knew all the answers. It's the questions that confused me.

I've got a scholarship to Harvard Medical School ... but they don't want me while I'm alive.

School just started and already they've voted him, "Most Likely to Recede".

He was halfback on the football team and way back in his studies.

SWIMMING AND BATHING

My wife was saying that Coney Island was swept by a breeze, and I said that was the first time it had been swept by anything in years.

It was so crowded at the beach, only bald-headed men got sunburned.

There I was barefoot, barefoot up to my chin.

Bathing suit: The little bit that isn't bare.

I didn't bathe much ... the pool was full of hard water and I bruise so easily.

Rub-a-dub-dub, three men in a tub ... that's sanitary?

To test the water for baby's bath, dip baby in tub ... if baby turns red, water too hot ... if baby turns blue, water too cold ... if baby turns white, the kid musta been dirty.

My last birthday present was a bathtub with a built-in ring. The first time I took a bath I said to myself, "Who knows, I might like it, and if I do I'll take another one some day."

TEETH

The girl I took out last night was called "Baby." That's because she didn't have any teeth. She lost them shifting gears on a hot-pastrami sandwich.

You bit into an apple and broke two teeth? Well, don't get excited, dear ... you still have one left!

That gal sure is homely! Her teeth stick out so far ... her nose looks like it's giving a piano recital.

She has Pullman teeth ... one upper ... one lower.

He's the careless type ... he's got his teeth in sideways.

He still has his original set of false teeth.

Her teeth have so many cavities, she talks in echoes.

I brought my girl some candy for her sweet tooth ... I wish she had a few more to go with it.

WIVES

Did you wake up with a grouch this morning, or did she wake up ahead of you?

I'm crazy about my wife ... I love every hair on her lip.

I got my wife a three-piece sweater set for her birthday ... two needles and a ball of wool.

I've got the most beautiful wife in the world. One of these nights I'm gonna go home and visit her.

My wife weighs 250 pounds and she's all mine ... every acre of her.

I don't know what I'd do without my wife ... she's never given me a chance to find out.

My wife is involved in a triangle. She can't decide which she likes better ... her right or her left profile.

My wife doesn't exactly snore, but she breathes a beautiful soprano.

My wife is a perfect lamb. Every time I suggest anything she says, "Baa!"

Last night my wife dreamed that I gave her a mink coat, so I told her, "When you dream again, wear it in good health."

WOMEN

She had her nose broken in three places ... Philadelphia, Chicago, and Hollywood.

She just turned 24. Before she turned it, it was 42.

Did you hear about the debutante who came out last year? All she has to do now is report once a month to her probation officer.

She was stood up more often than a bowling pin.

When she wears a sweater, it becomes occupied territory.

She's the kind of girl her mother doesn't want her to associate with.

She spends so much time in parked cars ... they're showing her on all the road maps this season.

She's so high brow, she thinks a bicuspid is a double-barreled spittoon.

She reminds me of an automobile ... knock-kneed action and floating kidney power.

She doesn't know where her next schlemiel is coming from.

She's an intellectual golddigger and just loves to read. In fact, she's a member of the Bankbook of the Month Club.

Men don't like her for her mind. They like her for what she doesn't mind.

In the first place she was too fat. Come to think of it, she was too fat in the second place too.

What a shape! She had six places you could hang your hat on. Four drunks looked at her and took the pledge.

She doesn't wear any make-up ... some people will do anything to attract attention.

I saw her at the track, yesterday, but I don't remember in which race.

Women should enjoy social life. For that reason I believe in clubs for women ... but only when kindness fails.

She was so skinny, that every time she yawned her dress fell down.

She had a speech impediment ... she couldn't say, "No!"

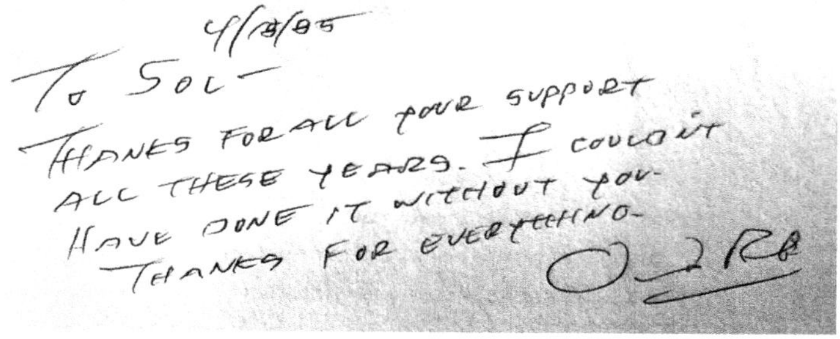
4/18/85
To Sol—
Thanks for all your support
all these years. I couldn't
have done it without you.
Thanks for everything.

To Sol,

Thanks for all your support all these years.
I couldn't have done it without you.
Thanks for everything.

David Roth ... April 18, 1985

Printed in Great Britain
by Amazon

82208063R00173